Lost
Demesnes

Irish Landscape Gardening, 1660–1845

Lost Demesnes

Irish Landscape Gardening, 1660–1845

Edward Malins &
The Knight of Glin

Foreword by Desmond Guinness
President, Irish Georgian Society

BELAN, CO.
KILDARE. *Lord Ald-
borough reviewing Volun-
teers: oil painting by
Francis Wheatley, c. 1780.*

BARRIE & JENKINS
COMMUNICA-EUROPA

© 1976 Edward Malins and The Knight of Glin

First published 1976 by
Barrie & Jenkins Ltd
24 Highbury Crescent, London N5 1RX

ISBN 0 214 20275 5

Printed in Great Britain
by W & J Mackay Limited, Chatham

To Desmond and Mariga

My grief and my affliction
Your gates are taken away,
Your avenue needs attention,
Goats in the garden stray.
The courtyard's filled with water,
And the great earls where are they?
The earls, the lady, the people
Beaten into the clay.

W. B. Yeats and Frank O'Connor,
from the Irish poem, *Kilcash*

Contents

List of Plates

Acknowledgments

We have received so much help from so many people that there may be omissions in this list of acknowledgements. We must apologise to those we may have forgotten. We are grateful to them, but our memories are shorter than they should be, and the book has taken a very long time to reach publication owing to the unfortunate decease of the Irish University Press which was to have published it some years ago. We would like to thank Tom Turley, late of I.U.P. for the great trouble he took in editing the book with Claire Craven during the death throes of I.U.P. It is also right to remember Captain McGlinchey, the publisher, who was recently killed tragically in a car crash. His optimism and enthusiasm will be much missed. The Irish Georgian Society has continually encouraged us during many dark months, and their Secretary, Audrey Emerson, retyped the entire manuscript. Both Desmond and Mariga Guinness were among the earliest enthusiasts to appreciate Irish eighteenth-century landscape gardens and their attendant buildings. The successful results of the work of the Society can be seen in the restoration of the Conolly Folly, the Dromana Gateway and the Belan obelisk among many others.

It is excellent to be able to record that certain County Councils are slowly awakening to the aesthetic value in the landscape as well as the tourist attraction of such structures as lodge gates, follies and demesne walls; thus fewer are being used for road material. But there remains a long way to go in the struggle against ignorance and prejudice, though many lectures on the environment inaugurated by An Taisce are doing much to clear the path; for example, since this book was written the Limerick Branch of An Taisce has restored an old terraced garden at Glenstal Abbey. We hope that all those who have helped us, to whom we are so grateful, will feel they have played their part with us in bringing to people's notice some of the Irish landscape and gardening heritage which has been saved or still can be. We are much indebted to Maurice Craig, Desmond Guinness and Rolf Loeber for their scholarly comments after reading our manuscript. Jon Stallworthy especially deserves our thanks for it was he who originally forged our collaboration, and Michael and Isabel Briggs made that collaboration possible by their endless hospitality. We are also deeply grateful to Michael Hodson and Nancy Duin of Barrie & Jenkins for all their editorial help. To the following we are most indebted in many and various ways:

The Earl of Altamont
Lena Boylan
C. E. B. Brett
The British Library
The County Archivist, Bury St Edmunds Record Office
The Earl of Caledon
Marcus Clements
Mrs Howard Colvin
John Cornforth
Anne Crookshank
John Lewis-Crosby
Lady Victoria Cuthbert
Ray Desmond
The Hon. Ethel Dillon
The Earl and Countess of Dunraven
The Earl of Erne
Syndics of the Fitzwilliam Museum, Cambridge
Christopher Gaisford St Lawrence
William Garner
Richard Green
John Hardy
John and Eileen Harris
Michael Hartnett
The Houghton Librarian, Harvard College
The late Dr T. R. Henn
The late Mr Frank Hilliard
The Librarian, Holkham Hall, Norfolk
Andrew and Gabrielle Holmwood
Arnold Horner
Lord Inchiquin

Major T. E. Johnston
Barbara Jones
Professor Walter Kaiser
John D. La Touche
The Duke of Leinster
The City Librarian, Londonderry Public Libraries
The Countess of Longford
The late Lord Talbot de Malahide
Anthony Malcolmson
The Governors and Librarian, Marsh's Library, Dublin
J. D. C. Masheck
Edward McParland
Niall Meagher
The Earl of Meath
The Paul Mellon Foundation
George Morrison
The Hon. David Nall Cain
National Gallery of Ireland
National Library of Ireland
The late Eoin O'Mahony
Lord O'Neill
Lord O'Neill of the Maine
Thomas and Valerie Pakenham
David Posnet
The late Viscount Powerscourt
Peter du Prey
Claud Proby
Public Record Office of the North of Ireland, Belfast
Miss Hilary Pyle
W. B. Rankin
The Duke of Richmond
The Earl of Rosse
Alistair Rowan
The Earl of Shannon
George Stacpoole
Denys Sutton and the Proprietors of *Apollo Magazine*
The Librarian and Keeper of Manuscripts, Trinity College, Dublin
Victoria & Albert Museum
Francis Warner
The County Librarian, West Suffolk County Council
Dr Peter Willis

The authors would also like to express their thanks to the following owners, institutions, photographers and publications for permission to reproduce the following plates:

By Gracious Permission of Her Majesty the Queen *132*, A & C Photography, Belfast *121*, *166*, *167*, Aerofilms *112*, Baron Alexander Albrizzi *77*, The Hon. Mrs. Herbrand Alexander *21*, Mr Walter Armytage *203*, Mr Christopher Ashe *199*, Ashmolean Museum *75*, *101*, *102*, *111*, *120*, *133*, *182*, *183*, *199*, *200*, Mr David Bailey *181*, Bodleian Library *5*, *89*, Bord Failte (Irish Tourist Board) *199*, British Museum *53*, *176*, *191*, The Hon. David Nall Cain *8*, *10*, *63*, *64*, *70*, *71*, Christies, London *206*, Condé Nast Publications Ltd *181*, Mr Sean F. Cooke *171*, Major E. A. S. Cosby *26*, Country Life *12*, *13*, *15*, *29*, *56*, *57*, *93*, *130*, *131*, Courtauld Institute of Art, London *139*, Mrs Dominic Daly *124*, *125*, *127*, Major John de Burgh *39*, The Earl of Erne *82*, *83*, Fitzwilliam Museum, Cambridge *117*, *118*, Mr Jonathan M. Gibson *12*, *13*, *15*, Green Studio Ltd, Dublin *21*, *22*, *32*, *33*, *35*, *36*, *37*, *55*, *64*, *70*, *71*, *73*, *128*, *159*, *160*, Major Richard Gregory *198*, The Hon. Desmond Guinness *52*, *62*, *66*, *67*, *90*, *103*, *115*, The Hon. Mrs Desmond Guinness *201*, Mr John Harris *25*, *40*, *68*, *197*, J & S Harsch, Dublin *9*, *28*, *104*, *199*, Mr W. O. Hassell *11*, The Marquess of Headfort *104*, Mr Norman Ievers *27*, Mr Charles J. P. LaTouche *141*, Earl of Leicester *11*, The Duke of Leinster *58*, *60*, Dr Colin Lewis *7*, Mr W. D. G. Mackie *105*, *106*, Manning Galleries Ltd, London *172*, Mr and Mrs Paul Mellon *151*, Mr George Morrison *180*, National Gallery of Ireland *43*, *44*, *45*, *47*, *54*, *65*, *97*, *122*, *149*, *189*, National Library of Ireland *2*, *4*, *16*, *17*, *23*, *42*, *59*, *74*, *91*, *96*, *116*, *143*, *152*, National Portrait Gallery, London *150*, National Trust *frontispiece*, National Trust of North of Ireland *144*, Mr Michael and the Rev. Thomas Nicholson *165*, Mr John O'Callaghan *205*, Cian O'Carroll *46*, Lord O'Neill of the Mayne *87*, The Lord O'Neill *84*, *85*, *86*, Mr William O'Sullivan *150*, The Hon. Thomas Pakenham *22*, PDI Photography, Dublin *63*, the late Viscount Powerscourt *32*, *33*, Sir Richard Proby *5*, *6*, Public Record Office of North of Ireland *105*, *106*, *147*, *Reader's Digest 49*, The Earl of Roden *139*, Lord Rossmore *24*, *48*, *51*,

69, 76, 79, 123, 126, 135, 137, 161, 162, 168, 169, 170, 202, Mr Alistair Rowan *195, 196,* Royal Irish Academy *20,* Sabin Gallery *174,* Mr Christopher Gaisford St Lawrence *28, 31, 41,* Mrs Ralph Slazenger *35, 36, 37,* Mr George Stacpoole *171,* Canon J. J. Stevenson-Dean of Clogher *148,* E. E. Swain Ltd *11,* Lord Christopher Thynne *1,* Trinity College, Dublin *50,* Ulster Museum *6, 8, 14, 26, 62, 67, 84, 85, 86, 90, 113, 124, 125, 127, 129, 165, 203,* Victoria & Albert Museum, London *114, 140, 177, 178, 194,* The Marquis of Waterford *49,* Dr and Mrs Donald Weir *98, 99,* The Yale Center for British Art and British Studies *156, 190,* The Earl of Ypres *157, 158.*

Plates *7, 19, 30, 34, 38, 63, 107, 108, 109, 110, 129, 146, 153, 155, 163* and *164* are in the possession of The Knight of Glin.

The authors extend their apologies to any who, through an oversight, have not been acknowledged.

Foreword

The life expectancy of a garden is short, shorter by far than that of the building in whose shadow it may chance to lie. And memory of it is shorter still, for if those who described Irish country houses are few and far between, fewer still are those who had anything at all interesting to say about their gardens. Edward Malins and The Knight of Glin have set down for posterity a mass of hitherto unpublished material, patiently collected over many years. They have traced the history of the development of the Irish garden with particular emphasis on the use of natural beauty to embellish the prospect, a characteristic they find peculiar to this country.

In the late seventeenth and early eighteenth century the old-fashioned 'grand manner' of garden layout was generally found, faithfully chronicled by the French cartographer, John Rocque.

> Grove nods at Grove, each Alley has a brother,
> And half the platform just reflects the other.

Straight canals, straight vistas – even the flowers were planted in regiments, hedges were pleached, and yews carved in topiary figures to 'people' the walks.

Symmetry, however, was soon to disappear. 'Kent has leapt the fence and finds all nature is a garden,' wrote Walpole. It is he who also relates the story of 'Capability' Brown's invitation to remodel the park at Carton, and his proud rejoinder, 'I haven't finished England yet.' The ideal landscape from the middle of the eighteenth century was one where 'art and nature in just union reign'. Judging by Rocque's map of County Dublin in 1760, not many demesnes had been deformalised then, but when the Countess of Kildare persuaded her husband to cut down the great avenues that radiated from Carton so that she could indulge her passion for spotted cows and see them from the house, she was unconsciously sounding the death knell for the formal garden in Ireland. The few that remain, such as Howth and Kilruddery, are therefore all the more important.

Flowers were swept out of sight and locked up in a walled garden, some distance from the house – in some cases, for example Bowenscourt, surprisingly far away. The practical Victorians, who were perhaps employing a dozen or so gardeners, without so much as a hint of a flower visible from their houses, fell once again to digging up beds outside the windows. The wheel had come full circle, and there was a return to formalism, at least as regards flowerbeds and paths. William Robinson, whose book *The English Flower Garden* was all the rage at this time, was, incidentally, an Irishman, who had worked as Head Gardener at Ballykilcaven, County Leix, before his dramatic row with his employer, The Rev. Sir Hunt Henry Johnson-Walsh, Bt.

Walpole said that if the proprietor were a man of taste, he was best fit to lay out his own park, and the best designer of his own improvements. He sees the site through all the seasons of the year, at all times of the day. 'He knows where beauty will not clash with convenience, and observes in his silent walks, or accidental rides, a thousand hints that must escape a person who in a few days sketches out a pretty picture, but has not had leisure to examine the details and relations of every part.' The concoctions of the amateur architect are a peculiarity of the Irish countryside, whether pedimented houses of sham cut stone, or of the castellated breed, wearing a permanent frown and of equally pasteboard construction. In landscape design the amateur was successful, and professional landscape and garden designers during the Georgian period were thin on the ground. The natural beauty of the countryside, mountains, lakes and rivers, forms a magnificent backdrop to the 'nicer scenes of art' within the demesne wall.

Much of the English countryside has been altered out of all recognition by giant industrial undertakings which have scarred and blackened the landscape. Ireland has been more fortunate. Oil refineries, smelter plants and chemical waste will be ours in the future, however, if plans being mooted at present are permitted to materialise. Parks have been ruthlessly divided by wire and concrete with no aesthetic considerations. Sir John Betjeman compared the desecration of Moore Park, Fermoy, to the gashing of a Gainsborough landscape. The State has yet to be brought to realise that Irish gardens and parks are in themselves works of art worthy of preservation, and that in hard financial terms they represent a considerable national investment. Much has been lost through neglect, poverty, bureaucracy and a lack of understanding on the part of our planners. Much more will be lost because of the cost of upkeep and the pressures of housing and industry. The appearance of this work is therefore fortunately timed, and it is to be hoped that those concerned with physical planning in Ireland will look to it for guidance and inspiration.

Introduction

Large Elizabethan and Jacobean mansions like Burleigh, Hatfield and Audley End, with their extensive gardens, were never built in Ireland. Such was the troubled state of the country there was little gardening even inside castle walls, and outside these the landscape was stripped bare of trees. In England, statutes in the reigns of Henry VIII and William III ensured the planting and replacement of trees; but in Ireland these acts did not apply. Consequently, acres of native trees – oak, elm, birch, holly and alder – were ruthlessly felled and whole tracts laid waste.[1] The superior quality of Irish oak, especially from Shillelagh, caused timber to be sent abroad or wantonly cut for iron forges and furnaces. Early in the eighteenth century the Dublin Society, realizing the seriousness of the position, gave rewards for planting trees. Despite these bounties, planting in Ireland compared with a similar period in Scotland was negligible. Yet a few Irish landlords in creating their landscapes altered the face of certain parts of the country, and among these the marquesses of Waterford at Curraghmore preserved unrivalled forest trees and planted thousands more.

Such landscapes were never created nor preserved by absentee landlords. For example, Richard Boyle, 3rd Lord Burlington, Pope's friend, and the creator of the landscape at Chiswick House, Middlesex, was one of the richest landlords in Ireland, yet never visited the country. In contrast, Lord Charlemont, although he had strong cultural and social ties with England, decided in 1760 that 'Ireland could not be served in England', so he created a landscape of much beauty at Marino just outside Dublin. Similarly, Lady Louisa Conolly and her sister the Duchess of Leinster created settings for the two great Palladian houses, Castletown and Carton, adjacent to each other in County Kildare, and there they lived. Likewise, Richard Lovell Edgeworth, as his daughter relates, determined to dedicate his life to the improvement of his estate at Edgeworthtown, setting to work at 'fencing, draining, levelling, planting, though he knew that all he was doing could not show for years.' More important, he was doing work 'with the sincere hope,' he said, 'of contributing to the melioration of the inhabitants of the country from which he drew his subsistence.'

The English parliament neglected many of the social and economic problems of Ireland throughout the eighteenth century, and the period has left a legacy of hatred for the Anglo-Irish heritage which lasts into our own times. In this book we are not concerned with political problems except in so far as they concern the social side of landscape gardening. Maybe landlords did benefit from cheap Irish labour, yet it was often essential for the landlords to take special measures to alleviate their tenants' economic distress in times of famine, and the best did not fail to help. The building of an obelisk, the draining of a lake or bog, the enclosure of an estate by a perimeter wall, the planting of woodlands and extension of lawns all provided employment, and these works must not be dismissed as frivolous activity. Even in England such work was regarded by foreigners as one of the chief virtues of landscape gardening.[2] In Ireland, from the Battle of the Boyne (1690) for the next ninety peaceful years, landscaping became a social and economic necessity.

The historical development of landscape gardening in Ireland is initially the same as in England. Some fine baroque formal gardens, exactly similar to those in England, after the pattern of André Le Nôtre, were laid out in the late seventeenth century, and are discussed in Chapter 1. Nearly contemporary with these are gardens laid out in the Dutch manner, with clipped hedges and straight canals, their development having been carried out by the loyal supporters of the Dutchman, William III. Then follows the most important event, the arrival of the gardening ideas of Alexander Pope and William Kent at Twickenham by way of their friends, Dean Swift and Dr Patrick Delany. Their gardens (Naboth's Vineyard in St Patrick's Cathedral Liberties, and

Delville, Glasnevin) are discussed at some length as, with Lord Orrery's landscaping at Caledon, they are the curtain-raisers to the more free romantic-poetic landscaping which was to prevail throughout the century. The gardens at Delville and Caledon are contemporary and were similar in form to those at Stourhead, Hagley and Painshill in England.

It was Lord Orrery who noticed there was 'indeed a great Difference in the Complexion of the two Islands. Nature has been profusely beneficent to *Ireland*, and Art has been as much so to *England*. Here, we are beholden to nothing but the Creation; there, you are indebted to extensive Gardeners and costly Architects.'[3] This is indeed the prime difference in landscaping in the two countries: Ireland was little tamed by art as the milder climate and higher rainfall produced profuse horticultural growth. In addition, the much indented coastline, the many natural loughs amid mountainous scenery provided material for landscaping which was readily incorporated. These prospects, in which water played so large a part, created a very special harmony, unique to Ireland. Therefore it was fortunate that none of the best known English landscapers worked in Ireland during the eighteenth century, for they were not used to this type of terrain in which water did not have to be brought in nor hills artificially created. Humphry Repton was a government official rather than a landscape gardener when he was in Dublin in 1783, yet he was undoubtedly much influenced by what he saw going on and by the special characteristics of the Irish terrain. The estates at Castletown and Carton, to which we devote a chapter, were landscaped in this typically Irish manner: none of the vast, bare lawns of Capability Brown stretching to the very front door of the house, but a formal or balustraded terrace to set off the building in the landscape, as well as the eclectic use of certain Picturesque features, usually cottages ornés, in wooded places in the grounds. Repton's subsequent work in England much resembles these Irish landscapes in these respects, so it may be said that Repton, who was willing to accept the best of the Brownian landscaping, and also appropriately use features from the Picturesque school, was carrying on much of what he had seen in Ireland.

It is easy in Ireland to be lulled into a conceptual appreciation of the Picturesque, similar to that expressed by William Gilpin or Uvedale Price, as the many evidences of the past – round towers, ruins of abbeys, monasteries and houses – are evocative overtones of past grandeur when combined with holy mountains and wells of ancient high kings and native saints. There was little opportunity to view these in England from a landscaped estate, and in some cases, such as at Hagley, Worcestershire, a ruined hermitage had actually to be built.

The creative peak in landscaping is undoubtedly the last twenty years of the eighteenth century, the period of Grattan's Parliament. During these years, the Irish, in Elizabeth Bowen's words, 'began to feel, to exert, the European idea – to seek what was humanistic, classic and disciplined.' After the Act of Union (1800) there were but a few instances of splendid gardening as the country never recovered from the absenteeism of many of the landed proprietors. Mr James Fraser of the *County Survey*, the guidebook writer and gardener, remarks on the decay at Rathfarnham Castle, County Dublin: 'not a solitary instance, but one out of many, where a magnificent greenhouse, on the same plan as those at Hampton Court and Kew, has been turned into a cow-shed, and the fine old Dutch garden is now a total ruin.'[4] The fabric of a house can be repaired, but a garden cannot be exactly reproduced in the life of a man.

Similarly Lady Morgan brilliantly describes the scene of melancholy desolation at the ancient seat of the Fitzadlem family, in her undeservedly forgotten Irish novel *Florence Macarthy* (1818), pages 196 and 201:

The massive stone pillars on either side, overgrown with lichens, still exhibited some vestiges of handsome sculpture; the capital of one was surmounted by a headless eagle, the other showed the claw and part of the body of a gos-hawk – both natives of the surrounding mountains, and well imitated in black marble, drawn from their once worked quarries. Two lodges mouldered on either side into absolute ruin, and the intended improvement of a Grecian portico to one, never finished, was still obvious in the scattered fragments of friezes and entablatures, which lay choked amidst heaps of nettles, furze-bushes, and long rye-grass . . . The precipitous declivities which swept down from the rocky foundation of the house to the river, had been cut into terrace gardens, a fashion still observable at the seats of the ancient nobility of Munster: and it was melancholy to observe the stunted rose-tree, and other once-cultivated but now degenerate shrubs and flowers, raising their heads amongst nettles and briers, and long grass, and withered potatoe-stalks. Many fantastic little buildings were also seen mouldering on romantic sites along the river's undulating banks; some of shells, some of rock-work; all alike monuments of the bad taste of the day in which they were raised, and of the wanton caprice of the persons who projected them.

The tale has not been altered substantially in the last 130 years. Troubles, civil war and absenteeism have ruined more houses and landscapes than anywhere else in these islands. Too often on visiting the sites of these demesnes[5] we regretted we could find little; in others we rejoiced to find a ruined house, an obelisk or temple. After reading about those which have gone, and seeing those which remain it is easy to sense that special quality of Irish landscaping for the last two hundred years, and to realize the influence it has had on English landscaping, through that great English landscape gardener, Humphry Repton. The Irish union of man-made landscape with innumerable natural loughs, rivers, mountains and sheltered harbours is an achievement unique in European art.

1. See A. C. Forbes, 'Tree Planting in Ireland', *Royal Irish Academy Proceedings*, vol. XLI, sect. C, 25 August 1933, p. 175.
2. See Owen Cambridge's article in *The World*, 3 April 1755.
3. To Tom Southerne Dublin, 28 May 1737. *The Orrery Papers*, Harvard College, MS Eng. 218.2, vol. 7, p. 113.
4. 'On the Present State of Gardening in Ireland', *The Gardener's Magazine*, vol. I (1826), p. 13 ff.
5. Originally meaning the enclosed park round a great house, including the deer park or enclosure and the 'pleasure grounds' as the Irish called them which were the ornamental planting and garden immediate to the house. From *dominicus*, the lord's house.

1 The Baroque

There's statues gracing this noble place in __
All heathen gods and nymphs so fair;
Bold Neptune, Plutarch, and Nicodemus
All standing naked in the open air!

Richard Millikin,
The Groves of Blarney

It was in 1790 that Joseph Cooper Walker, a prominent member of the Royal Irish Academy, contributed his seminal 'Essay on the Rise and Progress of Gardening in Ireland' to the *Transactions of the Royal Irish Academy*. He begins his work with true Augustan enthusiasm, by discussing the state of Irish gardens in the seventeenth century:

Soon as the English had subdued the martial spirit of the Irish, and obtained for themselves the peaceable enjoyment of the lands which they had won with their reeking swords, they introduced the formal style of gardening, which then, and for some years before, prevailed in England. Of this style several specimens remained till very lately in this kingdom. 'At Bally-beggan, in the county of Kerry (says Dr. Smith) there are some good old improvements which escaped the universal devastations of the times, particularly some fine avenues of walnut, chestnut and other trees; with a large, old but thriving orchard, planted in a rich limestone ground, beneath which are several subterraneous chambers, lined with stalactical exudations'. The same author informs us, that at Bangor in the County of Down, 'there are gardens which are large and handsome, and filled with noble ever-greens of a great size, cut in various shapes'. At Listerne, in the County of Waterford, we are also informed by Dr. Smith, that 'there was a large and beautiful canal, at the further end of which is a *jet d'eau* that cast up water to a considerable height'. And a learned friend, in a letter now before me, says that he saw some years since, in the County of Cork, a very old garden carefully preserved, which he thus describes: 'It consisted of fourteen acres enclosed with an high wall; two acres were appropriated to a nut grove. It had a large fish pond, a bathing house, monstrous high yew hedges, and some laurel ones; these were cut into fantastical forms, obscuring the rays of the sun. Here were also large green plats in various figures'. Nor should I omit the pensile gardens of Thomastown in the County of Tipperary, which were laid out in the reign of Charles II. They lie principally on the gentle declivity of a hill, resting on terraces, and filled with 'statues thick as trees'. A long fish pond, sleeping under 'a green mantle' between two rectilineous banks, appears in the midst. And in another corner stands a verdant theatre (once the scene of several dramatic exhibitions) displaying all the absurdity of the architecture of gardening. . . .

He then firmly declares, as would be expected from a late eighteenth century commentator: 'Thus did our ancestors, governed by the false taste which they imbibed from the English, disfigure, with unsuitable ornaments, the simple garb of nature'.[1]

Cooper Walker based his account on Dr Charles Smith's various mid-eighteenth century Irish county histories, the gardens he discussed having nearly all disappeared. The 'very old garden' in County Cork, which he alluded to, was that at Palace Anne, a noble brick house of the late seventeenth century; unfortunately both garden and house have been swept away.

Another garden mentioned, at Thomastown, had most of its formal layout fashionably turned into a natural park in the late eighteenth or early nineteenth century, when a magnificent baronial castle, designed by Sir Richard Morrison, clothed with a Gothic mantle George Mathew's 'mansion hotel', to which Swift was a visitor. This house seems to have been an unusual establishment where the guests could either take their meals in their suites or join the company at a communal table. Mathew had lived on the Continent and was obviously *au fait* with the newest fashions in both accommodation and garden layout. The gardens, which in 1732 were considered by an English visitor to show 'more improvements than anywhere in Ireland',[2] were patronizingly described in 1778 – by which time they seemed old-fashioned:

Here are all the capabilities for a terrestrial paradise; and yet one thing is wanting that mars the whole. Every violence, that she is capable of suffering, has been done to Nature.

Behind the house is a square parterre of flowers, with terraces thickly studded with busts and statues; before it, a long and blind avenue, planted with treble rows of well-grown trees, extends its awkward length. In the centre of this, and on the acclivity of the hill, terminating the vista, are little fish ponds, pond above pond. The whole park is thrown into squares and parallelograms, with numerous avenues fenced and planted; where a hillock dared to interpose its little head, it was cut off as an excrescence or at least cut through; that the roads might be everywhere as level, as they are straight. Thus was this delightful spot, treated by some Procrustes of the last age.[3]

There are still at Thomastown remains of the terraces and formal 'Procrustean' beds, and an enormous walled garden with the significant feature of mammoth *oculi* (now partially walled up) on all four sides (Plate 1). This reflected the current French fashion for prolonging the axes of the garden into the surrounding country, and no doubt these *oculi* were originally furnished with wrought iron. These features were probably similar to the *clairevoie*, a common feature of contemporary English gardens.[4] In a sense, their predecessors were those artificial mounts, erected to provide a view of the surrounding landscape, which are found in early seventeenth century layouts. In Ireland these mounts were uncommon, yet in 1697 John Dunton, a London bookseller, significantly described the remains of one in a very remote area:

Six miles beyond Galway is a place called Lynches Folly from the extravagant designs of the owner, who endeavoured to raise a mount in his garden to such a height as to overtop a high mountaine at the foot of which is is situate, soe as to have a view of the sea and the neighbour-ing country; and he raised it to considerable height but by devouring time it is much crumbled down.[5]

At Kilkenny Castle, the seat of the Duke of Ormonde, the use of water in an exotic, yet practical, French fashion was commented upon by Thomas Dineley during his visit to Ireland in Charles II's reign.[6] Next to a square bowling-green was

a delightfull Waterhouse . . . which with an Engine of curious artifice by the help of one horse furnisheth all the offices of the Castle with that necessary Element. The Waterhouse hath a pleasant summer banquetting room, floor'd and lin'd with white and black marble,[7] which abounds here, with a painted skye roof with Angells; in this is seen a fountaine of black marble in the shape of a large cup with a jet d'eau or throw of water ariseing mounts into the hollow of a Ducall Crown [Plate 2], which but hangs over it, and descends again at severall droping places around.

1 THOMASTOWN, CO. TIPPERARY. *Oculus in garden wall.*

2 KILKENNY CASTLE, CO. KILKENNY. *Fountain in waterhouse from* Journal of Thomas Dineley . . . *in the reign of Charles II.*

3 BURTON HOUSE, CO. CORK. *A reconstruction by Rolf Loeber.*

4 RATHCLINE, CO. LONGFORD. *From an estate map in the National Library of Ireland MS 8646 (6).*

Ormonde employed a French gardener at Kilkenny, for in a letter from the Earl of Orrory to Ormonde on 2 July 1664 he mentions 'Carrie, your French gardiner, is very laborious, and hath undertaken to make a fountain in the centre of the court-yard where the alleys meet at Kilkenny which shall perpetually rise 24 foot high.'[8] Another fountain in the form of a Triton and shell spouted water from its mouth and there was also a grotto.

These gardens at Kilkenny were mentioned later by John Dunton, after a visit in 1699. By then the garden next to the bowling-green had gone to seed, but was being repaired by 'a young gardiner from England, and will in a few years, be as pleasant as the Spring Gardens near Foxhall [Vauxhall]'.[9]

The development of Irish gardens went on apace during the Caroline period and many English gardeners are mentioned in the contemporary letters of 'improvers' all over the country. Rolf Loeber[10] notes that all the new seats were surrounded by deer parks, decoys, pleasure gardens, bowling-greens and waterworks, going on to say that the pleasure gardens often comprised an integral part of the fortified enclosures such as at Burton House, County Cork and Rathcline, County Longford (Plates 3 and 4). Their design was usually made up of rectangles or squares, intercepted by gravelled walks sometimes bordered by box hedges and close walks of ash. The walls provided ornament and shelter for a variety of trees, and flowers in flower pots of Dutch or Irish manufacture were not uncommon.[11] Radiating avenues and rows of trees, compass-like, led off into the distance sometimes on axis with the local church. Canals and ponds besides being ornamental were, of course, stores for carp, trout and roach. Most gardens were also furnished with a pigeon house, aviary and ice house, buildings that often added to the ornamentation of the layout. All this Caroline development was unfortunately curtailed and much was destroyed in the subsequent Williamite war.

The Dutch school of gardening had its adherents in Ireland, and J. C. Loudon, writing in the nineteenth century, mentioned that 'in King William's time, knots of flowers, curious edgings of box, topiary works, grassy slopes, and other characteristics of the Dutch style had come into notice.'[12] This Dutch style was designed chiefly for the cultivation of fruit, flowers and vegetables, and its essence consisted of a compart-mented privacy which did not lead the eye to outside views and lengthy vistas. In fact these 'frittered enclosures', as Horace Walpole called them, were not unlike rooms adjoining the house, and were decorated with turf, gravel walks, fountains and statues. Loudon also mentioned that two Englishmen, Rowe and Bullein, who successively had nurseries near Dublin, were the chief propagators of the style in Ireland.[13] This is borne out by a description, obviously partially based on Loudon, of the gardens at Stillorgan, County Dublin, which were said to have been laid out in the Dutch style by Bullein for Colonel John Allen in 1695:

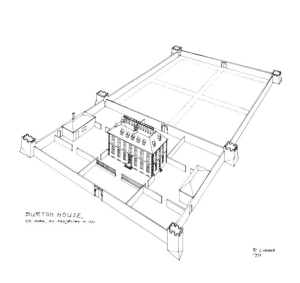

BURTON HOUSE, CO. CORK, AS PROJECTED IN 1671

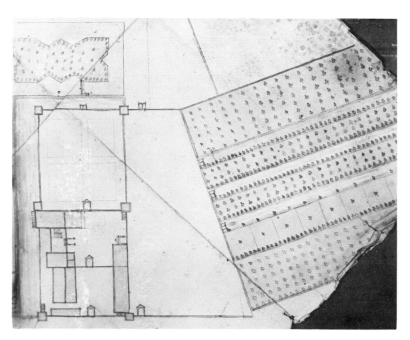

The gardens abounded in straight avenues and alleys with curious edgings of box, carefully clipped yew trees, knots of flowers, topiary work and grassy slopes, and possibly there might have been, as there was in Bullein's nursery, the representation of a boar hunt or hare chase cut out in box. Three artificial fish ponds, laid out, like everything else, on strictly rectangular lines, lay to the south of the house.[14]

The French Huguenots brought new horticultural expertise to Ireland after the Williamite wars.[15] Sir Erasmus Borrowes[16] relates that at Portarlington for instance these colonists 'exchanged the sword for the plumb-rule, the pruning hook, and the plough share'; and the houses backed on to the street, looking over gardens arranged in plots and departments for vegetables and fruit. They planted black Italian walnut trees and 'Jargonelle pears', and the walls contained bricked niches for beehives. Borrowes quotes a bill for seeds and plants brought from The Hague by a Portarlington refugee in 1722: 'Esparagus, raadishes, tamotas, sencitive plants, several sorts of latices, and about 60 sorts of flower seeds, leamon or citron trees, yppaticas, orange trees, mhirtle balls in pots, and turnip seed'. They tried growing vines, and in the 1720s these Huguenots formed a florists' club in Dublin.

5 STILLORGAN, CO. DUBLIN. *Formal layout: Elton Hall plan.*
6 STILLORGAN. *View of house and garden: oil on canvas by Gabriele Ricciardelli.*
7 STILLORGAN. *Sir Edward Lovett Pearce's obelisk: engraving by Brooks, c. 1730.*

However, it would seem that the French baroque style of Le Nôtre soon took over, for an anonymous early eighteenth-century drawing, from an album of drawings for Stillorgan, at Elton Hall, Northamptonshire,[17] shows the way in which the entrance front of the Dutch-influenced house with its Palladian wings was approached by an enormous oval forecourt and three radiating avenues in the Versailles tradition (Plate 5). A mid-eighteenth century painting (Plate 6)[18] also at Elton Hall, by the Neopolitan painter, Gabriele Ricciardelli (1722–93), conveniently portrays the rear façade and also the clumps of approximately forty-year-old trees which make up a series of radiating vista-like gaps. One of these is closed by Sir Edward Lovett Pearce's magnificent obelisk (1727) on a Berninesque rock-work base (Plate 7). Pearce also designed an elaborate grotto approached by rigidly formal cut banks and rusticated walls, part of which also survives.

The best picture of a late seventeenth-century garden in the French baroque style, complete with crow's foot avenues, parterres and clipped yews, can be seen in Johann van der Hagen's bird's-eye view of Carton, County Kildare, circa 1730 (Plates 8 and 9). In this painting the prospect tower is on the hill in the right foreground, and straight avenues radiate from a semi-circular parterre in front of the house. In the far distance on the left, to the north-west, is the keep of Maynooth Castle. Between that

8 CARTON, CO. KILDARE. *Oil on canvas: attributed to Johann van der Hagen, c. 1730.*

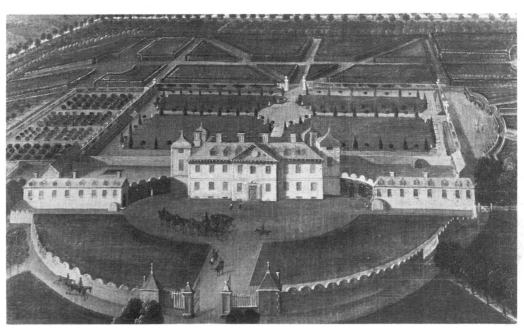

9 CARTON. *Detail of Plate 8 showing the formal gardens.*

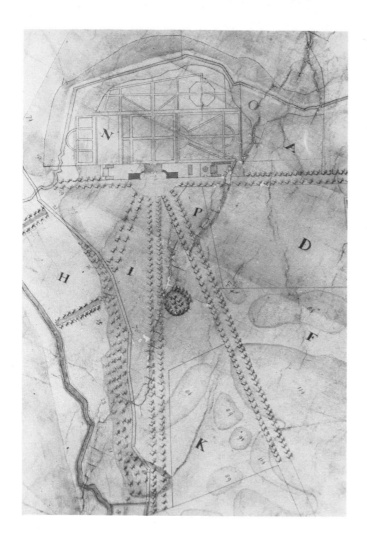

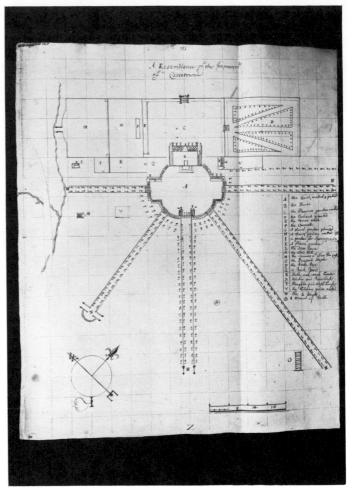

10 CARTON. *Baylie & Mooney Estate map, 1744.*
11 CARTON. *Late seventeenth-century plan at Holkham, Norfolk.*

12 KILRUDDERY, CO. WICKLOW. *The two long canals.*
13 KILRUDDERY. *The Angles.*
14 KILRUDDERY. *The Kilruddery Hunt: oil on panel, c. 1730.*

and Carton runs the Ryewater that was to become the main feature of the Brownian landscape which was developed on the south-east side of the house from which van der Hagen has taken his perspective view: in fact, this was on the opposite side of the house to the landscaping prior to 1720. Although the hills to the southeast in the far distance are artistic licence, the detail in the foreground is accurate, as can be seen from a comparison with Charles Baylie's and John Mooney's survey map of 1744, some fourteen years later (Plate 10). The bones of this layout are also clearly portrayed in a drawing at Holkham, dating from the end of the seventeenth century; it appears to show the Jacobean house before the addition of the Dutch Palladian pedimented block which appears in Plate 11. During this period the estate was meadow and pasture, with fine gardens round the substantial mansion-house. It remained in the family of Ingoldsby until 1739 when it was sold to the Earl of Kildare for eight thousand pounds.

Fortunately, at Kilruddery, County Wicklow, the seat of the Earls of Meath, there still exists intact the most complete late seventeenth- or early eighteenth-century formal garden in the country. In front of Sir Richard Morrison's Tudor revival house are two long canals that train the eye to a lime avenue leading uphill through the park (Plate 12). To the left are cut lime, hornbeam and beech hedges, long since known as the 'Angles' (Plate 13), with statues at the intersections and enclosed by further hedges of yew. These are shown fully grown in a charmingly naïve topographical painting of the early eighteenth century, still in the house, of the original building and layout, the view of which also depicting the Kilruddery Hunt in full cry (Plate 14).[19] In another part of the garden, to the right of the canals, there is an enormous round pond with a surrounding fifty-foot-high beech hedge, cut into arches and niches for statues (Plate 15). This must be of a later date, for it does not appear in the painting. Though many of the statues, fountains and ornaments in the garden are nineteenth century, they happily carry on the French baroque tradition, and there is no reason to doubt that many of them replaced similar ornaments from an earlier period. Cut banks surround flowerbeds, and a small amphitheatre, used for amateur theatricals (reminding one of the description of Thomastown already quoted), silently broods behind its attendant laurel hedge. Monckton Milnes, visiting the Meaths in the mid-nineteenth century, especially noted these gardens with their groves of ancient ilexes and 'yews planted before the flood'.[20] The gardens must date from the late seventeenth century, for a newspaper sale advertisement of 1711[21] describes the property as having 'a new Summer House . . . with 4 rooms on a Floor well wainscotted, and in good order, with pleasure Garden, cherry Garden, Kitchen Garden, New Garden, Wilderness, Gravel Walks, and a Bowling-Green, all walled about, and well planted with Fruit Trees, with several Canals or Fish Ponds . . .'.

15 KILRUDDERY. *Beech hedges and round pond, c. 1900.*

Another important Irish garden of this type, still partially remaining, is at Antrim Castle, County Antrim, where lime hedges, a canal and a Danish mound survive alongside the empty shell of the house.

Mrs Delany visited Antrim Castle in October 1758 and noted that 'the garden was reckoned a fine one forty years ago – high hedges and long narrow walks.'[22] This tells us that the garden was already in its prime as early as 1718. When James Boyle was collecting material for the Antrim *Ordnance Survey Memoir* between 1835 and 1840, he made particular note of this important Irish garden, and his description of the 'wilderness', terraces and mount, is worth quoting in full:

The 'Wilderness' is at once unique and curious in its arrangement being a perfect specimen of the French style of gardening in the 17th century. And though almost flat and extending over no greater extent than 37 acres it is so laid out as to seem more than double its real size.

It consists of a grove thickly wooded with very tall and tapering elms, interspersed with a few other trees and some shrubs, traversed by numerous perfectly straight alleys and walks, and these again intersected by several curiously contrived vistas cut through the planting and bearing on some interesting object such as the round tower, the church spire, the chapel etc. and at the termination of two of them are handsome bases [vases] supported by pedestals.

The grounds are also ornamented by some beautiful ponds. One of these is 220 yards long and 10 yards broad, a walk and a splendid lime hedge 18 feet high extends along each side of it. There are two other ponds which are circular, the largest of these is 186 yards in circumference.

Towards the western side of the Wilderness is a curious little parterre [indecipherable] yards square surrounded by a beautiful lime hedge 20 feet high and laid out in the most fantastic manner. Some of the beds contain flowers but numberless little ones laid out in every variety of shape, enclosed by boxwood edging contain only gravel, each containing a different colour. In the centre of the parterre is a yew tree 14 feet high in the form of an obelisk.

A little to the north and nearly opposite the castle are the terrace gardens which consist of a beautiful range of flower beds extending along three sides of a square 110 × 108 yards. They are 16 feet wide and raised 9 feet above the adjacent ground, a high wall encloses them from a kitchen garden in the centre and a lower one from the grounds on the outside. They contain a choice selection of flowers and shrubs, among which are some fine myrtles.

Close to the north side of the castle is a mount 37 feet high and 51 yards in diameter at the base and 12 at the summit. It seems to be one of the old Danish mounds commonly met with in the country.

It is planted with a variety of trees and shrubs and a well-constructed spiral walk leads to its summit.[23]

Then, as now, these gardens were open to the 'strangers' and 'the people of Antrim'.

Fragmentary sections of this type of garden survive at Birr Castle, County Offaly in the form of a thirty-five-foot-tall box hedge *allée*, and there was a maze there until this century (see page 98). At Saunders Grove, County Wicklow (Plate 16) one could still see until recently the sad ruin of a splendid, long, stepped, Marly-style waterfall on an axis with the house (Plate 17).[24]

There were certainly others, for John Rocque's maps of the environs of Dublin,[25] dating from the 1750s, show many of them, a typical example being Santry Court (Plate 18). Further evidence can be unearthed from an unpublished account of a tour dated 1709 that noted 'improvements'. The author, Samuel Molyneux, saw ample proof of the rage for French formal gardening, describing Gaulstown, County Westmeath, as:

A most notable improvement designed by Mr. Rochfort, part of which is to be a canal already almost finished, tis ye most noble canal by far I ever saw and cousin Dopping assured us as fine as any he had seen in England. It has three noble large Basons one at each end and one in the middle. Tis twenty one yds broad and 1000 long. A Terras Wall on each side planted with Lime trees. In the furthest Bason from the House stands on an Island a Pretty Summer House which very agreeably Determines your view . . .[26]

Elsewhere, Molyneux saw in County Carlow at Garrihunden 'a very pretty new improved garden of grass, greens, gravel, etc. A large Bason and fountain in the middle of the garden and a noble Canal at the end of it'. The gardens at Burton Hall in the same county he described as being 'after the new manner. Grass and Gravel and [they] are indeed handsome, particularly the Bowling Green and a large gravel Walk at the end of the wood. On either hand is prettily cut into Walks and Avenues to the

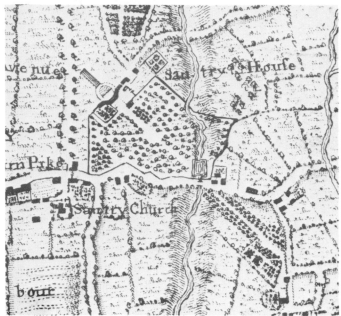

Garden.'[27] This estate was described in 1749 by William Chetwood: 'The Avenue that leads to the beautiful House is at least an English Mile long . . . a wood not forty years old, cut into a variety of Vistas. The house is much the same age as the wood.' He also saw a stone wall nine feet high surrounding the estate, and at the end of a vista a statue of a gladiator, 'a Good Copy of that finished Original now in Hampton Court Gardens'. He went on to say the woods were 'illuminated (memorable day) with a large number of Lamps, placed in regular rides, after the manner of Ranelagh. The beautiful Cascade is adorned with elegant statues, some of which are Originals brought from Italy.'[28]

Swift, who knew Thomastown and Gaulstown, also used to ride on Lord Moles-

18   SANTRY COURT, CO. DUBLIN. *Detail of Rocque's map of Co. Dublin, 1757.*

14

worth's estate at Breckdenstown near Swords, County Dublin.[29] Molesworth had brought the Italian architect, Alessandro Galilei, to Ireland to work on his garden, in 1716. It is not certain what part the Italian played in it, for Molesworth had been planning and making his formal layout as early as 1709. His partially published correspondence[30] gives us more information about the laying out of an eighteenth-century formal garden than exists elsewhere in Ireland, or almost anywhere else in the British Isles.

Robert Molesworth wrote to his wife on 12 July 1709, giving her instructions as to the planting and laying out of the grounds. Talking of the design for the 'wildernesses' he said: 'Remember to leave rounds or ovals in the middle of each [wilderness] for a basin and also near the corners for four small ones. The walks must be very narrow and close, yet the principal ones a little broader than the others.' These wildernesses seem to have been relatively formal, for in 1709 there was little taste for irregularity in garden design. However, Molesworth may well have known Sir William Temple's famous essay and been aware of the irregular implications of the word 'sharawadgi', as it would seem plausible to suggest that Swift was responsible for introducing him to this essay, as Swift had not only been living at Moor Park, Surrey, when working for Temple, but had imitated the gardens there on a small scale of two acres at Laracor, County Meath, in 1699.

On 18 November 1710, Molesworth sent another letter from his English home, Edlington, concerning a water-house and cistern: 'This may be a handsome open summer house upon pillars under it facing the sea and Sword's Steeple.' He was constructing fishponds, canals and a pigeon house in 1711, and on 29 November 1712 he again informed his wife about plans for further improvements:

When the water from the river is brought up, and the long canal 40 yds wide made, the sides of which planted as it ought to be [presumably with lime allées] and the overplus water (which would be great in winter) conveyed by cascades down the hill again to the ponds. What a sight this would be! Yet all this, with the fine water summerhouse and the leaden large cisterns upon it, and the 5 or 6 basins in the gardens and wildernesses with pipes would not stand in 500 £ sterling, a small sum for so great a beauty . . . but nature has done its work so well that it would do. All this water on the very top of a hill, with the sea, ships, rocks and steeples beyond it in view, would be such a sight that I doubt to whether the world would afford the like.

His enthusiasm for the work and the surrounding view increased and soon further plans were made. Mrs Molesworth scribbled to her husband on 12 June 1714:

Mr. Stew.[art] has been in the north at Mrs. Hamilton's of Tullamore [County Down] where he saw a most noble canal 300 or 400 yards long made by her gardener, an Englishman and a very understanding man . . . whenever he heard it (our canal) was to be begun, he would come into this country to assist us. He says that there are as many very understanding workmen of this country to be had, so that you need not be at the expence of bringing anyone out of England for it, at least before you hear and see these here. What I apprehend you will most want is a mason for your stoneworke, I think men of skill in that trade are very scarce here.

They imported 'flowers and flowering schrubs' from England and he bought apple and pear trees from the fashionable royal gardener 'Mr. Wise of Brompton Park'. Elsewhere, Molesworth talked about the plans of his friend, Mr Secretary Johnston, for the garden, and referred to Johnston's buying elm trees for him at Twickenham.[31]

The name of Alessandro Galilei appears in connection with the garden in 1716 and 1717. On 7 June 1718 Molesworth (by then a viscount) discussed with his wife Lord Blessinton's garden in County Wicklow. The print reproduced in plate 147 shows that the house was a typical seventeenth-century Dutch-inspired pile, similar to Stillorgan, Eyrecourt and Beaulieu. Rocque's map[32] reveals that a few radiating avenues led from it, and that the old village church was used to close the main vista. Molesworth smugly commented: 'I thought you had known my Lord Blessinton's gardener: if your acquaintance of him be but at second hand (though it be Secretary Johnstons), I rely not a bit on it . . . in truth I would wonder how a good gardener could find matter to work upon and show his skill in such a mountain as

Bessinton [*sic*]. I think I shall send to Holland for a Kitchen gardener.'

By 1719 in an unpublished letter[33] to that great improver, Lord Coningsby,[34] he summarizes all his gardening activities. This letter is of such interest that it is reproduced here almost in its entirety:

Breckdenstone near Dublin
Tuesday May the 26th 1719

My Lord

On this day was sevenight I safely reached my own house, from whence I have the honour now of writing to y^r L^{d}p & in the first place to return my thanks for all y^r favours, in the next to desire you to remember me when you have got ye designs of ye water contrivances at Bushy Park: I found my hop yard much beyond any (in growth & prosperity) of what I left in England: my hop vines as thick as my finger had already (on ye 20th instant) reached above ye topps of their Poles. & in my gardens & orchards such a plenty of all sorts of fruits (except Apricots) that I never expected the like. but what surprized me most agreably was ye quantity of apples, more than ever I saw at one time & likely now to be out of Danger being for Y^e most part as big as small walnuts. I acquainted out 2 Ld Chief Justices & some other gentlemen improvers with Mr Switzers[35] ability, & his design to visit Dublin they seem very fond of him & really I believe his comeing over (assisted by what favour & countenance I can give him) will answer his end. but by his not meeting you at Hamptn Court I suppose my Ld Cadogans departure has made him alter his project of seeing this country. . .

I amuse my self with ye business of my estate & the diversions of my Grounds & gardens. I dare averr that I have by much the finest Canal near compleated in the Kings dominions, with regard to ye situation, in respect to ye house & gardens & to ye Sea & to all ye prospects, tis not much less than that in St James's Park. but tis infinitely more beautifull & herein I do not exaggerate & I shoud be glad y^r L^{d}p had such a just occasion as I wish for, to view it upon ye spott & disprove me if you coud: I have a great many chimerical designs of my own & of others for y^r large parterre wch leads down to it from whence I have ye noblest prospect of the main ocean, of ye Harbour of Malahide, & ye Sand Downs beyond it of Severall rising rocks & Islands, (such as Lambay, Hoath, Irelands Eye, Feltrim Hill, Malahide Hill, with many castles & churches & Wind mills &c), that I my self who have bin so long used to it am charmd with it. I can see ye Fleets of Shipps pass by to ye Bay of Dublin as I lye in my bed: yet I am above 3 miles from ye Wide Sea & have no manner of ill influence from it lying so much above it as I do, with a gentle descent all ye way to it, & ye harbour. (wch is within 2 long miles of my house) & where at this instant I have a Ship of 80 tunns laden wth Coales for my use lying ready to be unloaded to morrow so that y^r L^{d}p may see I do not intend to lye idle this summer but shall be deep in mortar & other work too chargeable for a purse like mine, wch gett's nothing to speak of from a Government I have served all my Life. however I can not refrain doing, tho I spend my whole income, & I coud wish for Mr Switzer to joyn his maggots to mine, & I am vain enough to think he woud learn as much here as he woud teach us. I have & shall manage a little water to as great advantage as any man in Britain, tho I want proper workmen & instruments for the execution of my designs. this Kingdom affording none good . . .

I had brought to my house on fryday last (immediately out of ye Sea for my Dinner) a turbott larger then any dish in my kitchen & 4 inches at least in thickness. I had our 2 Ld Chief Justices & other worthy gentlemen my neighbours to the eating it, it was ye most delicate morsel I had tasted of for these many years past. & I had ye honour to begin y^r L^{d}ps health & to see it pledgd with good affection by everybody for no Tory approaches my house or table. But tho we have now gotten Carp among us wch breed very well yet I want such as youres, & we have no Perch graylings or Crow fish, as yet in this kingdom. but I have most excellent perch & trouts, & Pike, & shall soon have plenty of Carp, so that w^t with these & what ye Sea constantly furnishes us with we make a shift to indulge in fish. indeed I think y^r mutton is better th^n ours, wch is too Large. we can get none of that very small size wch is sweetest & best for a gentleman's own table. & is so rare to be had even at London.

Thus my Lord I have given you an ample account of my self, what we do, what we have. what we want. You will think by ye Length of this letter that I am very Idle, & imagine you to be so too, when I propose to give you ye trouble of reading it. but ye heat of ye day is not to be endured abroad, & I cannot pass it over better then in discourseing with a good friend. I wish y^r gardiner's brothers were as good & skillful as he is. I shoud not be long without one of them, principally for my kitchen & fruit, tho I have mellons now bigger then my fist in pretty plenty. but my hedges & greens are not near so well clipped as your L^{d}ship's. one may see at Hampton Court that ye Owner of it neither wants Genius nor mony nor heart to lay it out; the middlemost of these 3 particulars is what cannot be braggd of by my Lord

y^r most faithfull & affec^t humble serv^t
Molesworth

In 1720, the garden at Breckdenstown was still progressing, and Molesworth describes it with obvious pleasure on 27 December 1720: 'A great circular or oval basin is a most beautiful thing. The elms about it shall be planted 30 or 40 foot asunder, in double rows, by which means all the fine prospect will appear under their branches and between the intervals of trees till they grow exceeding old.' Again one is reminded of the regimented formality of it all.

Molesworth's son, John, had been dispatched on an extensive Grand Tour. Evidently his father had sent him glowing accounts of his gardening activities, for, replying from Turin on 10 December 1721, John wrote: 'I rejoice to see so many authentic attestations to the beauties of Breckdenstown, which even in description make a great figure, and must in reality be a Paradise . . .' He also made suggestions about the purchasing of statues and urns:

It is of them as of pictures that good copys are better than scurvy Originals: 500^{tt} would go but a little way if such were made by the best hands here, besides which, freight would mount very high; whereas there are very tolerable things to be purchas'd at Hyde-park corner [the Cheere workshops], near at hand, & of which the very lead will yield something in case the figures chance to be spoiled. I remember some Niches at the corners of the walls in the parterre: if Yr Ld. intend to place any Statues there I suppose they will be Fauns & Satyrs or at least some of those Pastoral figures of Shepherds & Shepherdesses wch I see in the road to Hyde Park: the same will also fit the centers in the Wildernesses, for I do not know whether any *Dii Termini* are to be had ready made.

He also thought a Venus would do well for the middle of a grass plot. Interestingly, he advised that 'cornice is cheap at Bristol for the edging of basins'. It has been common practice in Ireland since medieval times to import stone already cut from Bristol. Later in the letter he sent an inscription for the garden, saying: 'the Greek motto will agree very well with the other fountain under the house, upon the side of a hill, the situation in a gloomy grove authorizing an air of mystery'.

Lord Molesworth replied on 27 February, 1722:

If you meet with any choice books relating to fine gardening and waterworks, fountains etc. of the manner of conveying and collecting water, pray purchase such at my expense: I am grown a great water-monger. . . . I once saw some French Folios of this sort . . . The Cutts & draughts in them were very fine . . . I thank you for your sketches for fountains, but they are much too costly for me, & besides we have no workmen or materials to make such things. Shells indeed & rotten rocks we have enough of: I must think of some cheap yet pretty ornament & bring my spring thro a grotesque or mask face into a Shell Bason . . .

Writing to his son again on 5 March 1723, in a particularly illuminating letter he revealed how much he had already spent on his gardening projects:

I never exceed above £150 per annum [in estate improvements] whatever you may hear to the contrary, except when the canal was digging, & then I believe it stood me in £300. There is neither bench, statue, fountain of stone, stairs, urn or flower pot here as yet, so that you may judge that meer grass, trees, hedges cannot cost much. Yet there have not been wanting envious fooles who gave out I had spent £1,000 here . . .

Unfortunately, Molesworth's gardening achievements, like so many others in Ireland, have been swept away, though it is still possible to see the remains of the long canal, and a fairly clear view of the formal layout is provided in John Rocque's invaluable map (Plate 19).

Formal gardens were being planned throughout Ireland. We find that as far afield as Ardfert, County Kerry, 'Sir Maurice [Crosbie] has a fine lawn behind his house and beautiful heights to fifty feet like those at Kensington.'[36] The remains of his 'lawn' with cut banks still survive. The old Castle Bernard, County Cork, which was built in 1715, was described as having a 'fine garden on three sides of the house, adorned with fountains, statues, and other decoration. That on the north is a most delightful spot, called the water garden, with cascades, *jet d'eau*, etc.'[37] Templeogue, County Dublin, boasted a Doric rotunda on a ramped mount (Plate 20). This was moved to Santry Court, where it stood until the end of the nineteenth century.[38] Also at Templeogue were 'artificial cascades in the Marly style with statues and urns on

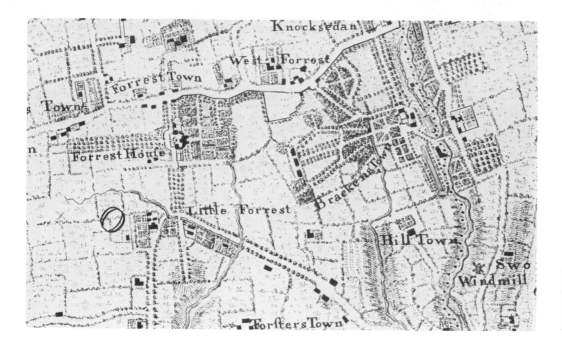

either side'.[39] An interesting portrait by the Irish artist, Anthony Lee, of Sir Compton Domville, Bt., shows him pointing at the ground plan (Plate 21) of his formal garden, centred on a canal of exactly the same shape as the Kilruddery examples. Presumably the canal terminated with the cascade, which appears in the background of the painting. The inspiration for this rockwork waterfall probably came from the elaborate plates of French and Italian gardens shown in Stephen Switzer's *An Introduction to a System of Hydrostatics* (1729).

Evidently complaints about not being able to find garden ornaments were to become unwarranted, for such ornaments were soon being advertised in the Dublin papers. Thomas Greenway, the Bath mason and architect, found it worth his while to come to Dublin in 1730, advertising himself as:

Thomas Greenway, Stone-cutter from Bath having lately imported a large number of Flower Potts, urns and Vases, of the newest and most fashionable pattern, and also several other ornamental pieces, fit for Gentleman's Houses in the City, or Seats in the Country, all curiously wrought in Freestone, proposes to sell the above Pieces at very reasonable Prices; and if during his stay here any Gentleman or Other are pleased to make use of him he is ready to wait on them with a great Variety of Draughts, of all kinds, and will forward such Pieces as they shall please to be speake, with Care and Dispatch. He is to be spoke with, or directed by

Letter, at Mr. Housewalls, Trunk Maker, at the Lower End of Wine Tavern-Street, Dublin.[40]

Another provincial example from Cork reads:

Just imported from London, by John Daly, Marble-Mason, a large quantity of Ornaments of Stone and Lead, such as Statues, Urns, Flower-potts, Vases, Pines, Lions, Eagles, Foxes, Hares, Rabetts, and Sun Dial Pedestals, which goods he will sell cheaper than any gentleman can import.[41]

The formal landscape at Pakenham Hall, County Westmeath, survived until the late eighteenth century (Plate 22). George Pakenham shows some of the details which are mentioned by him in his diary for 1736, now in the possession of Thomas Pakenham:

My brother's house is situated in the declivity of a hill from whence descending by variety of slope-works you come to a basin of 300 foot wide; from this is a cascade falling into another basin at the head of a canal, 150 foot wide and 1,200 foot long. On each side a large grass walk planted with trees. From this canal there runs in a direct line another near a mile in length, equal in breadth to the first, and terminates in a large basin at the foot of three or four beautiful hills . . .

So, although the cascade was wild and natural, it was formally set in a layout of basins and straight canals.

An exactly similar situation must have existed at Woodstock near Gowran, County Kilkenny, the seat of Sir William Fownes. In 1736 Henry Brownrigg wrote to Sir William from Orleans where he had been buying trees for him from French nurseries:

I'm delighted with the account you give of yourself and your Improvements . . . It surprizes me how you could do so much in so short a time. I have your new walk in my mind's eye and find it delightfull; the Cascade opposite the house is so wild and natural that everybody of Taste must like it . . . Your fruit trees are now at Rouen and lest they might suffer, I desired

21 TEMPLEOGUE. *Sir Compton Domville, Bt.: portrait in oil by Anthony Lee, c. 1740.*

19

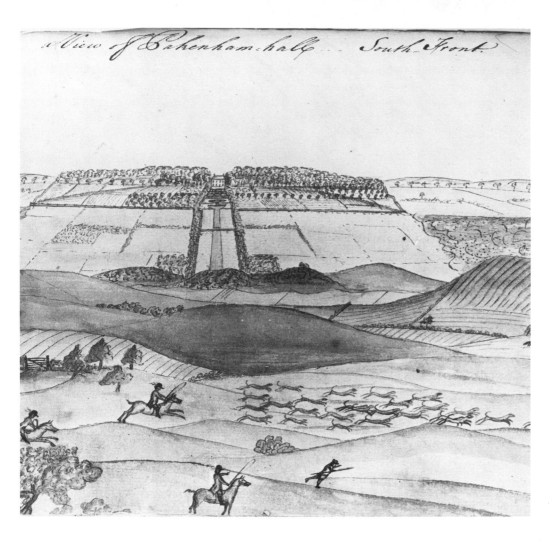

a View of Pakenham hall . . . South Front .

22 PAKENHAM HALL,
CO. WESTMEATH. *South
front: watercolour by
George Pakenham, 1736.*

the Gentleman I sent them to . . . to send them off by the first ship bound either for Dublin or
Corke . . . Orleans is the Nursery of France for fruit trees, and.'tis from thence the Carthusian
furnishes himselfe as well as most of the Gard'ners in France. This is a truth I'm convinced of,
but as you desir'd I would apply to him I did so, from the extravagant demands he made, and
knowing he has his trees from hence I made use of a Nursery Man here, who I believe is
very knowing and has the character of an honest man, his name is Vincent Transon and must be
known to the Gardner recommended by Miller;[42] he goes every year to London with Trees,
furnishes most of the Nobility and in particular Ld Burlington some of whose Letters he shew'd
me . . . I have muster'd up 74 dwarfe Peaches; don't believe by the number I send that they
are easily had. I knew they would please so took what pains I could to procure them. The
Gardners assur'd me that there are not so many in all France . . . I have sent you some of the
true Maroniers de Lyons, Vines red and white to be stuck down by the Rocks, 4 bundles of
Paradise Stocks for your Nursery . . . I have since made up a small baskett containing 4
pomegranate trees which bear fruit and which only bear a double flower and are curious, and
two Cypress trees which I would have you plant by the Cascade, and if they take plant a row or
two on each side. I think they are common in Ireland, but if you cant have them I'll send some
over; there is no tree that has a more solemn or venerable air. I think they will add greatly to
the beauty of the Cascade.[43]

Certain Irish landlords' enthusiasm for formal improving and planting increased
even during the second quarter of the century. For instance John Bourke of Palmers-
town, County Kildare, later first Earl of Mayo, wrote of his activities to his fellow
Irish parliamentarian, Henry Boyle of Castlemartyr, County Cork – a descendant of
the great Earl of Cork – who, in his turn, after being Speaker of the Irish House of
Commons, was later created Earl of Shannon. Bourke apologizes for not having
written, in a letter dated 30 June 1729: 'You should have heard from me much sooner,
but that I waited to be able to give you a full account of my Elms, I believe scarce the
half of them are vigorous, and there are some even now pulling out, but I doubt they
will not live; I just filled my Canal in order to discover the level exactly . . . and fancy
when you see it next you will like it.' He then elusively mentions, before talking of

his wall going on 'briskly', that 'Caesar travelled very well, but was a little stiff for a week after his journey'. One wonders whether he was joking about an imported statue or mentioning a horse! Two months later he wrote again hoping that Mr Boyle and his wife Lady Harriet would pay him a visit on their way to parliament in Dublin, 'tho' to be sure, Planting would be a much more agreeable entertainment this Winter, than sweating at Elections in a House of Commons'.

The Shannon Papers, from which these two letters and the following ones are quoted, are at the time of writing only beginning to be catalogued; but these further letters to Henry Boyle throw some light on his estate management at Castlemartyr.[44] Boyle was 'improving' as early as 1718. For instance trees and fishponds were being planted and formed in the demesne, as an encouraging letter from his brother, William, from London dated 27 November attests:

I sincerely retract from what I said in relation to y[ou]r trees and fishponds. 'Tis certain y[ou]r works will not go on nor the designs be so well executed, if you have not a watchful eye, nay two, therefore since you have so great an undertaking in hand, I think you absolutely in the right not to absent yourself from the workmen. I have experienced what it is to leave one's affairs to other people, having paid for what they ordered, and been forced to the expense of demolishing what they had done to make all new again. This has happened to me within these two months and in the compass of three acres; how might you suffer in 250. I wish you success in what you are about and may you long enjoy the pleasure of those innocent country amusements . . .

Later he states: 'I have now made myself acquainted with some of the most noted nurserymen and gardeners, so that if you want anything that this country affords, command me and I will soon find out some ship bound for Cork.'

One of his stewards, Garratt Fleming, gives detailed accounts of the purchase and planting of trees; for instance in March 1728, Fleming talks of 'Dutch elms in the walk', French and English cuttings for the nursery, Dutch alder from Mr Croker (of Ballnagarde) in County Limerick and that 'the bowling green is planted with sycamore'. He also bought 'a thousand fir trees for Col Maynard' (of Curryglass) and noted that 'the chestnut walk is finished and the grass in it is very fine', adding: 'I have planted a great many yew and laurel on both sides of the walks for underwood and have left holes between the laurel and yew to plant holly in them'.

A letter from his 'most Humble and most Obediant nurseryman Alexander Bucks from Ballynacurra ye 5th November 1731' informed him that

most part of ye Large Ash is taken up and now we are about Taking up the smaler sort. Mr. Robert Bettesworth ordered me to take up Every tree little and bigg that is in the Strand Avinew and that I should not Lave a tree in the North part of the Grove where ye Chestnut trees are. We have mostly thin'd ye rest of ye Grove as was don last year but they are two thick still to stand for they are not above 6 ft. asunder. I want to know whither yr. honr. would have the Chestnut trees, wallnut trees, Horsechestnuts, Maples, Duch Elm, Wichezol, Filbud Hezol, and several other trees taken up. I was speaking to Mr. Bellew about them but he did not resolve me. There is a greydale of ash backward of ye Old Church and the Nursery of tal trees Eastwards of ye house . . .'

Later it becomes apparent that the agents, Bettesworth and Bellew, are unwilling to let him have any grass for his cows, and he adds sadly, 'I have noe bysness to Expect any faver or friendship of you when yr. Honr's trees are all taken up.' A letter from Robert Bellew in Dublin, dated 26 October 1732, talks about thinning the nurseries at Ballynacurra and mentions planting ash, oak and birch 'about 3 foot asunder . . . Please God the weather holds Fair'. Bellew frequently wrote to Boyle when he was away in Dublin at 'Lucuses' Coffee house', and in a letter of 5 October 1731, he tells him that 'we mounted 9 Pots for the walk'. Trees and shrubs were commonly set out in pots at this time, along walks or terraces.

Boyle, as described in the last edition of Eustace Budgell's book on the family,[45] was noted for his 'hereditary Taste for Improvements', and Dr Smith[46] describes the layout at Castlemartyr as having a 'large and beautiful canal' in front of the house and many trees; but the most important feature was a serpentine, artificial river which surrounded the demesne and the town of Castlemartyr. This was 'one of the greatest Undertakings of this kind in Ireland', and Smith describes it as being 'regularly Bank'd, it's Sides adorned with fine plantations'. Near the east end of the town it was formed into a series of cascades, and pleasure boats sailed on it. Work went on in a formal fashion until a much later date, for in a letter of 2 December 1760, Robert Pratt tells Boyle, now Earl of Shannon, that 'Mr. Halfpenny staked out the Parterre so as to rise 3 inches in the Centre, and declined to almost nothing at the drains.' The formality of the planting can be seen from the report that 'one tree was wanting in the walk from the elm to the Bowling green, 3 or 4 beyond the fruit house not in the line but back of it.' Two years later Pratt was reporting leaks in the canal. For the history of the sad decline of this interesting demesne, see page 99.

The French formal style surprisingly was still being recommended by George Semple, the builder of Essex Bridge in Dublin, in his *Treatise on Building in Water* as later as 1776. Here he lists various practical recommendations, for when 'a gentleman had an elegant Visto, terminated by a spacious Canal . . . and he requires a foundation . . . whereupon he intends to erect an obelisk', etc. Another recommendation gives directions on how to build 'an elegant octagonal pavilion or Pleasure-house' in the middle of a lake, for viewing the 'natural Landscapes'. This suggests an awareness of the spirit of the late eighteenth century, though his pavilion would have been more in fashion fifty years earlier. He cheerfully adds that 'when the windows are fully illuminated, a Band of Marshall Music etc. on rejoicing Nights will contribute greatly toward the amusement of the Nobility and the ajacent Neighbourhood.'[47]

To return to the 1730s: the sunk ditch or 'ha-ha' became commonly used. In England it had been first seen at Stowe in about 1725.[48] The first mention of an Irish one is in an unpublished description of the Bishop's Palace at Kilmore, County Cavan, in 1739, where an elaborate garden had been laid out in the previous two decades. This garden boasted a 500-yard-long canal opposite the hall door, the middle of which was widened into a basin. On the garden front, facing west, lay a parterre:

agreeably diversified with Verdour Sod, gravel walks, small Fruit Trees, Elms and Arcades of Beech and Hornbeam. The sides are enclosed with High Brick Walls covered with choice Fruit. This parterre terminates in a Deep Ha-Ha, which is the whole length of the Front, on each Angle of the Ha-Ha looking into the centre of the parterre is a large Shell seat, adorned with stucco.[49]

Then, from the parterre, in line with the house, lay an avenue composed of a triple row of elms on either side, terminating 'at the High Road in another Ha-Ha with piers'. Not a sign of this garden survives. For its later history, see page 126.

Views of the formal Irish garden are rare, and a complete plan for the layout at

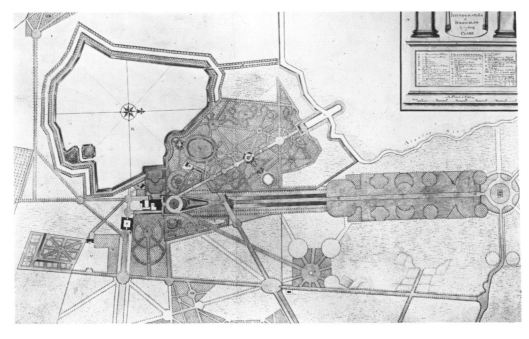

23 DROMOLAND, CO. CLARE. *'Ichnographia' of the entire layout*, c. 1740.

24 DROMOLAND. *The Rotunda.*

25 DROMOLAND. *The Belvedere.*

26 STRADBALLY, CO. LEIX. *Bird's-eye view: oil on canvas by unknown artist, c. 1740.*

Dromoland, County Clare is the most elaborate surviving example (Plate 23).[50] It is on vellum, by an unknown hand, and shows avenues, vistas, terraces, *ronds points* and the superimposition of a formal character on a large lake. The Irish architect, John Aheron, the author of Ireland's first architectural book, worked here for Sir Edward O'Brien, Bt., and designed some of the ornamental buildings on the estate as well as the original house. A fine lead-domed rotunda, complete with a Mercury, in the Vanbrugh Duncombe Park manner (Plate 24), survives, with its vista exactly as is shown on the great 'Ichnographia' as the map was called. A belvedere (Plate 25), for viewing racing, also stands on a hill, though it is off the map. Unfortunately, the plan seems to be by a hand other than Aheron's, though a close collaboration between architect and gardener must have taken place. Certain other features of this baroque garden still remain but now are almost totally masked by a natural late eighteenth-century layout. A whole volume of garden plans with details of cut banks, fences and ornamental features of all kinds still survives.[51]

Aheron also built a large residence at Stradbally, County Leix, and there still hangs in a later house on this site an enormous, primitive bird's-eye view of the estate dating from about 1740 (Plate 26).[52] It shows an extensive formal layout of a compartmented type on either side of a central vista. Statues, temples and other garden structures, even including an outside wooden privy, are dotted over the garden. The significance of this view lies in its exceptionally old-fashioned character, for, except for the main axis of the house and garden vista to the rear, the planning is composed entirely in compartments in the Dutch style, without any French influence. Very little survives.

Two modest, anonymous, overmantel paintings, of about 1740, depict the gardens at Mount Ievers, County Clare (Plate 27), and Howth Castle, County Dublin (Plate 28). Both remain in these houses. At Mount Ievers, the main vista, dovecot, winding stream and canal are in good condition, though nature has softened all the outlines beyond recognition. Howth Castle, however, still shows many traces of its formal garden, including some of the highest beech hedges (Plate 29) in the British Isles.[53] Rocque[54] is again useful, the detail from his map (Plate 30) clearly depicting the composition of the French *bosquets* behind the house, formally intersected by angled walks. An aerial view of Howth shows these woods, vistas, hedges, pond and canal much as they were in the eighteenth century (Plate 31).

At Powerscourt, County Wicklow, Richard Castle, Ireland's most prolific Burlingtonian architect, built between 1731 and 1741 a magnificent Palladian mansion on the site of an earlier house and castle, superbly situated in the Wicklow Hills. The garden front looked down a steep slope, and here an elaborate terraced layout was created. This garden is always considered a purely extravagant nineteenth-century creation of the sixth and seventh Viscounts Powerscourt, made between 1843 and 1875.[55] The pebble terrace, great zinc horses, urns and ironwork certainly date from this period; but, if one looks closely, one sees the skeleton of the original garden in a series of curved amphitheatre-like stepped terraces terminating in a round pond. Two early photographs show the original pond and formal banks before most of the later accretions (Plates 32 and 33). Prior evidence appears on a detail in John Rocque's map of 1760 (Plate 34),[56] and therefore they must be of eighteenth-century date. Fortunately, additional information in the form of a very cursory sketch plan, of about 1740, has recently come to light in a folio of drawings still in existence.[57] This shows a vast formal garden plan with the pond, terrace and a series of crow's-foot vistas. A key notes a 'Laberinth' [sic], a grotto, decoy water, etc.; though the plan is unsigned, mention is made of 'Mr. Townsend and Mr. Ross's work'. The plan is preserved with many other designs including one for a cold water bath, parterres (Plate 35), obelisks, gates (Plate 36) and an amphitheatre (Plate 37). Significantly, bound up with these, are drawings by Richard Castle himself, so it seems that all the plans might originate from his office.[58]

During the year of the great frost of 1741, a great deal of work was going on at Powerscourt. A newspaper report states that 'Richard Wingfield of Powerscourt Esq., so remarkable for employing great Numbers of Labourers, from his unbounded Charity, feeds 150 poor People every day.'[59] Five years later the work may have been finished, as in another newspaper we read:

George Dean who was lately Gardener to Lord Viscount Powerscourt undertakes surveying, designing and laying out all sorts of plans in the Garden Way and other Improvements viz Pleasure Gardens, Parterres, Wildernesses, or Woodworks, Labyrinthes, Kitchen Gardens or Waterworks in their various kinds, bringing the water for the use of Gentlemen's Seats, at the most reasonable expence.[60]

Richard Castle probably oversaw the whole plan, and perhaps the unsigned designs owe their origins to the hand of the George Dean referred to in the quotation. Castle also created cut banks and a formal pond behind Russborough, in the same county, the spade and shovel work alone costing, according to tradition, £30,000 (Plate 38).[61]

All these gardens[62] have one element in common: essentially they reflect the baroque theory that man was overwhelming nature. Nevertheless, by the second quarter of the eighteenth century, this theory had lost its impetus. One of the consequences of the anti-formal movement was to arrest the progress of these pompous and ambitious layouts. Long before 1750 a new conception of man's place in nature was increasingly seen at work. The remaining chapters of this book attempt to record the progress of this movement. Too often, when one today visits the sites of these formal gardens, one

29 HOWTH CASTLE.
Beech hedges.
30 HOWTH CASTLE.
Detail of Rocque's map of Co. Dublin, 1757.

27   MOUNT IEVERS, CO.
CLARE. *Bird's-eye view of
layout: wall painting, c.
1740.*

28   HOWTH CASTLE, CO.
DUBLIN. *Bird's-eye view
of gardens, c. 1740.*

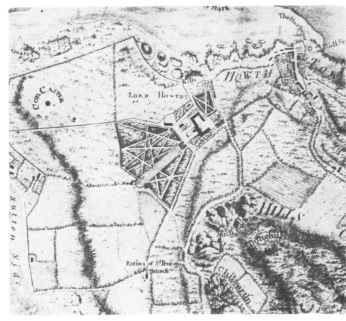

31 HOWTH CASTLE.
*Aerial view: modern
photograph.*
32 POWERSCOURT, CO.
WICKLOW. *The pond:
photograph, 1860.*
33 POWERSCOURT. *The
banks: photograph, 1860.*

34 POWERSCOURT.
*Detail of Rocque's map,
1760.*
35 POWERSCOURT. *A
design for the parterres, c.
1740.*
36 POWERSCOURT. *A
design for the gates.*
37 POWERSCOURT. *A
design for an amphi-
theatre.*
38 RUSSBOROUGH, CO.
WICKLOW. *Detail of
Rocque's map, 1760.*

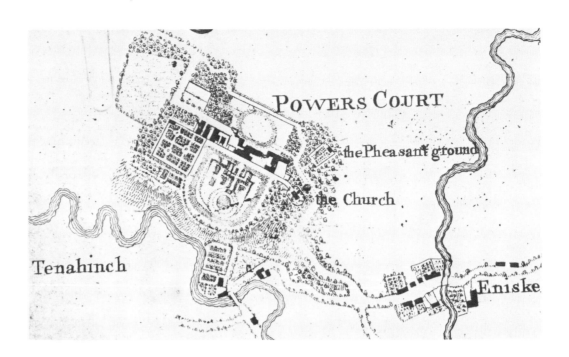

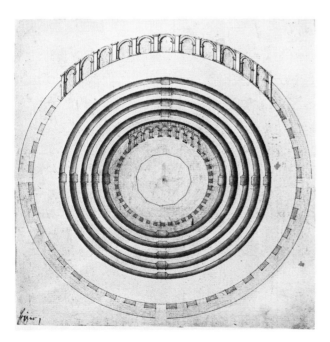

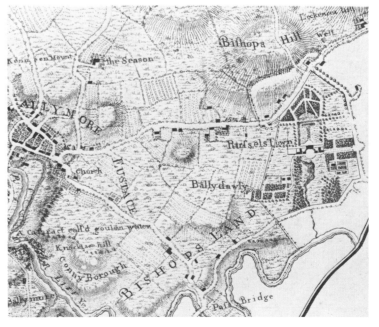

27

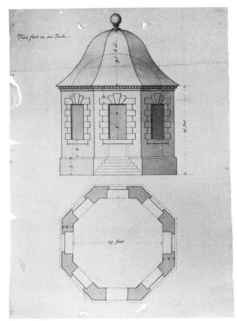

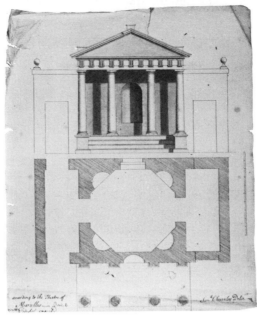

39 OLDTOWN, CO. KILDARE. *Gazebo and temple. The temple drawing is signed 'Sam^e Chearnley Delin'.*

40 GLOSTER, CO. OFFALY. *The Arch.*

follows choked paths to devastated spots, where an undergrowth of nettles and brambles remains triumphant within the confines of ruined and ivy-clad walls. Nature has had her revenge on man.

1. *Transactions of the Royal Irish Academy*, 1790, vol. IV 'Antiquities', pp. 3–19.
2. J. Loveday, *Diary of a Tour through Ireland*, 1732, p. 43.
3. Reverend Thomas Campbell, *A Philosophical Survey of the South of Ireland*, 1778, pp. 169–70.
4. Celia Fiennes called them 'grates'. See Christopher Hussey, *English Gardens and Landscapes*, p. 18. It is curious how similar the Thomastown *oculi* are to the moon gates of the Chinese. See Osvald Sirén, *China and the Gardens of Europe in the Eighteenth Century*, plate 72.

5. Quoted by Edward MacLysaght, *Irish Life in the Seventeenth Century*, 1950, p. 329.

6. 'Journal of Thomas Dineley,' *Kilkenny Archaeological Society*, vol. IV (new series) 1862–63, pp. 105–6. Christopher Wren and Hugh May were asked by Ormonde for advice concerning the construction of this fountain.

7. Kilkenny marble which, until a few years ago, was being quarried.

8. Bodleian Library, Oxford, Carte MS 220 f 102.

9. *Some Account of my Conversation in Ireland*, pp. 51–54.

10. 'Irish Country Houses and Castles of the late Caroline Period; an unremembered past recaptured', *Quarterly Bulletin of the Irish Georgian Society*, vol. XVI, nos. 1 and 2, January–June 1973, pp. 44–48.

11. Quoted by Loeber, 'Irish Country Houses and Castles', p. 46. Dr Loeber in a letter to us states that 'Anthony Tylman, the gardener' at Charleville Castle 'in 1670 was paid by the Earl of Orrery "for 24 fortnights allowance 1669–1670, at £3 10s per fortnight": £84 (NLI. MS 13,197, Orrery MSS) which amounts to £99 10s per year, a high salary for a gardener at that time. He obviously must have been able to offer a lot for such an amount of money. This appears true, for two years later, on 4 February 1672, he appears on the payroll of Sir Philip Perceval who by then was finishing Burton House. The entry reads: "4 feb. 72, Anthony tillman [*sic*] the gardener for planting trees and setting out walks in [the garden] £4.19s". (BM Add. MS 46,949, f.139). To my knowledge this is the first instance of a gardener in Ireland of whom documentation exists that he laid out a garden.'

12. J. C. Loudon, *Encyclopedia of Gardening*, p. 273.

13. Loudon, *Encyclopedia*. Serious interest in shrubs and plants was becoming common. For example, Sir Arthur Rawdon of Moira, County Down, in the early eighteenth century was stimulated by Sir Hans Sloane's collecting of Jamaican plants, and sent his gardener, James Harlow, who had already travelled in Virginia, to Jamaica in search of exotic plants. He built the first hothouse in Ireland to receive them. See Cooper Walker, 'Rise and Progress of Gardening', p. 14. Walter Harris, *A Topographical and Chorographical Survey of the County of Down*, 1740, p. 35, mentions 'the gardens . . . in Good Taste, the Walks, Vistas, the Espaliers regular . . . Here is a pretty Labyrinth, and several Ponds and Canals . . . a wood cut into several Vistas'.

14. F. Elrington Ball, *The History of the County of Dublin*, 1917, p. 122.

15. Albert Carre, *L'influence des Huguenots Français en Irelande*, 1937, pp. 130–31.

16. 'The French Settlers in Ireland – no. 5', *Ulster Journal of Archaeology*, 1855, vol. III, p. 66.

17. See Howard Colvin and Maurice Craig, *Architectural Drawings in the Library of Elton Hall by Sir John Vanbrugh and Sir Edward Lovett Pearce*, where this album, dated 1731, is briefly mentioned in the introduction. Most of the drawings in the album are by Pearce or his office, though the one reproduced here seems to be in an earlier and more primitive manner than the others.

18. See *Irish Houses and Landscapes* (exhibition catalogue), Dublin 1963, pp. 27–28. The picture, with two others, was previously attributed to Dominic Serres.

19. *Irish Houses and Landscapes*, pp. 31–32 and reproduced in plate 3 of that book. J. N. Brewer noted the gardens at Kilruddery in *The Beauties of Ireland*, vol. I, pp. 284–5, contrasting them with the site. 'From the natural grandeur of the surrounding country, the formality of this mode stands revealed with peculiar distinctness. The enclosing mountains rise boldly and at once, with all their brilliance of purple and brown colouring, above the long avenues of stately elms, the close-cut yew hedges, and regular terraces of this little St. Cloud.' The long ponds and circular pond surrounded by a twenty-foot-high beech hedge and the alleys are described in George Petrie and G. N. Wright, *A Guide to the County of Wicklow*, pp. 10–12.

20. James Pope-Hennessy, 'The Flight of Youth', *Monckton Milnes*, London 1951, p. 68.

21. *Dublin Intelligencer*, 14 April 1711, Gilbert MS, Public Library, Pearse Street, Dublin. This was kindly communicated to us by Dr Rolf Loeber.

22. Llanover, *Mrs Delany*, vol. III, p. 517.

23. Republished by the Public Records Office, Belfast 1969, pp. 26–27.

24. The Birr hedges date from the late seventeenth century. They are reproduced by Lanning Roper, *Country Life*, 1964, CXXXVI, p. 1,157. Saunders Grove (now rebuilt) dates from 1718 – *Georgian Society Records*, 1913, vol. V, p. 107.

25. *Carte Topographique de la Comté de Dublin . . . 1757*. This was in four sheets and John Rocque started surveying in 1754. See J. H. Andrews, 'The French School of Dublin Surveyors', *Irish Geography*, 1967, vol. V, no. 4, p. 278, for further information on him and his influence.

26. Samuel Molyneux, MS I.I.3, Trinity College, Dublin, p. 103. For later developments, see p. 34.

27. Molyneux, pp. 89 and 91.

28. William R. Chetwood, *A Tour through Ireland*, 1748, p. 208.

29. F. Elrington Ball, *The Correspondence of Jonathan Swift*, 1912, vol. III, p. 2.

30. Historic Manuscripts Commission, *Report on Various Collections*, 1913, vol. VIII, p. 242. We have, however, also used the original letters now in the collection of Marcus Clements, of Lough Rynn, County Leitrim, and supplemented the Commissioner's report with further extracts. We have not, therefore, footnoted each transcription hereafter.

31. Mr Secretary Johnston lived in a house at Twickenham which was famous for its gardens and an octagon summer house, an especially beautiful room overlooking the Thames. John Macky, *A Journey through England* (1722), p. 61, writes: 'He has the best Collection of Fruit, of all Sorts, of most Gentlemen in *England*. His Slopes for his Vines, of which he makes some Hogsheads a Year are very particular, and Dr. Bradley of the Royal

Society, who hath wrote so much upon Gardening, ranks him amongst the first rate Gardeners in *England*.'

32. Rocque, *Carte Topographique*; J. C. Loudon, op. cit., p. 273, singled out Blessington with Thomastown as being among the most important late seventeenth-century gardens in Ireland: 'Blessington gardens, if tradition may be relied on, were laid out during the reign of Charles I, by an English gentleman who had left his estate at Byfleet in Surrey to escape the persecution of Cromwell.' The house was burnt and demolished in the '1798'. This 'English Gentleman' was Austin Cooper born at Byfleet, Surrey, c.1620. See Richard A. Cooper, 'Genealogical Notes on the (Austin) Cooper Family in Ireland. 1660–1960', *The Irish Genealogist*, vol. iii, no. 9, October 1964, p. 351.

33. PRONI (Belfast) MS D638/82/2. This was kindly brought to our attention by John Cornforth.

34. For his improvements to Hampton Court, Herefordshire, see John Cornforth, *Country Life*, 22 February, 1 and 8 March 1973.

35. See Chapter 2, p. 33.

36. Pádraig O Maidín, 'Pococke's Tour of South and South-West Ireland in 1758', *Journal of the Cork Historical and Archaeological Society*, vol. xxiv, no. 199, June 1959, p. 48.

37. Charles Smith, *The Ancient and Present State of the County and City of Cork*, vol. i, pp. 240–41.

38. *Georgian Society Records*, vol. v, p. xciii. It is now at Luggala, County Wicklow. The watercolour by Gabriel Beranger reproduced in Plate 19 is taken from his 'Rambles Thro' the County of Dublin', RIA 3c 31.

39. Ball, *History of the County of Dublin*, part 3, p. 25.

40. Faulkner's *Dublin Journal*, 15–19 December 1730.

41. *Munster Journal*, 5 February 1750.

42. Philip Miller, *The Gardener's Dictionary*, 1732.

43. Tighe Papers, National Library of Ireland, MS 8802/5.

44. PRONI (Belfast) D2 707/A/I/I – 13296–7.

45. *Memoirs of the Lives and Characters of the Illustrious Family of the Boyles*. The last edition of 1754 gives an account of Lord Shannon.

46. *State of the County and City of Cork*, pp. 127–28.

47. Page 94.

48. C. Hussey, *English Gardens*, pp. 35–36, gives a summary of its origins. See also Peter Willis, 'From Desert to Eden: Charles Bridgeman's "Capital Stroke"', *Burlington Magazine*, March 1973, p. 150 ff.

49. Henry MSS, p. III–12, Public Records Office, Dublin (The Four Courts).

50. In the possession of Lord Inchiquin. See *Irish Architectural Drawings* (exhibition catalogue), Dublin and London 1965, plate 47 and pp. 4–12.

51. Also in the possession of Lord Inchiquin.

52. See *Irish Houses and Landscapes*, p. 31 and illustration on the cover.

53. See F. Elrington Ball, *Howth and its Owners*, 1917, p. 133. The castle was restored in 1738 and the garden dates from about then.

54. Rocque, *Carte Topographique*.

55. The garden architects involved were the English Francis Cranmer Penrose and the Irish Daniel Robertson. See Royal Archaeological Institute of Great Britain and Ireland, *Programme of the Summer Meeting 1960 at Dublin*, p. 34, in which Dr Maurice Craig states that Robertson used to 'be wheeled about the place in a wheel barrow grasping a bottle of sherry; when the sherry was finished Mr. Robertson ended his designing for the day'.

56. Rocque, *Carte Topographique*.

57. Folio I, p. 32.

58. Folio I, pp. 7, 11–13.

59. Faulkner's *Dublin Journal*, 5–9 May 1741.

60. *Dublin Courant*, 6–10 January 1746.

61. *Georgian Society Records*, vol. v, p. 70.

62. Other baroque gardens exist at Oldtown, County Kildare. Drawings in the possession of Major de Burgh show a six-columned Doric rotunda, a gazebo and a Doric porticoed temple, this last signed by Samuel Chearnley (Plate 39). Arch Hall, County Meath, a house possibly by Sir Edward Lovett Pearce, faced a rustic pedimented arch and was flanked by a canal and bridge. Gloster, County Offaly, also has a Vanbrugh-style arch flanked by obelisks terminating a vista to the left of the garden front of the house (Plate 40).

2 Jonathan Swift, Mrs Delany and friends

I often wish'd, that I had clear
For Life, six hundred Pounds a Year,
A handsome House to lodge a Friend,
A River at my Garden's End,
A Terras Walk, and half a Rood
Of Land set out to plant a Wood.

Jonathan Swift, *An Imitation of the
Sixth Satire of the Second Book of Horace*

The emancipation of eighteenth-century landscaping in England from the chains of French and Dutch rules and restrictions was initially the work of writers and artists, chief among whom were Pope and William Kent. It might be thought that their influence would take some years to cross the Irish Sea; but such was not the case. The work of Irishmen, principally Jonathan Swift and Patrick Delany, was simultaneous with that of their English counterparts, with whom they were in close touch. They did not possess the financial resources of the English landscapers, but their aims were the same, as they also had been influenced by the pleas of Shaftesbury and Addison for a more natural landscape. Their own landscaping was on a smaller scale, but their friends' was equal to any in England. Mrs Delany is a remarkable and unique link between this period of vital transition and the later eighteenth-century writers on the picturesque, Uvedale Price and William Gilpin. She was amazingly versatile: a watercolourist, painter in oils, *collagiste*, maker of shell grottoes, *stuccodore*, practical gardener and admirable diarist (her flower paintings and drawings can be seen in the British Museum, and in the National Gallery, Dublin). Her long life (1700–88) therefore links the landscaping views of Swift with those of Jane Austen. As an artist she unfailingly saw landscape in pictorial terms, as did Pope at Twickenham and also Vanbrugh when at Blenheim, as well as poets such as Denham in 'Cooper's Hill' and Thomson in 'The Seasons'. She is an enduring reminder that the theory of the picturesque in its simplest terms has never died; and that parts of Ireland, as can be seen from Mrs Delany's descriptions, are a particularly suitable terrain for the expression of picturesque landscaping.

September 1713 was the month that Swift, aged forty-six (Plate 41) and Pope, aged twenty-five, started that most famous of literary friendships. In that month also an article appeared in Steele's *Guardian* ridiculing topiary work and extolling a more free landscape. It was unsigned but was Pope's work. Before that date, Swift must have read Addison's articles in the *Spectator*[1] in which he described landscaping with 'a little rivulet which runs through a green meadow', a work of nature which was 'more delightful than artificial shows'. Swift certainly would have known the passage in Shaftesbury's *Characteristiks* stating that 'rude *Rocks*, the mossy *Caverns*, the irregular unwrought *Grottos*, and broken *Falls* of Waters, with all the horrid Graces of the *Wilderness* itself, as representing Nature more, will be the more engaging, and appear with a Magnificence beyond the formal mockery of princely Gardens.' Swift must have been struck by the contrast between these sentiments and the practical working out of a garden which he knew well – Sir William Temple's at Moor Park. This garden had been laid out in the 1680s and as a young man Swift had lived there on and off from 1691 until Sir William died in 1699. Nothing could have been more regular than the four large parterres and bowling green which flanked the house, and the remainder of the layout was exactly symmetrical including the canalized River Wey.[2] Only in the wilderness on the other side of the river was there one path which

41　HOWTH CASTLE,
CO. DUBLIN. *Full length
portrait of Jonathan
Swift: oil on canvas by
Francis Bindon, 1735.*

meandered slightly.[3] Although Sir William Temple wrote of a more free Chinese method of landscaping which he called 'sharawadgi',[4] his own garden was as symmetrical in its compartments as the rooms of his house. In fact it was perfectly Dutch, copied from many he had seen when he was ambassador at The Hague. In no way can this garden have influenced Swift to such ideas as art being perfect 'just when it resembles nature'. The nearby Mother Ludwell's Cave, a natural wonder of Surrey, appealed to Swift more. He makes this quite plain in his verses which are so picturesque and 'Cooper's Hill' in spirit: 'A Description of Mother Ludwell's Cave (1693?):

> Consider, Ludwell, what to him[5] you owe,
> Who does for you the noisy court forego;
> Nay he a rich and gaudy silence leaves,
> You share the honour, sweet Moor parke receives.
> You with your wrinkles admiration move,
> That with its beauty better merits love.
> Here's careless Nature in her ancient dress,
> There she's more modish, & consults the glass.
> Here she's an old, but yet a pleasant dame;
> There she'l a fair, not painted Virgin seem.

. . . .
Thus nature is preserv'd in every part
Sometimes adorn'd, but nere debauch'd by art.[6]

These views, which might also be Pope's, were further reinforced in practice after the arrival back in England from Italy of William Kent in 1719, and by the publication of Stephen Switzer's *Ichnographia Rustica* (1718). Although Swift had not then met Kent he would have read Switzer's advocacy as a gardener of *in utile dolce* – the combination of cultivation with pleasure, for this is exactly what Swift was to achieve in his garden in Dublin. In 1719 Pope started to garden in earnest at Twickenham, and in a short time achieved gratifying results. Two years later Lady Mary Wortley Montagu pleased him by remarking on the fineness of his trees in the Great Walk, and in April 1722 she wrote that Pope had made a 'subterranean Grotto' which he had 'furnish'd with Looking Glass'.[7] Before that date she had acknowledged a copy of Pope's verses. 'To Mr. Gay, who wrote him a congratulatory letter on the finishing his House':

> Ah friend, 'tis true – this truth you lovers know –
> In vain my structures rise, my gardens grow
> In vain fair Thames reflects the double scenes
> Of hanging mountains, and of sloping greens.

On 5 October 1725, Pope wrote to the Earl of Strafford he had completed 'a Theatre, an Arcade, a Bowling-Green, a Grove'; but he regretted he had only such a small area to landscape. It was 'like the fellow that spent his life in cutting the twelve Apostles in one cherry-stone'.

Swift's gardening activity was simultaneous with Pope's. On 8 January 1721 as Dean of St Patrick's he obtained the lease of his future garden which he called with his customary plain-spokenness, Naboth's Vineyard.[8] As this name shows, he had brought pressure on a previous leaseholder to part with this section of the Liberties of St Patrick's before his lease had run out. Although the actual Deanery had a small garden of about half an acre round it, Swift also needed more space in which he could take exercise, as well as a paddock for his horses. According to Lord Orrery he quickly made his power felt as Dean: he had endeavoured at an earlier date to obtain land by ending a lease made by the Vicar's Choral to Lord Abercorn on land between the Deanery and the west side of St Stephen's Green, but he had been unsuccessful. Unlike Pope, who concentrated more on Switzer's second tenet for the perfect garden – *simplex munditiis* of Horace – the noble elegance and decency in the parts of the garden – Swift was concerned with more practical horticulture. In the summer of 1724 he spent £400[9] on enclosing Naboth's Vineyard with a high wall because his fruit was being stolen and his horses worried. After lining the wall facing south with bricks (a common eighteenth-century practice to hold the sun's heat), he used to have excellent crops of peaches, nectarines, pears and paradise apples. When he was away from the Deanery it was looked after by the Dean's Vicar. In July 1725 Swift thought the garden was being neglected so he wrote to the Reverend John Worrall, the incumbent, that he was told that Worrall had contrived to lose three hundred apples by bad management, and had saved only 1200 pounds. By that date Swift must have planted many trees successfully. As early as 1721 he had planted elms in the actual Deanery garden as well as in the cathedral churchyard, thereby disturbing the dead and angering the living 'by removing tombstones'.[10] These trees also grew well and a year later he told Thomas Sheridan proudly, 'You will make eight thousand blunders in your planting, and who can help it, for I cannot be with you.' There is no exact detailed plan of the layout of Naboth's Vineyard, but from Swift's approval of the work of his friend, Knightley Chetwode, at Woodbrook near Portarlington, where he was constructing a river walk, 'winding and meandering', we know it cannot have been in any way formal. By February 1723 he was writing to Chetwode that he knew 'nothing so well worth the enquiry of an honest man' as landscaping, and he added, 'I am as busy in my little spot of a town garden, as ever I was in the *grand monde*.' Naboth's Vineyard was a rectangular plot with a fine open view to the Wicklow Mountains on the south and, except for a slight drop on the west side toward the river Poddle, it was flat. This stream, flowing into the Liffey, would sometimes flood part of the garden (and even the cathedral), and was lined with willows: no trace of it remains. If Deane Swift, his cousin and biographer is to be believed, Jonathan Swift was not over-generous in giving presents to his family, but these trees seem to have provided at least one such gift: 'The only presents which Doctor SWIFT ever made in his Life, beside what hereafter shall be acknowledged to any Man of his Name and Family, were a Bundle of Osiers, and Half a Dozen young Cherry Trees to his cousin DEANE SWIFT [the father of the biographer] when he was planting his Garden . . .'[11]

Roger Kendrick's plan (Plate 42), drawn less than four years after Swift's death, gives us the exact size of Naboth's Vineyard and Sheba's Garden adjoining it, with its gate also on the Long Walk. (It is now covered by the Meath Hospital.) Undoubtedly a disadvantage of Naboth's Vineyard was its entry nearly two hundred yards south of the Deanery, on the other side of St Kevin's Street, and beyond the burial ground called by the curious name of the Cabbage Garden because of its previous usage before the Chapter annexed it into the Liberties. By the summer of 1725 his garden was well planted, and Swift was able to entertain the Vicereine Lady Carteret to an al fresco meal which he describes in 'An Apology to the Lady C – R – T':

> He'd treat with nothing that was Rare,
> But winding Walks and purer Air;
> Wou'd entertain without Expence,
> Or Pride, or vain Magnificence;
> . . . .
> Instead of Spoils of *Persian* Looms,
> The costly Boast of Regal Rooms,
> Thought it more courtly and discreet,
> To scatter Roses at her Feet;
> Roses of richest Dye, that shone
> With native Lustre, like her own . . .[12]

Amidst this planting of roses and shrubs, through which gravel paths meandered, Lady Carteret was 'fatigu'd to Death' by half a walk, and apparently started at the 'Rustling of the Trees'. But Swift is exaggerating to emphasize his point in contrasting her attitude with his own feelings on accepting an invitation to the Castle by the Vicereine. When Swift wrote to Pope on 8 July 1733, endeavouring to persuade him to come to stay with him at the Deanery, he gave his gardens as an attraction, and estimated their size fairly accurately: 'the immediate garden' (the actual Deanery garden of about half an acre) was 'as large as your green plot that fronts the Thames' and another two hundred yards further on was another garden 'larger than your great garden and with more air; but without any beauty'. As can be seen from examining Kendrick's plan, Naboth's Vineyard, excluding Sheba's Garden to the north, was exactly 106 yards long by 53 yards broad, and therefore nearly one and a quarter acres. By Pope's 'great garden' Swift must have been referring only to the central area, from obelisk to shell temple including the small mounds, bowling-green and groves. Without the flanking shrubberies with their irregular walks, or the vineyard, kitchen garden and stoves, this central strip was about the size which Swift estimated.

In these years Swift, like Pope, eagerly assisted his friends to landscape in theory, and sometimes, unlike Pope, with actual physical help. *The Journal* (1721)[13] des-cribes detailed activities, with his friends, Dr Patrick Delany, Thomas Sheridan and the Reverend Daniel Jackson, while staying at Gaulstown, County Westmeath, the Rochforts' estate. They spent much time in boating on the canal (into which Swift fell on one occasion),[14] and he was often 'deep among the Workmen'.[15] Rochfort had been 'improving' for some years, but in a formal manner. This formal landscaping survived for more than twenty years, as Isaac Butler wrote of the 'curious groves, fine Avenues and enclosed paths' which 'all open with a well-turned arch of cut stone'.[16]

Among Swift's personal friends with whom he exchanged visits was the Reverend Patrick Delany, a young Protestant Fellow and Tutor of Trinity College – a good-natured and benevolent man. Swift described him to Pope as 'a man of the easiest and best conversation I ever met with in this Island, a very good list'ner, a right reasoner,

42 NABOTH'S VINE-YARD, ST PATRICK'S LIBERTIES, DUBLIN. *Roger Kendrick's plan, 1749.*

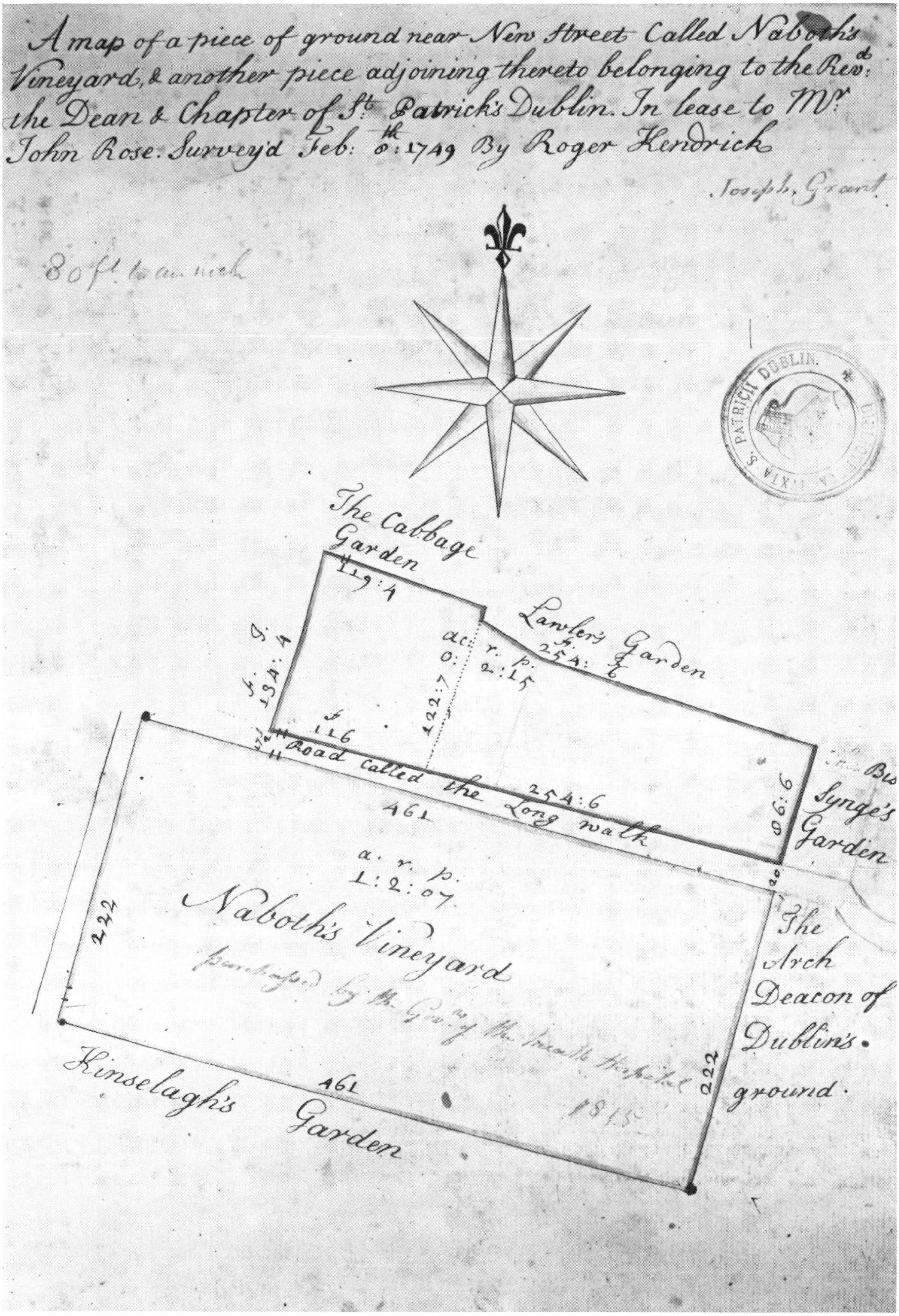

A map of a piece of ground near New Street Called Naboth's
Vineyard, & another piece adjoining thereto belonging to the Revd.
the Dean & Chapter of St. Patrick's Dublin. In lease to Mr.
John Rose. Survey'd Feb: 8th 1749 By Roger Hendrick

Joseph Grant

80 ft. to an inch

The Cabbage
Garden

119:4

Lawler's Garden

ac. r. p.
0: 2:15

254: 8

134:4

116

122:7

Road called the Long walk

254:6

461

Synge's
Garden

a. r. p.
1: 2:07.

Naboth's Vineyard

purchased by the Govrs. of the Incurable Hospital

222

The
Arch
Deacon of
Dublin's.

222

ground.

Kinselagh's
Garden

461

1815

35

neither too silent, nor talkative, and never positive'.[17] During his conversations with Swift he must have discussed his views on gardening, and in 1724 he himself began to improve a small estate which he called Delville, at Glasnevin about two miles from the centre of Dublin. Soon both Swift and he were swept into the full tide of landscaping by Pope and his friends when they stayed at Twickenham in 1726 and 1727. From 'not ten sticks when he took over', Pope planted trees which soon grew like 'new acquaintance brought happily together'; and his three rules – Contrasts, the Management of Surprises and the Concealment of Bounds – were exemplified by irregular patterns in planting, the tunnelled entry to the grotto and the uninterrupted view to the Thames and beyond.

While Swift was in England from March to August 1726 and from April to September 1727 he stayed with many of Pope's friends who were busy landscaping. He walked along Lord Bathurst's new avenues through Oakley Wood at Cirencester; saw Lord Bolingbroke's *ferme ornée* at Dawley, four miles from Twickenham; visited Mrs Howard's new garden at Marble Hill on the Thames, planned by Lord Peterborough and Pope; and viewed the Royal Gardens at Richmond in the making of which Pope and William Kent had recently had a hand. Patrick Delany was also in England staying with Pope at Twickenham during some of this period,[18] so it is not surprising that when he returned to Ireland he should have put into practice some of the ideas which Swift had already given him and which he had seen brought to life by Pope and his circle.

Delville was an estate of about eleven acres on rising ground on the other side from Dublin of a stream called the Tolka. On a bright day the masts of the ships of Dublin harbour could be seen, and the few spires and towers of the city pierced the skyline, with the Wicklow Mountains as a backdrop to the south. Round the house was a small parterre on which he successfully grew orange trees, and on the north-west side was a large kitchen garden, with a wall of good fruit,

in which there is a door that leads to another very large handsome terrace walk, with double rows of large elms, and the walk well gravelled, so that we may walk securely in any weather. On the left hand, the ground rises very considerably, and is planted with all sorts of trees. About halfway up the walk there is a path that goes up that bank to the remains of an old castle from whence there is an unbounded prospect all over the country; under it is a cave that opens with an arch to the terrace-walk, that will make a very pretty grotto . . .[19]

The walks, which ran across the valley in which flowed a stream with cascades, were lined with fruit trees, flowers and sweet-briars. Aged elms and evergreen oaks, rustic bridges, and seats enlivened the scene. It is an oversimplification to describe it as a *ferme ornée* in its initial state, for it was certainly not of sufficient acreage to farm.

The prototype *ferme ornée* of Philip Southcote at Wooburn, Chertsey, Surrey (1735) had about thirty-five acres of gardens and a circumambient path which led through one hundred and fifty acres of pasturage, even through that which was arable. The walk *was* the garden while everything else was the farm including tillage, cattle, sheep and poultry.[20] In a hitherto unpublished account, William Robertson (1770–1850), an architect of Kilkenny, during a tour in England in October 1795 describes, among other landscapes, Blenheim, Claremont, Esher, Persefield and also Wooburn Farm. In order to emphasize the differences between this *ferme ornée* and the Delville estate, parts of Robertson's account are worth quoting:

From the Lodge attended by the porter I went strait forward along a grass walk seperated from the Cornfield by a fence. Whether twas originally so or no I cant tell, but at present this fence is so high as to prevent your seeing over it; not that there are any objects worth looking for but that it has a confined appearance, makes me think 'twas not originally so. By the side of the walk a narrow border . . . filled with annual flowers & Herbaceous Holly, shut the Country out entirely. The cornfields are entirely surrounded by the same enclosure which prevents them from being seen at all from the House.[21]

He goes on to describe arable grounds, rich meadows, a walk of much variety; an octagon building; 'a canal of water the banks parallel and quite tame, about ten feet broad'; a Chinese bridge; too many ornaments and sculpture; but, on the positive side, fine planting of *Magnolia glauca* and a splendid *Liriodendron* (tulip-tree), as well as vistas down the Thames to Walton and Chertsey.

The estate at Delville indeed had a perimeter walk from which one could have different vistas into the central valley in which deer and cattle grazed, but it could not be said to be a farm, for there were too many formal terraces and artificial levellings at the tops of mounds. Pope's garden at Twickenham also had certain formal features such as a quincunx, a mount and *ronds points* from which *allées* led axially, yet, as at Delville, there was a freedom of confinement in the bounds, and a range of wild planting. There was in both, as Addison said of Kensington Palace grounds, 'the beautiful wilderness of nature, without effecting the nicer elegancies of art'. Neither Delville nor Twickenham was entirely shut off from the countryside by walls, hedges or formal planting, although, as can be seen in Mrs Delany's drawings, 1744–59 (Plates 43, 44 and 45), there was a high perimeter wall round Delville, but it did not shut out the distant views. The hay rick seems to be the sole evidence of agricultural activities. In a much-quoted passage, Cooper Walker says that Delany introduced the 'modern' style of gardening into Ireland, 'a style by which Pope, with whom he lived in habits of intimacy, taught him to soften into a curve the obdurate and straight line of the Dutch; to melt the terrace into a swelling bank, and to open his walks to catch the vicinal country'.[22] It was as much to Swift that he owed his inspiration, for Swift was a constant visitor to Delville and he had known Delany longer than Pope had. Unfortunately Swift never had sufficient money to put his ideas into practice as Pope did at Twickenham.

The neighbourhood at Delville much resembled Twickenham in that the houses and villas were lived in by an intellectual community of friends who were all within easy reach of a capital city. Addison, when secretary to the Viceroy Lord Wharton, had had a house there; and Thomas Tickell, the poet and literary executor of Addison, lived in what is now called the Professor's House in the Botanic Garden. In his poem 'On the Death of Addison' Tickell refers to Holland House (since demolished) in lines which seem to have a wider yet renewed relevance today:

> How sweet were once thy prospects fresh and fair,
> Thy sloping walks and unpolluted air!
> How sweet the gloom beneath thy aged trees,
> Thy noontide shadow, and thy evening breeze!

In the centre of the Delville circle was Patrick Delany, and many were pleased to receive invitations to visit him. The beautiful young Lætitia Pilkington showed pleasure in the doctor's 'lovely arbours', and an accompanying admiration for his virtues, by composing some verses when seated by the garden temple at the end of the terrace walk[23] (Plate 46):

> Hail, happy *Delville*! blissful Seat!
> The Muses's best belov'd retreat!
> With prospects large and unconfined;
> Blest emblem of their master's mind!
> Where fragrant gardens, painted meads,
> Wide op'ning walks, and twilight shades –
> Inspiring scenes! – elate the heart!
> Nature improved, and raised by Art,
> So Paradise delightful smil'd,
> Blooming, and beautifully wild.
>
> Thrice-happy sage, who safe retir'd
> By Heaven and by the muse inspir'd;
> In polished arts, or lays sublime,
> Or God-like acts employ your time.
> Here Nature's beauties you explore,
> And, searching her mysterious store
> Through all her operations, find
> The image of the Sovereign Mind;
> And in each insect, plant and flower
> Contemplate the creating Power:

43 DELVILLE, CO. DUBLIN. *Mrs Delany's view of the Swift and Swans Island in Delville gardens, 1745.*

44 DELVILLE. *Mrs Delany's view of the Beggar's Hut in Delville gardens, 1745.*

45 DELVILLE. *Mrs Delany's view of part of the little grove of ever-greens with the country and Bay of Dublin beyond it, 1744.*

Nor is thy love of Him alone
In fruitless speculation shewn;
Through life you happily exert
The Christian virtues of your heart,
To give new schemes of culture, birth,
And bless and beautify the earth;
To raise th'afflicted from despair,
And make the friendless wretch thy care:
To thee the highest bliss is given,
A soul to praise, and copy heaven.

On the entablature of this temple, which survived until the 1940s, were the punning words attributed to Swift – 'Fastigia despicit urbis' – the temple literally and metaphorically looking down on the roofs of the city. On the rear wall was a medallion of the bust of Stella.

After his visit to England in the summer of 1727 Swift never again left Ireland, so he often wrote to his friends inquiring of their improvements in landscaping. In March 1730 he wondered whether Lord Bolingbroke had 'taken down the mount, and removed the yew hedges', thus evidently ridding himself of two features of the older style of gardening. With the country opened up by the abandonment of perimeter walls for a ha-ha it was no longer necessary to have a mount from which to survey a prospect. For many months at a time Swift used to visit Sir Arthur and Lady Acheson at Market Hill (now Gosford Castle), County Armagh; and if his satiric verses reflect a true account of the situation, his interests were much concerned with landscaping in the modern style. He shows these clearly in 'My Lady's Lamentation and Complaint against the Dean' (1728).[24]

How proudly he talks
Of zigzacks and walks;
And all the day raves
Of cradles[25] and caves;
And boasts of his feats,
His grottos and seats;
Shews all his gew-gaws,
And gapes for applause?
A fine occupation
For one of his station!
A hole where a rabbit
Would scorn to inhabit,
Dug out in an hour
He calls it a bow'r.

46 DELVILLE. *The Temple: photograph, 1940s.*

47 MRS DELANY: *engraving by Joseph Brown, c. 1730.*

In 1731, the final shot, disposing of parterres, walls and parallel walks, was fired by Pope in his 'Epistle to Lord Burlington. Moral Essays IV'. The ostentation of a palace of a vulgarian, described as 'Timon's Villa', was so like the Duke of Chandos's House at Edgware that the town was set into a furore, and Pope was forced to deny any special reference to the Duke.[26] Among those who were outraged was Dr Delany who was in London at the time and immediately wrote to his friend, Sir Thomas Hanmer, enclosing a copy of the poem:

There is a general outcry [he wrote] against that part of the poem which is thought an abuse on the Duke of Chandos . . . One thing I regret with all my heart, that Mr. Pope was not acquainted with Mildenhall, because I am persuaded the united elegance and simplicity of your gardens had supplied him with a better standard of true taste than any he had yet met with; & methinks a just and proper praise of taste where it is, had been the best satire on the want of it . . .[27]

This admiration for the gardens of Sir Thomas Hanmer at Mildenhall, Suffolk, was indicative of Delany's taste, for the bowling-green, ringed by *bosquets* through which there were intersecting *allées* to buildings, was similar to Pope's at Twickenham and resembled the work of William Kent at Rousham. The gardens at Mildenhall, round the house on the north side of the church, also exemplified *in utile dolce* of Switzer by orchards and a vineyard from which each year Hanmer used to send a present of grapes to Queen Caroline.[28] As in Chandos's case, there was no shortage of money.

About this time a young lady known to Swift set sail for Ireland and, except for Horace Walpole and Mary Wortley Montagu, has given us a longer set of letters and autobiography than any other writer in the eighteenth century (Plate 47). As Mary Granville her background and family connections were aristocratic, her uncle being George Granville, Lord Lansdowne, and her cousin Lord Carteret, one-time Viceroy of Ireland. Unfortunately her father was implicated with the Tories when Lord Lansdowne was thrown into the Tower for suspected treason on the accession of George I. This resulted in her family being forced to live in the country at Buckland near Broadway, then in Oxfordshire. Perhaps it was during their time there, when they received few visitors and lived in comparative poverty, that her love of the countryside and landscaping was encouraged. She later describes Buckland as having

a front which faces the finest vale in England, the Vale of Evesham, of which there is a very advantageous view from every window . . . Nothing could be more fragrant and rural: the sheep and cows came bleating and lowing to the pales of the garden. At some distance on the left hand was a rookery; on the right a little clear brook ran, winding through a copse of young elms (the resort of many warbling birds), and fell with a cascade into the garden, completing the concert. In the midst of that copse was an arbour with a bench, which I often visited and I think it was impossible not to be pleased with so many natural beauties and delights as I there beheld and enjoyed around me.[29]

At the age of seventeen she was forced by her uncle into marriage with Alexander Pendarves, a rich but aged Tory landowner. Seven years later he died, and after a short period in London she decided to go to Dublin where she had relatives and friends, the Claytons. On 10 September 1731 she found herself waiting for a passage to Dublin at Park Gate in the Dee estuary, and as it was a fine day and the boat was not immediately due in, she visited Eaton, Sir Richard Grosvenor's estate in Cheshire. Her description of it reveals her attitude to landscaping: it was 'laid out in the old-fashioned taste, with cut-work parterres and wilderness enclosed in hedges'.[30] She may well have seen the start of Kent's work for Lord Burlington at Chiswick House in the 1720s when she was living in Chelsea; and although at Chiswick there were Bridgeman's 'rows of trees, paled in gravel walks, fine cut hedges . . . statues, fountains', such as noted elsewhere by Celia Fiennes at an earlier date,[31] there were not grass squares and exact uniform parterres. At Stowe in 1724, Lord Perceval, an Irish friend of Mary Pendarves, had remarked of Bridgeman's landscaping that 'nothing is more irregular in the whole, nothing more regular in the parts, which totally differ the one from the other. This shows my Lord's good taste . . . What adds to the bewty of the garden is that it is not bounded by walls but by a ha-ha which leaves you the sight of a bewtifull woody country . . .'[32] This was the type of landscaping that Mary Pendarves also thought the best.[33] By 22 September 1731 she was staying with Mrs Clayton, the wife of the Bishop of Killala, at their house, 80 St Stephen's Green, which had just been built by the Bishop with Richard Castle as architect. She walked much on the Green and rightly guessed it to be the largest square in Europe. It was a fine expanse of turf on which cattle grazed, and round which were gravelled perimeter walks under lime trees. Mary Pendarves soon visited Delville where she was charmed by it and its owner, but she did not then enter into detail about it. Nor, unfortunately, does she describe Naboth's Vineyard though she met Swift on more than one occasion at Delville.

As the spring brought better weather she went further from Dublin. One such visit in 1732 was to Dangan, the Wesleys' estate near Trim, County Meath, where in a flat and bare countryside Mr Wesley was making improvements by planting trees and digging three canals – evidently still formal landscaping.[34] On another visit she described models of a yacht, barge and yawl, one in each canal and went on to say:

In his garden there is a fir-grove dedicated to Vesta, in the midst of which is her statue; at some distance from it is a mound covered with evergreens, on which is placed a temple with the statues of Apollo, Neptune, Prosperine, Diana, all have honours paid to them and Fame has been too good a friend to the master of all these improvements to be neglected; *her* Temple is near the house, at the end of a terrace near which the Four Seasons take their stand, very well represented by Flora, Ceres, Bacchus, and an old gentleman with a hood on his head, warming his hands over a fire.[35]

Isaac Butler in his 'A Journey to Lough Derg',[36] circa 1744, mentions the lough into which by then the two canals had been converted, and goes into more detail concerning the quaint naval follies, such as the embattled fort with forty-eight pieces of cannon on it. When these were fired, the vessels riding at anchor in the lough returned the fire – a practice which must have been alarming for a civilian visitor, though Isaac Butler found it all 'agreeable'. On his visit he counted twenty-five obelisks, all 'whitened', two of which on arches still survive (Plate 48).

By 1747 the lough had obviously been made out of the canals; so, as at Stowe and elsewhere in England, the softening process had started. Mrs Delany (Mary Pendarves) notes the changes:

. . . six hundred Irish acres, which make between eight and nine hundred English. There is a gravel walk from the house to the great lake fifty-two feet broad, and six hundred yards long [still recognizably the old canals]. The lake contains 26 acres, there are islands on the lake for wild fowl, and great quantities of them embellish the water extremely . . . The part of the lake that just fronts the house forms a fine bason, and is surrounded by a natural terrace wooded, through which are walks cut, and a variety of seats placed, that you may rest and enjoy all the beauties of the place as they change to your eye. The ground as far as you can see every way is waving in hills, and dales, and every remarkable point has either a tuft of trees, a statue, a seat, an obelisk, or a pillar.[37]

After a call at Sir Arthur Gore's at Killala, County Mayo,[38] she arrived at the bishop's palace at Killala. There she indulged for the first time in what was to become a life-long hobby – the construction of grottoes of shells. Every morning at seven o'clock she would make her way to a natural grotto in the grounds where she would adorn the walls and roof with shells in elaborate and intricate patterns; and one day she exclaimed in a letter to her sister, 'I am now going to build a pyramid for the grotto'.[39] The Bishop, like many other landscapers, had a collection of shells, some from local beaches, others from the Mediterranean and the tropics. The finest of these shell houses (which still exists) was made by Lady Tyrone at Curraghmore from 1752 to 1754. It is in the form of a grotto encrusted with shells and crystals including rarities such as mother-of-pearl. A marble statue in the centre, by John van Nost, Jr, shows Lady Tyrone, in flowing garments, shell in hand (Plate 49). Lady Ferrard's less elaborate grotto in the demesne of Oriel Temple, Collon, County Louth, built for John Foster (1740–1829), Speaker of the Irish House of Commons, was typical,

48 DANGAN, CO.
MEATH. *One of the
obelisks.*
49 CURRAGHMORE,
CO. WATERFORD. *Grotto.
Statue of Lady Tyrone by
John van Nost, Jnr, c.
1751.*

being lined with shells, stained glass, coloured stones, etc.[40] Shell work became so
popular that Charles Smith, writing of County Waterford, had to admit: 'there are
many beautiful shells found on this coast, but which have been· of late pretty scarce,
since the making of shell-houses and grottos came in fashion, with other works of this
kind.' Then he goes on to describe one such example at Thomas Christmas's at
Whitfieldstown, three miles south-west of Waterford, where there was an hexagonal
grotto with statues in niches, and walls encrusted with shells:

. . . the vivid red of the *concha Corallina*, the bright yellow of the small Wilk, and the fine
azure of the common Muscle, which add an agreeable contrast to the pearly brightness of the
polished *Indian* shells. The *Jersey* Oyster, when polished, has also as bright a lustre as Mother-
of-pearl. The ranging, collecting, and polishing of so many shells, must have been very expensive, and it is said this grotto cost upwards of £500.[41]

In another of his county surveys, Charles Smith mentions a handsome natural
grotto at Ballybeggan House, County Kerry (1756), 'done up like an altar-piece,
covered with a pleasing variety of chrystals found in this county, with several bright
spars, and transparent pebbles of various colours, as green, yellow, brown, red and
purple, being tinged with different metalline substances, that reflect the light in a
very agreeable manner'.[42] This grotto seems to be similar to Pope's superb grotto at
Twickenham for which his friends sent him specimen rocks and fossils from distant
parts: yellow mundic; German spar; flint, crusted, pellucid and shot round a globe of
copper; lead ore; Cornish 'diamonds'; sparry marble and coral; lumps of amethyst;
Brazil pebbles; two stones from the Giant's Causeway; and many others. Shell
grottoes were the easier to construct, for there were many beautiful shells on Irish
beaches, and the Dublin newspapers sometimes advertised them, such as in the *Dublin
Courant* of August 1745: 'To be sold at Mr Levi Wolfes in Fleet Street all sorts of
India and Irish Shells for Grottoes and Shell works of all kinds.'

The fashion seems to have continued throughout the century, for Dr Haliday,
friend and physician to the Stewarts, wrote from Mount Stewart to Lord Charlemont
on 21 June 1788 of the extravagance of Lord Donegall who had '£10,000 of shells
not yet unpacked'.[43] This seems to be an excessive amount even for one who held the
Gilbertian title of Hereditary Lord High Admiral of Lough Neagh.

An earlier example, in England, was the Duchess of Richmond's exquisite shell
room at Goodwood, which can also still be seen. The initials S.R., C.R., C.F. and
E.K. are worked into the pattern on the wall: her own, her husband's (Charles Richmond, the second Duke) and those of her daughters, Caroline, who married Henry
Fox in 1744, and Emily who became Countess of Kildare in 1747.[44] The construction
of all these rooms required a sense of design, a knowledge of shells and a pertinacity in

completing the task. In addition to designing and drawing carefully, the cleaning of the shells and the mixing of the mortar, even with labourers' help, must have been hard work. Mary Pendarves thought shells were as interesting as flowers in their history and variety, and she was prepared to pay a sum of fifteen guineas for a rare tropical nautilus. During her long life (1700–80) she finished grottoes of Irish shells at Clogher for the Claytons when he was Bishop there; for her brother at Calwich Abbey, Ashbourne, Derbyshire; for her uncle, Sir John Stanley at 'Northend' near Fulham; as well as at Delville after she had married Patrick Delany.[45] The grotto at Killala had seats in it for four people, with an extensive panorama over the ocean and the islands. It must have been a delightful spot and very suitable for Mary Pendarves and her friends who admired the picturesque in landscape as much as subsequent Jane Austen heroines. Of another spot she later remarks, 'I walked over the bridge by moonlight along a walk of tall elms which leads to a ruined house they call the Black Castle, from a vulgar tradition of its being haunted; it lies over the Blackwater, has a vast number of trees about it, and seems to have been pretty.' At Cabra Castle, then County Meath, 'a rivulet that tumbles down from rocks in a little glen, full of shrub-wood and trees' pleased as much as did 'the copsewood which is cut into vistas and serpentine walks . . . and here and there overgrown forest trees, in the midst of them is jessamine, woodbine, and sweetbriar, that climb the trees',[46] at Cootehill (Bella-mont Forest), County Cavan. In fact she not only advocated a more free treatment of landscaping in the William Kent style but was ahead of her time in appreciating many of the features of the later picturesque.

In April 1733 she returned to England, but she did not lose touch with her Irish friends, including Swift to whom she wrote in October 1733, when on a visit to Bathurst's at Cirencester, that they 'did not forget to talk of *Naboth's Vineyard* and *Delville*'.[47] Nor did she cease to correspond with Dr Delany who continued to spend more money than he could afford on improving Delville, which could not be supported by his income. In 1729 he addressed to the Lord Lieutenant Lord Carteret a poem entitled 'An Epistle',[48] in which he complained of the poor revenues from his living in the north of Ireland:

> Add to this crying Grievance if you please,
> My horses founder'd on *Fermanagh* Ways;
> Ways of well-polish'd, and well-pointed Stone,
> Where every Step endangers every Bone;
> And more to raise your Pity, and your Wonder,
> Two Churches – twelve *Hibernian* Miles asunder!
> With complicated *Cures*, I labour hard in
> Besides whole Summers absent from my Garden!
> But that the World would think I plaid the Fool,
> I'd change with *Charly Grattan*[49] for his School –
> What fine Cascades, what Vistos might I make,
> Fixt in the centre of th'*Iernian* Lake!
> There might I sail delighted, smooth, and safe,
> Beneath the Conduct of my good Sir *Ralph* . . .[50]

Swift published a satiric reply to this poem, entitled 'An Epistle upon an Epistle' (1730)[51] in which he made fun of Delany's expensive hobby (see page 50).

But it did not involve Delany in any financial worry to help his friends to improve their estates. In the 1730s, as well as helping Sir Ralph Gore at Belleisle, he may well have had a hand in Dr Samuel Madden's garden at Manor Waterhouse in County Fermanagh, on the eastern side of Lough Erne, where there were 'shady walks, terraces, artificial cascades, labyrinthes, recesses, bowers interwoven of Branches of Trees' and 'pyramids of bones'. This description ends with a convenient summing-up of the attitude at this time towards gardening and nature: 'throughout all this wild-ness Nature appears in her native beauty and charming wildness.'[52] In Ireland, where so much rolling, lake-begirt natural landscape was available, it was popular and cheaper to lay out a garden by making use of these natural advantages, rather than create the expensive parterres and elaborate *allées* of the previous generation's baroque taste (Plate 50).[53] In December 1736 Lord Orrery wrote from Dublin to Tom Southerne

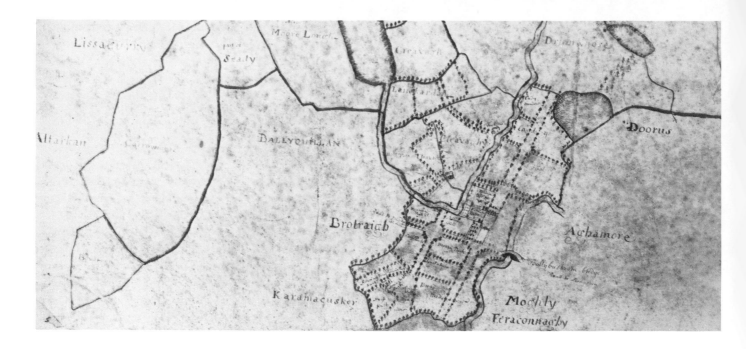

that 'Tickell and Dr. Delany perform Quarantine at Glassnevan. We must not hope to
see Them till longer Days and milder Weather. The World, I suppose, will reap the
Benefit of their Retirement. The Press will groan for it, and future Ages will revere
Delvil as much as the present Age honours Praeneste [Palestrina, near Rome]'.[54]

John, fifth Earl of Orrery, who was friend of Pope, Swift and Dr and Mrs Delany,
in June 1738 married Margaret Hamilton, the rich heiress of Caledon, County Tyrone.
Very soon he started to make a garden in the poetic-romantic style of Pope and Delany.
Loudon states that Stephen Switzer came over to Ireland, and as he worked for Lord
Orrery at Marston, Somerset,[55] dedicating *The Practical Fruit Gardener* (1724) to
him, it is likely that he also worked at Caledon.[56] From March 1739, when Lord
Orrery wrote from London to his wife at Caledon that he proposed 'vast Pleasure' in
their retirement at Caledon in making improvements, he grew more and more absorbed and increasingly fond of the demesne. In May 1740 he wrote to Tom Southerne:
'My trees flourish, my Lawn looks green, and my Walks rise. My gardens are encompassed by a River, whose Borders are covered with goodly trees, the boast and
glory of the County of Tyrone.'[57]

In March 1743 he told Lady Orrery from London to 'plant away as fast' as she could.
Then follows a gap in his letters about landscaping for some years, but his enthusiasm
had obviously increased as, when he was again in London, Lady Orrery took over. In
August 1746 she mentioned to him her 'Rustick Cascade' which was being constructed,
and described a visit of Dr and Mrs Samuel Madden and family from Manor Waterhouse, to whom she showed her new works. She also told her husband she was employing a kitchen gardener at ten pounds a year, as 'Joans could not do the Hill and
Caledon'.[58] This certainly implies the interchange of employees on Lord Orrery's
estates, for 'the Hill' was his house at Marston, Somerset. After Lord Orrery
returned to Ireland he became lyrical about his work when writing to Dr William
King of St Mary Hall, Oxford:

. . . my lot is fallen here, here is my treasure, and *where my treasure is there must my heart be*
also. In truth, *Caledon* itself is a most delightful place, and I am attempting to make daily
additions to its beautys. Gardens, Groves, and, above all, an hermitage! where I hope to have
your bust, that the image of learning may appear within the confines of *Orrery Hill* . . .[59]

In January 1747 he was 'going on in Mottos' and had placed a statue of Diana with
a Latin inscription

at the entrance of a wood, which by the turns of the river is formed into a Peninsula . . . To
tell you the truth, my tenants have a notion that I am atheistically inclined, by putting up
heathen statues and writing upon them certain words in an unknown language. They immediately suspected me for a papist, and my statues had been demolished, my woods burnt and my

throat cut had not I suddenly placed a seat under an holly bush with this plain inscription, SIT DOWN AND WELCOME. I have assured them that all the Latin mottoes are to this purpose, and that in places where they cannot sit down, I have desired them in the old Norman dialect to go to the lodge, and drink whisky.[60]

Some of these statues were still there in 1794, for in O'Connor's *Journal* he described the place:

Adjoining to the Road in the suburbs of Caledon is the Ruins of the Dwelling House of the Earl of Orrery in a hollow on the banks of the Rivulet nor far from the house of Lord Caledon. On the banks of the River Blackwater in a sort of Sloping Green the Statue of Minerva, having her right breast bare . . . she stands on a pediment on which rests opposite to her right knee her shield on which is portrayed the head of Medusa with her wide tongue out dropping saliva, a thick Roman nose, a flat haggard complexion, lank cheeks marked with furrows, large terrible eyes, as if staring out of their sockets – makes I thought the sight would petrify me.[61]

Writing to Lady Elizabeth Spelman a few months later in 1747, Lord Orrery told her that they spent most of their time at Caledon in the summer at a lodge in the park, about a mile and a half from the house. Concerning his 'noble grove of fir trees' beside the river he expressed sentiments similar to many of the picturesque writers later, in words that might have been used by Mrs Delany: 'like the tall cedars of Lebanus they are perpetually green, and afford us at this time of the year, a gloomy shade, that like the awfulness of a Cathedral, inspires us with a serious kind of reflection.' The next month he planned what alone remains, though ruined, of all these garden works – a bone house (Plate 51). To this end he wrote to a friend in England for particulars of Lady Curzon's bone house at Kedleston, Derbyshire:

You will, if possible obtain . . . an exact description of that ossified edifice. Let us know the size of it. The sort of bones. The method of putting them together. In short, all particulars relating to ossification. We intend to strike the Caledonians with wonder and amazement, by

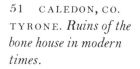
51 CALEDON, CO. TYRONE. *Ruins of the bone house in modern times.*

affixing an ivory palace before their view. We have already gathered together great numbers of bones. Our friends the butchers and tanners of Tyrone have promised to increase the number.[62]

In the same letter he described other garden structures, which were finished:

We have built, at the expence of five pounds, a root house, or hermitage, to which on Sunday the country people resort, as the Londoners to Westminster Abbey. For gayer scenes, I have a lodge near a mile distant from the hermitage, and large enough to contain a good number of friends at dinner or supper, or to entertain eight couples with a country dance. Behind this room are three little rooms, a kitchen, a bedchamber, and another room, besides a cellar. . . . These buildings are in the form of Buckingham house. And the courtyard is filled with various fowls, and admits the most lively and innocent scene imaginable. All the buildings command a view of the river, of groves and of various agreeable objects . . . Caledon has changed me into a Hibernian. It is a charming place indeed.[63]

Mrs Delany graphically summed up the effect made by the lodge and hermitage, though curiously did not mention the bone house, in a letter to Mrs Dewes. After stating that Lord Orrery 'is more agreeable than he used to be' and that his wife 'is very plain in person' but 'sensible, unaffected, good-humoured and obliging', she wrote:

I spent the day very pleasantly: it is a fine place by nature, and they are both fond of the country; *she* delights in *farming* and he in *building* and *gardening*, and he has very good taste. They have a lodge about a mile from their house where they spend most of their time; it has all the advantages of water, wood, and diversified grounds; and there the new house is to be built. Nothing is completed yet but an *hermitage*, which is about an acre of ground – an island planted with all the variety of trees, shrubs and flowers that will grow in this country, abundance of little winding walks, differently embellished with seats and banks; in the midst is placed a hermit's cell, made of the roots of trees, the floor is paved with pebbles, there is a couch made of matting, and little wooden stools, a table with a manuscript on it, a pair of spectacles, a leathern bottle; and hung up in different parts, an hourglass, a weatherglass and several mathematical instruments, a shelf of books, another of wooden platters and bowls, another of earthen ones, in short everything that you might imagine necessary for a recluse.[64]

In a letter of 20 July 1748, Lady Orrery described a visit from two similarly enthusiastic gardeners, who were themselves landscaping in the same style – Mr Justice Ward of Castleward (see p.111) and Mr Justice French. They were 'charmed with the Lodge, commended the proportions of the Room; but they declared they would not have lost sight of the Hermitage and Island on any Consideration. They were in raptures, and Mr Warde offered to get for you several rockwork and curious Stones from the Sea-coast on which he lives, and that you may command all his garden contains.'[65]

Dean Swift, Lord and Lady Orrery, Dr and Mrs Delany, and Dr Samuel Madden are undoubtedly the chief precursors of the romantic-poetic garden in Ireland, which is simultaneous with Pope's work at Twickenham until his death in 1744.

After 1733 Mrs Pendarves (Delany) never saw Swift again, and Dr Delany saw him less as the Dean's health deteriorated. For many years Swift had suffered from Ménières disease resulting in acute giddiness, sickness and deafness from a disturbance in the canals of the ear, and the only relief he obtained from this was by physical exercise. Therefore he often rode along the sands of Dublin Bay to the home of his friends, Lord and Lady Howth. Their improvements at this time in the garden layout at Howth can be seen in John Rocque's plan (Plate 30) and in an overmantel painting still in the house. The formality of design in walks intersecting *bosquets* was remarked on in Chapter 1. Despite this, the rest of the estate was most picturesque. From the square towers and stepped battlements Swift could have looked out over the estate where his host's family, the St Lawrences, had lived since the twelfth century. In the garden round the castle walls he would wander along beech *allées* from which he would gaze over the sea to the romantic St Nessan's Island (Ireland's Eye). Or if he continued his ride through the St Lawrence demesne up the rocky bridleways of the hill of Howth he would look over Dublin Bay whose shores were dotted with historic castles, or north to the pale mountains of Mourne on the horizon. The primeval oaks and ancient hollies under which he rode were as old as the cairn on the summit, reputed to be the burial place of Crimthan, High King of Ireland in earliest Christian times. The sublimity of the picturesque – the steep rocks, dark paths, pagan cromlechs, ivied ruins, hanging woods and mountain streams – formed the natural accompaniment to those overtones of ancient grandeur, the burial places of Irish saints. But from 1740 until his death in 1745, Swift no longer undertook expeditions to his friends, as he showed progressive signs of mental disturbance. Many years previously he had pointed out an oak tree to Thomas Sheridan, asking him whether he had seen it was dying at the top. That was how he would die, he said.

In 1743 Delany visited Rousham, Oxfordshire, his favourite garden, staying with the owner, Sir Clement Cottrell. Then he proposed marriage to Mary Pendarves, and was accepted despite opposition from the Granvilles. In June 1743 they were married and took up residence at Delville. For twenty-five years until Delany's death they divided their time between Delville and Downpatrick where he was Dean. A consistent love of the picturesque of Pope – a painter's picturesque – stayed with her: 'That Idea of "picturesque" – from the swan just gilded with the sun amidst the shade of a tree over the water on the Thames' as Spence reported Pope to have said. [66] This is not the gloomy awe-inspiring grandeur of the sublime, but nearer to the aesthetic reasons given by Vanbrugh for preserving part of Woodstock Manor in Blenheim Park: '... were the inclosure filld with Trees (principally Fine Yews and Hollys) Promiscuously set to grow up in a Wild Thicket; so that all the Building left (which is only the Habitable Part and the Chappel) might appear in Two Risings amongst 'em, it would make one of the Most Agreeable Objects that the best of Landskip Painters can invent.' [67] These words might have been written by Mrs Delany in 1731 or William Gilpin a century later, for an artist's eye for the picturesque never really closed.

In 1732 she had preferred 'an old mansion, dark and gloomy' to Mr Justice Donellan's 'finished with the utmost art, where the twirling of the salt mill had more charms' for her than 'all the nightingales singing near her window'. A day at Leixlip, County Kildare in June 1747 was described in similar terms in a letter to her sister: 'They [Mr and Mrs Lowe] have a pretty cabin there, and gave us some fine trout caught out of their brook just at their door. I wished you were there, it was so new a scene; and the men at work laying out the cloth, etc., on the grass in our view was very pretty, the machine for rinsing the clothes is very curious.' [68]

This is very Gilpinesque – a love of the scene for its human aspects associated with the local linen industry. On the same day she called at Mr William Conolly's, at Leixlip Castle, on the top of the hill round which the Liffey winds:

... laid out into fine grass walks well planted, and set with all sort of forest trees and flowering shrubs; openings here and there that show the river so far below you that it is almost horrible. A winding path and steps by degrees carry out down to a winding terrace by the river side above a mile long; every step there shows you some new wild beauty of wood, rocks and cascades [Plate 52]. [69]

At Delville her work continued: 'I am considering about a green house, and believe I shall build one this spring; my orange trees thrive *so well* they deserve one. I propose having it 26 ft by 13, and 13 high, and a room under it (with a chimney for my poultry-woman) that will open into a little back garden, which I intend to make my menagerie. Will you tell me if the chimney will be a disadvantage to my orange-trees?' [70]

Mrs Delany's passion for grottoes and picturesque landscape took the Dean and her to Ireland's most famous natural curiosity – the columnar basalt wonders of the Giant's Causeway. A discussion of this is not strictly concerned with landscape gardening in demesnes, but is so much the essence of the picturesque, as seen through the eyes of Mrs Delany, that we include her account as being relevant to an understanding of her attitude, which in turn affects her landscaping ideas. It was really the exquisite engravings, possibly by Vivares, after Mrs Susanna Drury's paintings (Plate 53), that caught the imagination of the Irish tourist, though earlier Dr Molyneux had been interested in the Causeway and its origins, and during the late seventeenth century he and the first Dublin Society had commissioned a painting of it which proved to be

52 LEIXLIP CASTLE, CO. KILDARE. *The Salmon Leap: engraving after Huet.*

singularly inaccurate.[71] Mrs Drury's drawings were more accurate, and William Hamilton says in his notable series of letters discussing the origins of the Causeway: 'the attention of the world was therefore again directed toward this antiquated subject'.[72] These paintings won a premium from the Dublin Society in 1740,[73] and the prints were elaborately dedicated to the Earl of Orrery and the Earl of Antrim, the local landlord. Mrs Delany must have seen these prints a few years after, as she wanted to go to the Causeway in July 1744. She mentions the prints and Mrs Drury's efforts, in a letter to her sister dated 8 October 1758:[74] 'I am still in an amazement at the stupendous sight,' she wrote, and she describes how she and her husband and a large party of ten went to visit 'one of the *world's wonders*', exclaiming,

I am now quite at a loss to give you any idea of it; it is so different from anything I ever saw, and so far beyond all description. The prints you have represent some part of it very exactly, with the *sort of pillars* and the remarkable stones that compose them of different angles, but there is an infinite variety of rocks and grassy mountain *not at all* described in the prints, nor is it possible for a poet of a painter, with all their art, to do justice to the awful grandeur of the whole scene . . . We walked along a path on the side of a hill that formed an amphitheatre, of a great height above us, and sloped down a vast way below us to the sea from the path we walked on . . . At the bottom, the sea foaming and dashing among the rude rocks; on the side of the hill, sheep feeding undismayed at the roaring of the sea and terror of its waves, and shepherds tending their flocks. Our next scene was a second amphitheatre, diversified with amazing rocks, and the pillars and loose stones which are peculiar to this place, the entrance guarded on one side by a range of rocky mountain, and on the other two pyramidal mountains of a singular form. From that point we walked round the semicircle that forms the second amphitheatre on a precipice that was very formidable indeed, persuaded by our guides that the lower way was not practicable; but D.D. was not so ambitious, and kept the low way on the rocky strand, and had the advantage of us, as our path led us a great way about, and was so frightful that we could not look about us. However, we got safely to the part that is called 'the Causeway', which forms a point into the sea, and begins the third amphitheatre; this contains the greatest quantity of the pillars, some so very exact and smooth that you would imagine they were all chiselled with the greatest care. After gazing, wondering, and I may say *adoring* the wondrous Hand that formed this amazing work, we began to find ourselves fatigued. Our gentlemen found out a well-sheltered place, where we sat very commodiously by a well (called the Giant's Well) of as fine sweet water as any at Calwich,[75] and cold mutton and tongue, refreshed us extremely after three hours' walking, climbing, and stumbling among the rocks.

I took an imperfect sketch of the place, which if I can make anything of you shall have a copy. Mrs. Drury, who took the draughts (of which you have the prints), lived three months near the place, and went almost every day. I can do nothing so exact and finished; in the last amphitheatre facing the entrance, about half-way up the side of the rocky mountain, the pillars are placed in such a form as to resemble an organ: you will see it in one of Mrs. Drury's prints.

What is called the Causeway is a most wonderful composition of pillars, which in some part form a mosaic pavement, in others appear like the basement of pillars, but when you are on the strand below, then you see they are all pillars closely fitted to each other, though the angles vary; they chiefly consist of hexagons. The sun shone part of the time and shewed the place to great perfection, but we had a sprinkling shower or two that made us wrap up in my brother's good lambswool cloaks, and shelter ourselves under some of the rocks.[76]

Three of her sketches survive, dated 1762, four years after her visit, so she probably recopied them then. One of these (Plate 54) shows her little band in single file walking along the path just as she describes in her letter and, though she calls the sketches 'imperfect', they form a pleasingly naïve contrast to the professional finesse of Mrs Drury (Plate 53). The Causeway for Mrs Delany was a natural 'folly' and she leaves any scientific musings to clerics like Dr Pococke or the Reverend William Hamilton. A postscript in this letter illustrates very well her attitude to travel and scenery: 'Much have we seen, much been hurried, but thank God all well, and pleased to have Delville now in view, which will be a perfect calm after the seas, rocks, torrents we have beheld!'[77]

During the later part of the eighteenth century, every tourist worth his salt visited the Causeway by sea and land; the Earl-Bishop of Derry (see page 144) public-spiritedly made a footpath there for travellers. As late as 1844, James Fraser

53 GIANT'S CAUSEWAY, CO. ANTRIM. *Engraving by Vivares (?) after Susanna Drury.*

54 GIANT'S CAUSEWAY. *Mrs Delany's drawing, 1762.*

complained how difficult it was to see the view, exclaiming, 'How different at the cliffs of Moher'[78] (see page 179). The romantic nature of the place was later vulgarized by railings, loquacious guides and an electric train; but the Causeway should be rightly numbered with the Wicklow Mountains and Killarney as the three best-known picturesque sights in Ireland.

Back at Delville the Delanys had eighteen head of deer in the fields, the orange trees thrived, and in summer they used to breakfast out of doors amid the roses, jasmines and pinks, or sometimes under the shade of the nut trees with an Irish harper playing old tunes to them. Such is the belt of mild climate, she could glean as late as 28 September, 'melons, beaury pears,[79] grapes, filberts, and walnuts', filling her basket with 'honeysuckle, jessamine, gillyflowers and pippins'. Among small improvements she constructed a ninepin-bowling-alley, 'a very merry exercise' along a terrace in a nook of the garden, with 'houses built up for blowing auriculas at the end'. By eighteenth-century standards Delville's eleven acres were small for an estate, and at his death Delany was said to be

> Quite ruin'd and bankrupt, reduc'd to a farthing
> By making too much of a very small garden.

Nothing remains; the Bon Secours hospital is on the site. Swift had predicted his financial ruin earlier in 'An Epistle upon an Epistle':[80]

> But you forsooth, your *All* must squander,
> On that poor Spot, call'd *Del-Ville*, yonder:
> And when you've been at vast Expences
> In Whims, Parterres, Canals and Fences:
> Your Assets fail, and Cash is wanting
> For farther Buildings, farther Planting.
> No wonder when you raise and level,
> Think this Wall low, and that Wall bevel.
> Here a convenient Box you found,
> Which you demolish'd to the Ground:
> Then Built, then took up with your Arbour,
> And set the House, to *R-p-t B-b-r*.[81]
> You sprung an Arch, which in a Scurvy
> Humour, you tumbled Topsy Turvy.
> You change a Circle to a Square,
> Then to a Circle, as you were:
> Who can imagine whence the Fund is,
> That you *Quadrata* change *Rotundis*?

After her husband's death in 1768 Mary Delany could not bring herself to live alone at Delville, so she went back to England. As a writer on landscaping for the greater part of the eighteenth century, with an artist's eye and feeling for the picturesque, she records the period between the work of Pope and Swift and the theories of William Gilpin, whom she helped and promoted. None but a practitioner of the visual arts could have achieved this. She lived her remaining years with vigour, and even at the age of seventy was prepared to make a detour in her chaise in order to climb Cooper's Hill to show the prospect to her life-long friend the Duchess of Portland.

> My eye descending from the Hill, surveys
> Where *Thames* amongst his wanton vallies strays.[82]

Then, having seen the fine view of Windsor Castle, they went on to their hosts where they read Denham's poem, which in 1640 had implied so much of the picturesque in its theme. Was it Denham's early days in Ireland that had given him this feeling for picturesque landscape which was so admired by Mrs Delany?

1. 12 April 1711 and 25 June 1712.
2. See C. Hussey, *English Gardens*, plate 3.
3. As did the paths of Marly-le-Roi through the *bosquets* of Louveciennes, shown in the plan of 1700.
4. *Upon the Garden of Epicurus* (1685).
5. Sir William Temple.
6. *The Poems of Jonathan Swift*, edited by Harold Williams, excludes this poem from the canon, but Joseph Horrell, *Poems of Jonathan Swift*, London 1958, vol. I, pp. 34–36, lines 59 ff., includes it.
7. To Lady Mar, *Letters of Lady Wortley Montagu*, edited by Robert Halsband, vol. 2, p. 15.
8. MS St. Patrick's Cathedral, 'Minutes of the Chapter, 1700–50'.
9. Letter to Charles Ford, 27 November 1724. Swift increased the figure to £600 when he wrote to Pope on 1 May 1733. Nevertheless the garden squandered all he had saved. Williams, *Correspondence of Swift*, vol. IV, p. 154.
10. Swift to Knightley Chetwode, 12 December 1721. Williams, *Correspondence of Swift*, vol. II, p. 412.
11. Deane Swift, *An Essay upon the Life, Writing and Character of Dr. Jonathan Swift*, London 1755.
12. Williams, *Poems of Swift*, vol. II, p. 374, lines 99–102 and 109–14.
13. Williams, *Correspondence of Swift*, vol. I, p. 278.
14. To the Reverend John Worrall, 14 September 1721. Williams, *Correspondence of Swift*, vol. II, p. 403.
15. To Archbishop King, 28 September 1721. Williams, *Correspondence of Swift*, vol. II, pp. 404 ff.
16. 'Journey to Lough Derg', 1744, MS Armagh Public Library, p. 104.
17. 2 May 1730. Williams, *Correspondence of Swift*, vol. III, p. 397.
18. Swift to Miss Martha Blount, 'Dr Delany is gone to England this morning.' 29 February 1728. Williams, *Correspondence of Swift*, vol. III, p. 269.
19. Mrs Delany to Mrs Dewes, Delville, 19 July 1744. Llanover, *Mrs Delany*, vol. II, pp. 314–16.
20. See Thomas Whately, *Observations on Modern Gardening* (1771), pp. 177ff, for a description of Wooburn Farm.
21. National Library, Dublin, MS 248.
22. Cooper Walker, 'Rise and Progress of Gardening'.
23. Lætitia Pilkington, *Memoirs, 1712–50*, London 1928.
24. Williams, *Poems of Swift*, vol. III, p. 851, lines 173–86.
25. 'That serves as a place of repose. (poet.)' *O.E.D.*
26. See George Sherburn, 'Timon's Villa and Cannons', *Huntingdon Library Bulletin*, no. 8, October 1935; Professor Kathleen Mahaffey, 'Timon's Villa: Walpole's Houghton', *Texas Studies in Literature and Language*, IX (1967), pp. 193–222; Maynard Mack, *The Garden and the City*, Toronto and Oxford 1969.
27. Sir Henry Bunbury, Bart. (ed.), *The Correspondence of Sir Thomas Hanmer, Bart.*, London 1838, pp. 216–17.
28. MS E 18/600, The Record Office, Bury St Edmunds, Suffolk.
29. Llanover, *Mrs Delany*, vol. I, pp. 17–18.
30. Llanover, *Mrs Delany*, vol. I, p. 287.
31. Christopher Morris (ed.), *The Journeys of Celia Fiennes*, London 1949.
32. To his brother-in-law, Daniel Dering, 14 August 1724. Hist. MSS Comm. Egmont, VI.
33. For more about her opinions see Edward Malins, 'Mrs Delany and Landscaping in Ireland', *Quarterly Bulletin of the Irish Georgian Society*, vol. XI, nos. 2 and 3, April–September 1968.
34. Llanover, *Mrs Delany*, vol. I, p. 348.
35. Llanover, *Mrs Delany*, vol. I, pp. 406–7.
36. MS Armagh Public Library.
37. Llanover, *Mrs Delany*, vol. II, pp. 500–2.
38. Llanover, *Mrs Delany*, vol. I, p. 353.
39. Llanover, *Mrs Delany*, vol. I, p. 363.
40. See p. 107.
41. *The Ancient and Present State of the County of Waterford*, pp. 97–98.
42. This is now nearly a ruin as, in 1787, was one made by Dr Delany at Mallow upon which there were verses, but which was 'so filled all round with ordure, that its exhalations are offensive'. Dr Beaufort, *Journal of a Tour through part of Ireland . . . in 1787*. Part 2. Trinity College, Dublin. MS K6, 57 (4027).
43. Charlemont Papers, 12/R/15, Royal Irish Academy.
44. See p. 56.
45. Her shell work in the oratory at Delville is noted by George Montagu in a letter to

Horace Walpole, 1 October 1761: 'all fitted up and painted by her own hand, the stucco composed of shells and ears of cort the prettilyest disposed imaginable'; and he compares it with Madame de Sévigné's chapel. Indeed Mary Delany's autobiography is like hers in many ways. All shell and plaster work was destroyed when Delville was demolished in 1951. It is described in C. P. Curran's *Dublin Decorative Plasterwork of the Seventeenth and Eighteenth Centuries*, London 1967, pp. 21–23, and plates 10 and 11.

46. Llanover, *Mrs Delany*, vol. I, pp. 375–77.
47. Williams, *Correspondence of Swift*, vol. IV, p. 200.
48. Williams, *Poems of Swift*, vol. II, p. 470.
49. Charly Grattan was master of Portora School.
50. Sir Ralph Gore owned the estate of Belleisle beside Lough Erne where he was busy landscaping; see p. 77.
51. Williams, *Poems of Swift*, vol. II, p. 475.
52. Henry MSS, p. 129. P.R.O. Dublin.
53. This estate map (1688) shows seventeenth-century planting, which Dr Samuel Madden must have inherited.
54. *Orrery Papers*, Houghton Library, Harvard College, MS Eng. 218.2, vol. 4, p. 85.
55. Loudon, *Encyclopedia of Gardening*, p. 273. Writing to Dr King, Lord Orrery mockingly mentions a series of disasters which had occurred after Dr King's departure from Marston; among them, 'Twitzer talks of planting Thistles and Crab trees'. Orrery, *Orrery Papers*, vol. I, p. 264.
56. His connection with Lord Molesworth has already been mentioned. See Chapter 1, p. 16.
57. *Orrery Papers*, op. cit.
58. Orrery, *Orrery Papers*, vol. I, p. 169.
59. *Orrery Papers*, Houghton Library, Harvard College, MS Eng. 218.2, vol. 5, p. 7.
60. See a similar reaction by Mr Wildgoose in Richard Graves, *The Spiritual Quixote*, 1773. This is discussed in Edward Malins, *English Landscaping and Literature*, Oxford 1966, pp. 73–75.
61. Trinity College, Dublin, MS 539.
62. *Orrery Papers*, Houghton Library, Harvard College, MS Eng. 218.2, vol. 5, p. 55.
63. Ibid.
64. Llanover, *Mrs Delany*, vol. II, p. 492.
65. Orrery, *Orrery Papers*, vol. II, p. 253.
66. Joseph Spence, *Anecdotes, observations and characters of books and men, collected from the conversation of Mr. Pope*, Oxford 1966.
67. *Reasons for Preserving Part of the Old Manor*, 11th June, 1709.
68. Llanover, *Mrs Delany*, vol. II, p. 469.
69. Llanover, *Mrs Delany*, vol. II, pp. 469–70.
70. To her brother, Bernard Granville, 19 January 1750. Llanover, *Mrs Delany*, vol. III, p. 7.
71. Reverend William Hamilton, *Letters concerning the Northern Coast of the County of Antrim*, part II, p. 14.
72. *Northern Coast of the County of Antrim*, part II, p. 16.
73. For further details see W. G. Strickland, *A Dictionary of Irish Artists*. Dublin 1913, vol. I, pp. 304–5.
74. Llanover, *Mrs Delany*, vol. III, p. 318.
75. Her brother's house on the Dove, Derbyshire.
76. Llanover, *Mrs Delany*, vol. III, pp. 519 ff.
77. Llanover, *Mrs Delany*, vol. III, p. 523.
78. James Fraser, *A Handbook for Travellers in Ireland*, 1844, pp. 395 and 639.
79. 'Beurré. 1714. Fr. buttered, buttery. A mellow variety of pear'. *O.E.D.*
80. Williams, *Poems of Swift*, vol. II, p. 475, lines 59–76.
81. Rupert Barber (1736–72), the miniaturist, and his wife, a poetess, were friends of Swift, and were given a house by the Delanys at the end of the garden at Delville.
82. Sir John Denham, 'Cooper's Hill', London 1642.

3 Carton, Castletown and County Kildare

The avenue was green and long, and green
light pooled under the fernheads; a jade screen
could not let such liquid light in, a sea
at its greenest self could not pretend to be
so emerald. Men had made this landscape
from a mere secreting wood: knuckles bled
and bones broke to make this awning drape
a fitting silk upon its owner's head.

Michael Hartnett,
A visit to Castletown House (1975)

After Swift became Dean of St Patrick's in 1713 he was followed to Ireland by Esther Vanhomrigh (Vanessa) to whom he had written the autobiographical poem, 'Cadenus and Vanessa'. She went to live at Celbridge, a small town about twelve miles from Dublin in County Kildare. In the gardens of Celbridge Manor which she had inherited from her father she soon started to plant and lay out walks, in a style similar to Pope's at Twickenham. The site was not dissimilar: a central area of lawn intersected by walks leading down to the river Liffey, but she could also extend her landscaping to an island, and to the far bank. Unlike Pope's garden at Twickenham, however, the Celbridge site was cut by a road which ran past the house on the other side. Whereas Pope's garden was mostly on the side away from the Thames, Vanessa's was on the river side. In the classic bower[1] which she built, Swift and she would spend many summer hours, out of sight of the house on an island in the middle of the 'Great River, which sometimes roars, but never murmurs'.[2] During the next ten years she continued to improve her landscape, from the time when Swift declared he had heard she had not one beech tree in all her groves 'to carve a name in',[3] until she had set out shrubberies on the perimeter which included a laurel planted each time Swift visited her[4] – and that was often. From the Deanery he used to ride out from Dublin along the Galway turnpike, turning off at Lucan to Celbridge, until one day in May 1723 when he quarrelled with her and never again saw her.

During these years he must have passed shire horses dragging carts with vast blocks of stone for the building at Celbridge of Castletown House. On 29 July 1722, writing to his friend Sir John Perceval from Trinity College, Berkeley mentions that

the most remarkable thing now going on is a house of Mr. Conolly's at Castletown. It is 142 feet in front and above 60 feet deep in the clear, the height will be about 70. It is to be of fine wrought stone, harder and better coloured than the Portland, with outhouses joining to it by colonnades, etc. The plan is chiefly of Mr. Conolly's invention, however, in some points they are pleased to consult me. I hope it will be an ornament to the country.

To which Perceval replied from Tunbridge, Kent, on 5 August:

I shall be impatient until you send me a sketch of the whole plan and of your two fronts. You will do well to recommend to him the making use of all the marbles he can get of the production of Ireland for his chimneys, for since this house will be the finest Ireland ever saw, and by your description fit for a Prince, I would have it as it were the epitome of the Kingdom, and all the natural rarities she afford should have a place there.

This was indeed the start[5] of the largest house in Ireland, designed by Alessandro Galilei,[6] with the direction of the building by Sir Edward Lovett Pearce. The Right Honourable William Conolly was a self-made man reputed by Swift to be worth sixteen thousand pounds a year, owning estates in ten Irish counties, nine times a lord justice, and Speaker of the Irish House of Commons from 1715 to within a few days of his death in 1729. After his death his widow lived on in the unfinished house, continuing his good works in the neighbourhood. When John Loveday, a touring Oxfordshire squire, visited Castletown in 1732 he saw thirteen uninterrupted bays of silvery limestone in the main block, with curved colonnades leading to wing pavilions on either side, like some great city palace in Rome, with Palladian additions. He also noted some planting, for he described the Liffey flowing 'below the Fruitery'. In the same year Mrs Pendarves also saw it, then wrote to her sister that the 'situation was very fine, and the country extremely pleasant – some wood and pretty winding rivers.' Yet in November 1734 Lady Anne Conolly, who had married the Speaker's nephew and heir, wrote to her father, Lord Strafford, from nearby Leixlip Castle, that Castletown was:

. . . unfinished outdoors, though the house is really a charming one to live in. The front is quite without ornaments of any sort, not even so much as pediments over the windows; and the offices are separated from it by a very handsome colonnade, that altogether it looks very well. At least here it does, where there are but few places any way like a seat; and, too, they all have one fault, and that is the want of trees, by which every place looks terrible, raw and cold.

Thus it continued until Mrs Conolly's death in 1752 in her ninetieth year. She was hospitable, religious, punctual and business-like, and the landscape at Castletown was improved by buildings, among which was the Wonderful Barn, 1743 (Plate 55), a strange conical structure closing the north-east vista, balanced by two towers of similar design but without external staircases. Nevertheless, it was practical as a barn, and A. Atkinson in *The Irish Tourist* (Dublin 1815) has been one of many visitors who have been fascinated: 'In the centre of each floor a square hold has been formed, through which a rope suspended by pullies, is let down from the top to the bottom, and thus the corn deposited in the great granary can, without much trouble, be carried to or removed from any part . . . This barn, if now erected, would cost 2 or 3000 pounds.'[7]

The radiating avenues, some of which still exist, must be of early origin. They appear on a plan circa 1739 (Plate 56) along with an irregular inverted T-shaped lake straddling a vista to the north-west. At the extremity of this was placed Mrs Conolly's greatest landscaping achievement – the unique and splendid obelisk (Plate 57) to the memory of her husband. In March 1740 her sister wrote that Mrs Conolly was 'building an obleix to answer a vistow from the bake of Castletown House, it will cost her three or four hundred pounds at least, but I believe more. I really wonder how she can

55 CASTLETOWN HOUSE, CO. KILDARE. *The Wonderful Barn.*
56 CASTLETOWN HOUSE. *Plan, c. 1739.*

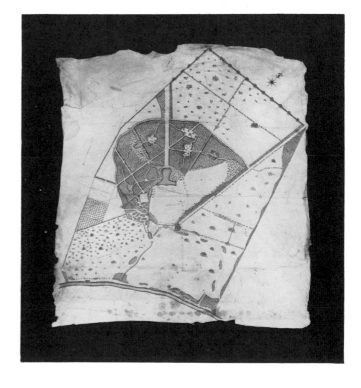

dow so much and live as she duse.'[8] Like the obelisk at Stillorgan (1727), the Conolly
Folly was built to help the poor in a hard winter when their crops failed. In fact it was
such a severe winter with such prolonged frosts that it was estimated by Charles
Smith in *The Ancient and Present State of the County of Kerry* (Dublin 1756) that a
third of the inhabitants of the southern counties died through the destruction of un-
protected potatoes. Caesar Otway in his *Tour of Connaught* (1839) rightly remarks
that such buildings 'are called follies in Ireland; to give such names only argues poor
taste and sense in those who bestow them. Would that there were many such evidences
in the land that the rich cared for the poor.' It was also appreciated at the time on
aesthetic and moral grounds, if the laudatory poems written about it are not to

be taken as sycophantic. Henry Jones's 'On Viewing the Monument of the Right Honourable William Conolly Esq' is typical:

> Still o'er thy shrine thy faithful Consort bows,
> Still to thy mem'ry pays her plighted Vows.
> See Grandeur here by social Virtue grac'd;
> The Manner noble, as refin'd the Taste!
> Nor Pride, but Piety there strikes our Eyes
> And Meekness lifts yon Pillar to the Skies.[9]

It stands as planned, on high ground, majestically closing a two-and-a-half mile vista from the west front of the house, although a series of further vistas all radiating from the house are not visible. The shaft soars from a point seventy feet above the Promethean arch which supports it, triumphantly flanked by double-tier smaller arches. Its sturdy baroque dignity can be seen thirty miles away, and its detail, as in the four pineapples and in the eagles perched on urns, is equally exciting close up. Whoever the architect and builder – and convincing claims have been made for Richard Castle[10] – it seems that the multi-arched build-up with smaller obelisks may have been influenced by the 'theatre' on the penultimate terrace of Isola Bella, as much as by the obelisk at Wilhelmhohe in Hesse-Kassel near Richard Castle's birthplace. This outstanding monument visually links Castletown with Carton, the neighbouring eighteenth-century landscape. When it was built, the Conolly Folly stood on land belonging to Carton.[11] Here it also forms a dramatic feature in the landscape, not at the end of a rising vista, but complementing a medieval tower as a focal point in an arc from the south-west side. Both houses were built of local limestone, in tranquil landscapes whose woods and little rivers presented no very bold natural features.

When, in 1747, Emily Lennox, at the age of sixteen married Lord Kildare, Carton House had already been rebuilt to the designs of Richard Castle, having been finished in 1739. He had repeated the centre block with two wings joined by colonnades like Castletown. But, as we said in Chapter 1, the landscape remained formal. In the Baylie and Mooney 1744 map (Plate 10) it can be seen that the avenues on the south side of the house have been retained, and the layout of *patte d'oie* and parterres nearest the house on the north side; but alterations had been made in nine neighbouring townland boundaries, incorporating them within the demesne, which became five times its previous size until, about eighty years later, the whole came to be called Carton Demesne. The subsequent naturalistic improvements concentrated on the southern aspects, with lawns falling to the Ryewater.[12] Arthur Devis's portrait of Lord and Lady Kildare (Plate 58), shows her examining a design for a bridge by

58 CARTON, CO. KILDARE. *Lord and Lady Kildare laying out the park at Carton: oil on canvas by Arthur Devis, 1753.*

Isaac Ware, subsequently executed differently by Thomas Ivory who also designed the gates (Plate 59); but as the Devis picture was painted in England in 1758, the landscape is an imaginary one, bearing no resemblance to Carton.

Four years after her marriage, Emily Kildare was joined at Carton by her two younger sisters, Louisa and Sarah Lennox, as both their father and mother had died. In these formative years Louisa must have been influenced by her elder sister's practical work on the landscape at Carton, which she carried out in the absence of Lord Kildare when he was on political duties in Dublin and London. For example, she had to arrange for a new head gardener from England at thirty pounds a year with seven shillings a week board. She had already had bad luck with the previous gardener, for on 19 May 1757 she wrote to her husband, 'That gardener is gone, but we are looking out for another. It's immense what people give them, but that you won't mind, I know, if it's a good one. They all object to living in Ireland. Everyone says those recommended by Miller [Philip Miller, see page 30] and Greenings etc, never turn out well.'[13] In choosing the new head gardener, who was obviously of great importance in the absence of a landscaper, she renewed her acquaintance with her father's old friend, Sir Peter Collinson F R S, the well-known botanist who had given advice in the planting at Goodwood in the 1740s before her father's death. Collinson promised to see the new head gardener before he set out for Ireland; and she persuaded Collinson to send Lord Kildare a set of instructions on planting, which she told her husband to 'read over three times every morning for three days following, for it's of infinite consequence to our plantations that *you* should be quite au fait of it all.'[14]

When her husband was away in the late 1750s and early 1760s, planting continued in both a 'formal' wilderness – in belts of protective trees round the estate – and in informally placed clumps. She often wrote to him of how the landscaping was going on: of how on one occasion she had to deal with an undergardener (before the arrival of her new head-gardener) who, instead of a little path to the kitchen garden, had constructed 'a great broad gravel road'. She also passed on to him the advice of her brother-in-law, Henry Fox (created Lord Holland, 1763), who at that time was erecting castellated follies and towers on his estate on the North Foreland, Kent, that she should get 'a vast quantity of horse-chestnuts and sycamore, as well as walnuts and common chestnuts'.

In 1758 Louisa Lennox, aged fifteen, married Tom Conolly of Castletown. So the subsequent creation of the Castletown landscape was the result of the skill and loving care of Louisa who also was responsible for the landscaping while her husband was absent on parliamentary business in Dublin and London. Had either of these two sisters, Emily and Louisa, been long absentee themselves or been ignorant horticulturally, or lacked an eye for landscaping, or wanting in practical sympathy for the

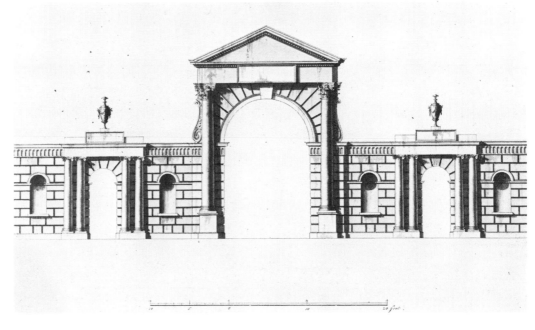

59 CARTON. *Thomas Ivory's design for the gates, c. 1770.*

local community in times of hardship, neither of these two landscapes would have worthily accompanied the two magnificent Palladian houses. We mentioned[15] the exquisite shell room of the second Duchess of Richmond at Goodwood. Caroline Fox and Emily Kildare, her two eldest daughters, assisted her, and both had absorbed many of the principles of landscaping with which they grew up at Goodwood.

Their younger sister, Louisa, after her marriage to Tom Conolly until her death in 1821, lived at Castletown, with only a few visits to England. In July 1761 she wrote to her sister, Lady Sarah Bunbury, that she was building a little 'dear, tidy' lodge of her own design which was a 'prodigious entertainment' to her, in addition to building a dairy, and she found it very pleasant to superintend work herself. In 1764 she again wrote she 'always hated London' and was glad to be back home again that summer and to be sitting in an alcove in her 'Cottage' (the lodge she had designed) with a porch before it, in the wood three-quarters of a mile from the house. The grass was very green, honeysuckle and roses were flowering well, mignonette was coming up, seringa was out. Mrs Staples (her sister-in-law) was playing her guitar on the porch, while she worked and read. It was more the fashion in Ireland than in England to have such a cottage, and in this case it was 'neatly fitted up with Tunbridge ware' which she used to drink tea during the summer. Louisa Conolly also planted many oaks and elms, though not on the scale of her brother at Goodwood who planted a thousand four-year-old Lebanon cedars in 1761.[16] That she had an eye for landscape is certain, for at the age of sixteen she had written from Wentworth Castle, Yorkshire, to her younger sister of 'the immense quantity of wood and vast command of water with the prettiest rising grounds that can possibly be', and further commented on the temples in the park. Undoubtedly it was she rather than Tom Conolly who carried out improvements at Castletown. While he was engaged in political duties in England (without any ability) or hunting in Kildare or racing at the Curragh (with little more

60 CARTON. *The cascade: oil on canvas by William Ashford, c. 1800.*

success), she interested herself in Castletown. Her lodge preceded the building at Carton of the shell cottage, buried in the woods beside the bridge over the cascade (Plate 60) down which the Ryewater tumbles. This charming thatched cottage still stands, with its shell room (Plate 61), but the mother-of-pearl linings of the shells are now a little lustreless and the old mirrors forlornly tarnished. Yet the design of the Gothic casements with rosy and blue stained glass;[17] the intricate patterns of egg-shaped Scots pine cones interlaced with larger cylindrical ones of silver fir; the mirrors set in frames of bark; the tufa dado; the Chinese bamboo chairs; the writhing stems of ivy; the coral strings; and, above all, the complex patterns of shells, from huge conches to tiny ormers, on wall and column, now radiate a melancholy charm in a room which once must have been as gay as the dancing light on the cascading river alongside.

In December 1762 George Barret (1732–84), the landscape painter, was at both Castletown and Carton. Plate 62 shows his painting of a liveried coachman driving Louisa Conolly with a small niece beside her, and her nephew, Charles FitzGerald, riding on a pony behind them as they bowl along in her curricle by the Liffey. The detail of Castletown House is not very accurate – he has painted the wrong number of bays and columns – but who would bother with this licence if the painting gives the feeling of the whole setting as well as this one does? When George Barret painted this he had experienced only picturesque landscapes in the Wicklow Mountains or Killarney. The rich masses of trees associated with the Dargle and the Powerscourt waterfall were his *forte*, so Emily Kildare thought he would have more difficulty with the Castletown landscape which was 'too flat ever to make a pretty picture'[18] compared with Carton where the scene was more diversified, especially after improvements had been made in the landscaping of the river. Emily Kildare wrote to her husband in England describing this:

New river is beautifull. One turn of it is a masterpiece in the art of laying out, and I defy Kent, Brown or Mr Hamilton[19] to excel it: this without flattery. And now that you may not be too vain, the shape of the island in its present state is not pretty; whether its rising so much above the water be the cause of it or not I can't tell, but it wants that grace and easy pretty turn . . . The end is extremely well hid at present, and when the banks are dress'd and green it will be altogether a lovely thing. I had great pleasure is seeing ten men thickening up that plantation between Dublin and Nine Mile Stone Gate with good, tall shewy-looking trees, elm and ash . . .[20]

This was evidently the climax of the work in widening the river, which had started four years previously, during which time Emily had been living at Carton. (The alterations can be seen by comparing Plate 63 with Plate 64.) The landscaping at both houses continued through the 1760s and there is no doubt that in all essential features it was only mildly Brownian: streams widened to pools at climactic visual points, gentle slopes of lawn, and much perimeter planting on a grand scale. The whole

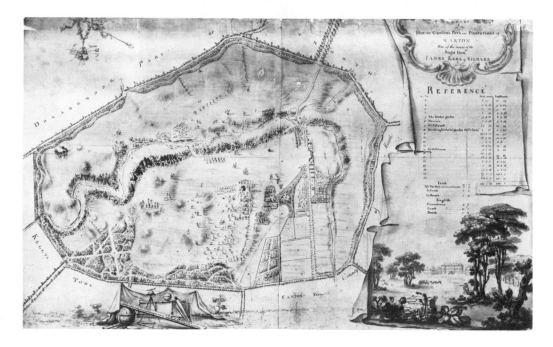

63 CARTON. *John Rocque's plan, 1760.*

64 CARTON. *Map of the glen and part of the park, c. 1776.*

natural layout can clearly be seen in John Rocque's decorative map of 1760 (Plate 63). Nothing remains of the formal garden except in the newly planted wilderness, south-east of the house, and the straight avenue to Maynooth. Had Brown worked there in person he would undoubtedly have carried out more extensive levelling of ground. For example, he would not have left the rising lawn on the south-west side of Carton House, which prevents the water from being seen from the ground-floor windows. But he would not have suggested certain romantic-poetic features named in a later 1769 map: the 'Chinese Bridge' over the river at its south-west extremity, or the 'Brides' Well' and numerous mock-Gothic towers.[21]

On one occasion when improvements were being carried out in the Castletown grounds and the house was being decorated, Louisa Conolly stayed at Leixlip Castle which was also owned by the family. It dominated a most romantic setting on top of a hill above the Liffey (Plate 65). Every day in the spring of 1766 Louisa Conolly used to walk over the fields to Castletown to superintend the making of a flower garden, which she thought was becoming very perfect, especially in the growth of the roses. Although she had previously grown roses in a hothouse she realized that those grown outdoors have a more lasting scent.

Fortunately, Capability Brown, whom Lord Kildare went to see in London in 1762, was too busy or too ill to accept an invitation to come to Carton.[22] A new flower garden called Waterstone in the area of the shell cottage was laid out, the fifty acres of gardens near the house were walled in, and with an approach through a magnificent yew avenue, it all added up to a princely setting, as Thomas Roberts' two landscapes so evocatively show (Plates 66 and 67); indeed, Lord Kildare was created Duke of Leinster in 1766.

Compared with Carton, the landscape at Castletown was modest. Louisa began in

65 LEIXLIP CASTLE,
CO. KILDARE. *Oil on
canvas by unknown artist,
c. 1740.*

66 CARTON. *The bridge
in the park: oil on canvas
by Thomas Roberts, c.
1770.*

67 CARTON. *Sheet of
water: oil on canvas by
Thomas Roberts, c. 1770.*

1767 a new piece of work 'dressing the Banks of the River', scooping in one place, building up in another to make 'a little rising ground, – for alas! that is what this pretty dear place wants'. By May 1768 she wrote to her sister Sarah that she had 'got a little addition of ground by the river side, 'tis a very little bit, but very pretty, and the having a new thing to do is pleasant'. In August 1772 she again wrote to Sarah that she had finished the building of 'a little cottage', although the ground in front of it was 'not yet dressed', but she hoped to have it 'beautiful and to stock it with pheasants and poultry of all sorts' the following year.

Then she took a small house near the sea at Blackrock, a fishing village four miles from Dublin, where she would go in the summer. This was in order that she could be near Emily and the FitzGerald children who lived in the summer months at the next-door estate in Blackrock, called Frescati. The Bray road ran between this house and the rocky beach, so an underground passage was constructed under the road by which the sea water could be brought for the younger children nearer to the house. It was set in a small park with a stream from the mountains running through it and was delightfully planted, with views over the sea to Howth Hill. Louisa Conolly still continued with her landscaping at Castletown: the lime avenue from Celbridge was planted, and in the summer of 1776 she was 'doing the Pond, which will be tolerably pretty as a river and very usefull for fish, Ice and manure.[23] I am going to begin the Hen yard, and have got all the Fowl and Turkeys to live all day in the back lawn, which I am sure is better than any Yard, and, so only put them up at night.'[24] When Arthur Young visited her in June he found:

a large handsome edifice, situated in the middle of an extensive lawn, which is quite surrounded with fine plantations disposed to the best advantage to the north, these unite into very large woods, through which many winding walks lead, with the convenience of several ornamental seats, rooms &c. On the other side of the house, upon the river, is a cottage, with a shrubbery, prettily laid out; the house commands an extensive view, bounded by the Wicklow mountains.[25]

She also continued to enlarge the kitchen garden and the grape house, where she was said to have the largest vine in the two kingdoms, except for that at Hampton Court. All the works concerned with making the pond continued through the summer of 1778 as it was essential to give employment to the local poor after a bad potato crop. She was always conscious of their distress, and constantly mentions it in her letters to her sister in France: 'Were he [her brother Richmond] to know the true state of poor wretches here, he would be one of the first to pursue some method for their relief . . . a vast neglect of duty not to do something for them,' and again, in the winter of 1777, she said it made her heart ache to see the distress everywhere. On her own estate she ensured that there was work by continuing her landscaping. By the spring of 1779 the pond had been turned into a river and three cascades had been made in a cut. She also

68 CASTLETOWN HOUSE. *The Gothic lodge.*

built garden buildings including a temple, now ruined, dedicated to Sarah Siddons, whom she had met in Dublin:

> To thee, O Siddons, in this calm retreat
> Approving judgement dedicates the seat.[26]

There is also a lodge[27] (Plate 68), in the Batty Langley manner, on entering the Leixlip drive, which resembles in design the gothicized Leixlip Castle.

At the same time, the second Duke enlarged the Leinster estates to about sixty thousand acres, enclosing eleven hundred at Carton in a five-mile wall, and planting extensively. Yet most of this planting was yet of no great growth as it had been carried out by the first Duke. Arthur Young was impressed by the scene, which by 1776 must have been most Brownian in character:

It is a vast lawn, which waves over gentle hills, surrounded by plantations of great extent, and which break and divide in places, so as to give much variety. A large but gentle vale winds through the whole, in the bottom of which a small stream has been enlarged into a fine river, which throws a chearfulness through most of the scenes: over it a handsome stone bridge. There is a great variety on the banks of this vale; part of it consists of mild and gentle slopes, part steep banks of thick wood; in another place they are formed into a large shrubbery, very elegantly laid out, and dressed in the highest order, with a cottage, the scenery about which is uncommonly pleasing; and farther on, this vale takes a stronger character, having a rocky bank on one side, and steep slopes scattered irregularly, with wood on the other. On one of the most rising grounds in the park is a tower, from the top of which the whole scenery is beheld; the park spreads on every side in fine sheets of lawn, kept in the highest order by 1,100 sheep, scattered over the rich plantations, and bounded by a large margin of wood, through which is a riding.

Often visiting nearby Celbridge Abbey, owned by his cousin Thomas Marlay, was Henry Grattan, the Patriot leader who was fighting for the independence of the Irish Parliament. For many months before the motion of April 1780 when Grattan urged this independence, he meditated at Celbridge on the rightness of his actions, until, as he later wrote: 'Along the banks of that river, amid the groves and bowers of Swift and Vanessa, I grew convinced that I was right; arguments, unanswerable, came to my mind, and what I then presaged, confirmed me in my determination to persevere.'

The speech he made in the House was one of the finest in his career, and its inspiration was evidently drawn from the spirit of Swift which haunted Vanessa's Bower, in the landscape now clothed in yew, cypress, box and laurels planted by Vanessa. As the United Irishmen, proposing revolution rather than reform, gained in strength, Grattan, the moderate Whig, lost influence and retired temporarily into private life. For Grattan, the revolutionary changes were perhaps similar to the rude alterations which took place in the Celbridge grounds after the death of Colonel Marlay. In a few lines entitled 'Vanessa's Bower to Dean Marlay',[28] Grattan regrets this violence:

> Oh, thou! too prompt at fickle fashion's call,
> For the sloped bank to change the useful wall;
> To break those clumps that in meet order stand,
> Planted by ancient skill's exactest hand,
> To mock the true old beauties of my isle
> With the forced fiction of your Gothic Pile,
> Oh! born like Swift to head this sylvan scene,
> Like him to live a wit and die a *Dean*.
> Oh! spare these shades where our first poet sung;
> Each vagrant bough with sacred wreaths is hung.
> So may each vicissitude of taste
> Spare thy trim lawns nor leave thy flowers to waste.[29]

During this time Louisa Conolly was putting the finishing touches to the Castletown landscape by completing the piers of the Celbridge gate. She employed local craftsmen, with whom she was well pleased. The piers are still in excellent condition and are similar to those at Osterley, Middlesex. The two sphinxes surmounting them were taken from a design in Sir William Chambers' *Treatise on Civil Architecture*

(London 1759) and cost £16. 18s. 6d., according to a bill paid to John Coates of Maynooth, which is still preserved in Castletown. She also finished the last part of the riverside landscape:

I found some very pretty rocks that the sods would never stay on in time of flood and therefore have left them bare which has good effect coming out of the grass, and will afford some pretty romantic seats close to the water-edge, where I am going to plant some willows, which I hope will weep the right way but sometimes they are so perverse as to bend quite the wrong way.[30]

In May 1793 Lord Edward FitzGerald, the Duke's younger brother, returned with his wife, Pamela, to Frescati. At once he was active in work outdoors 'dressing the little beds about the house, or having the green full mowed and rolled; the little mound of earth that is round the bays and myrtles before the house I have planted with tufts of gentianellas and primroses, and lily of the valley'. And in the spring of 1794:

I have got an undergardener (myself) to prepare some spots for flowers . . . I have been hard at work today and part of yesterday (by the by, weather so hot, I go without coat, and the birds singing like spring) cleaning the little corner to the right of the house, digging round roots of trees, raking ground and planting thirteen two-year old laurels and Portugal laurels . . . I am to have hyacinths, jonquils, pinks, cloves, narcissues etc. in little beds before the house, and in the rosery. Some parts of the long round require a great deal of pruning, and trees to be cut; if you trust me, I think I could do it prudently and have the wood laid by. There are numbers of trees quite spoiling one another.[31]

A month later he told her that 'all the shrubs are out, lilac, laburnum syringa, spring roses and lily of the valley in quantities . . . I believe there never was a person who understood planting and making a place as you do. The more one sees Carton and this place, the more one admires them.' Unfortunately, his plans were frustrated by his step-father, William Ogilvie, who disliked Ireland, deciding to sell part of the Frescati estate, and persuading Emily Leinster to live permanently abroad. So for a few years Frescati was let. During that period Lord Edward lived with his wife and family at Kildare Lodge, lent them by Tom Conolly. It was a small white house with a gravel court before it, surrounded by a charming walled garden with large old elms, adjacent to the fifteenth-century tower of Kildare Castle, and with views across the Curragh. Despite his involvement with the United Irishmen, Lord Edward, in the autumn of 1794, spent many happy months planting 'roses, sweet-briar, honeysuckles and Spanish broom' in the spring. In the winter months also he was well contented 'of a blustery evening with a good turf fire and a pleasant book, coming in, after seeing my poultry put up, my garden settled – flower-beds and plants covered for fear of frost – the place looking comfortable, and taken care of . . .'[32]

In February 1797 he and Pamela paid a visit to Frescati for a few months – the last he was able to enjoy there. Once again he wrote to his mother in England:

I can't tell you how pleased I was to see this place again. In a moment one goes over years; every shrub, every turn, every peep of the house has a little History with it. The weather is delightful and the place looks beautiful. The Trees are all so grown and there are a thousand pretty sheltered spots which near the sea at this Season is very pleasant. The Birds sing, the flowers blow and make me for moments *forget* the world and all the villainy and Tyranny going on in it.

The estate has subsequently been built over, the house divided, stripped of fittings of value and gradually becoming ruined. However, the small stream still flows through a municipal garden before it reaches the shore. Soon after leaving Frescati, as Commander-in-Chief of the United Irishmen, Lord Edward had to go into hiding. On the night of 3 June 1798 he died of wounds received when resisting arrest. Louisa Conolly, who had seen him two hours before his death, arranged his funeral. Later she wrote to her sister Emily:

I have had no time for indulgence, nor can I allow it myself yet, but go on like a machine from morning till night, catching at the little momentary enjoyments of fresh air, the smell of mown grass, and flowers. And now and then, a morning's attention to the harvest coming home. But the eagerness and delight that used to attend these occupations is so mixed with pangs of grief, that I sometimes fly from them . . .

In 1805 Tom Conolly died. In his will he had written: 'I hope and recommend to the persons who will be entitled to my estate, that they will be resident in Ireland, and will always prove steady friends to Ireland, as their ancestor, Mr Speaker Conolly, the original and honest maker of my fortune, was.'[33]

No one better than Louisa Conolly could have carried out his wishes, and she continued to live at Castletown, designing buildings and personally caring for the estate workers. She died in 1821, seated in a tent on the lawn in order that she might look at the landscape she loved.[34]

This landscape, unlike that at Carton, did not progress from formal to transitional to Brownian, as at Dangan, County Meath, which Mrs Delany visited in 1749 (see page 41), where there was a well-documented progression. By the time Arthur Young went to Dangan in 1776 there was no trace of the old-fashioned canalized lake, but plantations in the Brownian manner were extensive and the lake had grown from twenty-six to an hundred acres: 'he has formed a large water, having five or six islands much varied, and promontories of high land shoot so far into it as to form almost distant lakes, the effect pleasing.' There were also many obelisks (one of which was mentioned by Mrs Delany) and, as at Belan, they are supported on arched bases which makes their attribution to Richard Castle likely (Plate 69).

At Carton plans for widening the river had been made by 1824 (Plate 70) and achieved some thirteen years later (Plate 71) though this water could never be seen from the house. By the 1840s a so-called Italian garden, with statues and vases, ran the length of the south front, and was kept in high order. Not far off at Lyons, a similar parterre, linking the house with the natural landscape in the style of Humphry Repton[35] can still be seen; in this case, with an artificially formed lake at the foot of a hill rising to about six hundred feet. It dates from 1805–1810 when the second Lord Cloncurry spent about £200,000 enlarging house and grounds.[36] But it is not very successful. The lake runs abruptly across the main central vista, and although its extremities are undetermined in the best tradition, the eye is never led away to some imaginary source of the water nor surprised by its disappearance and reappearance, nor is there any variation in the width of the lake (Plate 72).[37] Despite the two cedars flanking the central path, which break the vista, the junction between parterre and lake is too abrupt. This can be said also of a comparable landscape at Emo Park, County Leix, a fine neo-classical house by Gandon with a terrace to the lake, but no subtlety in the view of the water from the house. Prince Pückler-Muskau, whose eye for

69 BELAN, CO. KILDARE. *The obelisk.*

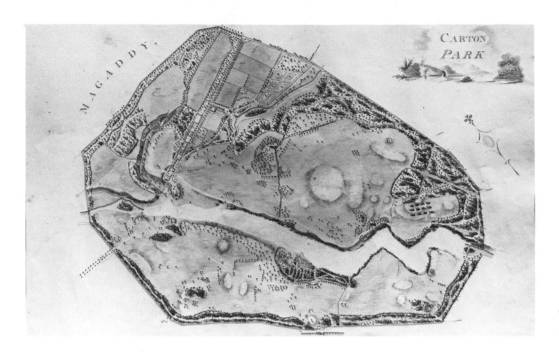

70 CARTON. *Plan, c. 1824.*

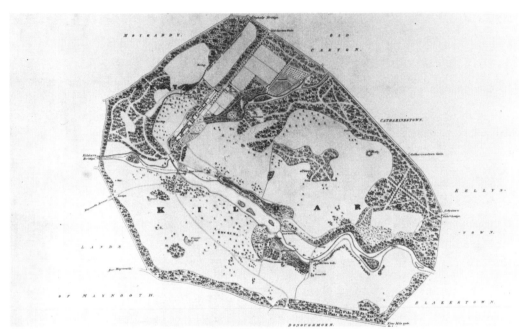

71 CARTON. *Estate map by Matthew Warren, 1837.*
72 LYONS, CO. KILDARE. *Aerial view of the parterre and the lake.*

landscaping was unrivalled, sums the matter up with reference to artificially created expanses of water:

the principal thing is never to suffer an expanse of water to be completely overlooked, or seen in its whole extent. It should break on the eye gradually, and if possible lose itself at several points at the same time, in order to give full play to the fancy – the true art in all landscape gardening.[38]

He is referring here to the landscape at Mount Bellew, County Galway (Plate 73) which was the work of Hely Dutton.[39] According to Pückler-Muskau, Mount Bellew afforded 'a perfect study for the judicious distribution of masses of water, to which it is so difficult to give the character of grandeur and simplicity that always ought to belong to them'. A comparison of the two plates referred to above will show the scene before and after Hely Dutton's work. An advertisement in the *Irish Farmers' Journal and Weekly Intelligencer*, vol. IV (2 September 1815 to 24 August 1816), page 70, gives the exact dates of the work.

Mr Dutton having completed the Lake of MOUNT BELLEW, which has occupied his time for upwards of three years, requests a renewal of the applications of those Friends whom he could not attend until the conclusion of his agreement. He has discovered a method of making Drains in CLAY SOILS, which is much cheaper than any at present in use; they cannot be injured by the plough or the tread of cattle, and will never require repairs. As usual, he thins Plantations, so as in most cases to unite utility with picturesque effect. Letters addressed to Mount Bellew Bridge, Castleblakeny, will be punctually noticed.[40]

Capability Brown in England had no need of such advertisements to augment his fame, as his skill in dealing with water soon showed in many famous examples; in his planting of trees and diverting the Thames at Nuneham round his plantations, or in a complete reconstruction of levels at Blenheim and Bowood, resulting in lakes which look entirely natural.

County Kildare is mostly flat, with less water and rivers than many other counties, so it might have been suitable for Brownian park landscapes. One such site, at Belan near Moone in the south of the county, belonged to the Stratford family who, as staunch supporters of King William, entertained him there once. In 1709 Samuel Molyneux thought the scene 'handsome and improved' with the river 'prettily cut into canalls and Fishponds'.[41] John Loveday, on tour in 1732, noticed 'large Plantations of trees in variety of shady walks, groves, several Ponds also new-stocked with Fish . . . Avenues on both sides of the house'; he also saw 'ye chief beauty' to be 'a noble Walk of Trees, of decent Width and Considerable Height so as scarce (take it

73 MOUNT BELLEW, CO. GALWAY. *Engraving by J. C. Varrall after J. P. Neale.*

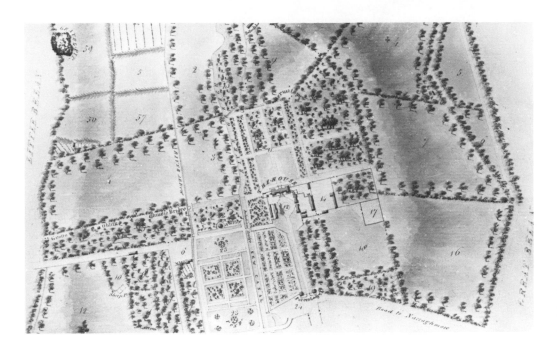

74 BELAN, CO. KIL-
DARE. *Plan of the
demesne, 1774.*

all together) to be parallel'd' (Plate 74).[42] The Stratford family prospered, and in 1743 the house was rebuilt by Richard Castle and Francis Bindon, until it became a three-storied structure with attic, about 120 feet by 44 feet, as can be seen in the background of Plate 75. By 1777 John Stratford had been given an earldom, and Belan had acquired a comparable grandeur. Perhaps no other painting sums up the splendour of the Anglo-Irish at this time than Francis Wheatley's superb picture of Lord Aldborough reviewing Volunteers in the park at Belan, which appears as the frontispiece of this book. Yet it seems that his younger son, Paul Stratford, was more interested in landscaping than his father as his letters often mention his purchases. In April 1772 he wrote to his brother-in-law, Mr Saunders of Saunders Grove, that he had been trying to get some spars, presumably for a grotto, as a spar is a lustrous crystalline mineral; but was not satisfied with the condition of the stone. On 26 August of the same year he wrote from Belan to his brother Edward that he had got up his 'temple and little Mercury' (Plate 76), as well as arranging for the cartage of a statue of Hercules, with some difficulty, and for which he was having a marble pedestal made. Then he added: 'I have frequently attempted to make some improvements, as I thought, here, but my Father, as often, Interrupts my Enterprize.[43] The Astler [Ashlar] Work at both ends has fallen down, and some of the front, which last has been repair'd, the place is just kept up, and that's all I can say for it, embellish-

75 BELAN. *Detail from
engraving by Thomas
Milton after William Ash-
ford showing Chinese
Bridge.*

76 BELAN. *The rotunda temple.*

ments are suspended until your arrival.' After Edward became second Earl of Aldborough he vigoriously pushed ahead with the repairs and improvements previously neglected by his father. His diary for 1792 shows his interest: [44]

Tuesday 3rd January 1792.

At home, walked out each morning before breakfast, read and wrote Forwarding the improvements of Eagle Park and St Patrick's Mead. It's soil limestone, is different clays, mould, marl, and mineral; and Turf 5 feet deep; dark mould, finest in Europe, and full of fine springs, suitably planted and ornamented. Aired in Caravan[45] last night; Gothic Temple begun and Hermitage. Top fence, terrace, and planting, drawing and swilling going on, and fences scoloping[46] etc.

3rd March

Sent to Belan 30,000 forest trees and folio books.

26th March

Settling papers, and despatching car from here [Dublin], sent the travelling case with books and toys, wax candles, hops, plaster, trees, plants etc.

And while on a visit to Bath in July:

30th. Walked out with Mr Simon to Lady Dudley, and Brook's Pheasant seller &c, then to a Statuary, Walcot Buildings for Diana and Vertumnus in marble, for 10 guineas.

These statues he sent off to Belan on 15 August, after they had arrived at Dublin by sea from Bristol. By 18 August he was back at Belan, where he set about building a grotto and a goldfish pond. On 19 September some shells came from Waterford for his grotto.

Monday 26th November

Works carrying on for erecting pedestals for two marble statues for Diana and Vertumnus,[47]

69

42. *Diary of a Tour through Ireland*, p. 28.
43. As can be seen from plate 20, it was still very old-fashioned in layout some forty years later. The siting of the grotto, the obelisk, the Chinese bridge, the dove house and the hermitage are clearly marked.
44. Diary quoted by Ethel M. Richardson, *Long-forgotten Days*, London 1928, pp. 297–300.
45. The summer house.
46. In the shape of convex rounded curves.
47. The Romans connected the god Vertumnus with the growth of plants. Gardeners accordingly offered him their produce at his festival held on 23 August.
48. A *camera obscura*. Pope described his at Twickenham: 'When you shut the Doors of this Grotto, it becomes on the instant from a luminous Room, a *Camera obscura*; on the Walls of which all objects of the River, Hills, Woods, and Boats, are forming a moving Picture in their visible Radiations.' To Edward Blount, June 1725. George Sherburn (ed.) *The Correspondence of Alexander Pope*, vol. II, p. 296.

    The *camera obscura* had been invented in the sixteenth century and consists of an arrangement of lenses and mirrors in a darkened room, tent or box. The view seen through the mirrors is reflected on to a large sheet of paper. Laurence Sterne, who lived in Ireland until he was ten years old, mentions a *camera obscura* in *Tristram Shandy*.

4 Elysiums by Lough and River

Trees are the best monuments that a man can erect to his own memory. They speak his praises without flattery, and they are blessings to children yet unborn. Every gentleman in Ireland is become a Planter. I doubt the spirit is not so universal in England.

Lord Orrery to Thomas Carew, 15 May 1749

Lancelot Brown was skilled in the management of ornamental water, placing it and shaping it in the enlargement of a river by forming pools at a bend, or altering its course or creating an artificial lake. At his best, in work at Harewood, Bowood or Blenheim, water is the life of the landscape; at its worst, from some of his followers, it appears as an insignificant trickle from a swampy stream. If there was not enough water, more had to be drawn in, and Brown, 'th'omnipotent magician', was notorious for achieving this. William Cowper pictures him at work:

> He speaks. The lake in front becomes a lawn;
> Woods vanish, hills subside, and vallies rise:
> And streams, as if created for his use,
> Pursue the track of his directing wand,
> Sinuous or straight, now rapid and now slow,
> Now murm'ring soft, now roaring in cascades –
> Ev'n as he bids! Th'enraptur'd owner smiles.
> 'Tis finish'd, and yet, finish'd as it seems,
> Still wants a grace, the loveliest it could show,
> A mine to satisfy th'enormous cost.[1]

But he had no experience in dealing with landscape in which there were to be incorporated vast expanses of natural water from lake or sea, to give full play to the imagination.[2] Therefore his influence showed less in Ireland than in England, for the Irish landscape, except in the flatter counties such as Kildare, could rarely be adapted to his style of work. One of his many followers was evidently a nurseryman and landscape gardener named Daniel Courtney, but we have been unable to trace his work. He advertised thus in the *Hibernian Chronicle* of 4 February 1773:

acquainting any Nobleman or Gentleman that intends to have their demesnes laid out in the modern taste, that he will design or execute the same according to the methods used at the Royal Gardens at Richmond by the direction of Mr Brown, Gardener to His Majesty at Hampton Court. N.B. said Courtney intends following the Nursery Business this season at Tralee . . .

This tradition of Brown, called 'modern' in 1773, was carried on in such flat terrains for the next seventy or eighty years in both Ireland and England. In villa gardens in the environs of towns and cities it soon became clichéd in its monotonous belting and clumping, and extensive boundary walls resulting in a lack of middle distance and vistas. However, in the flatter counties, where the terrain wanted mountains or water it was pleasing and satisfactory.

One of the examples in this tradition of landscaping and gardening was at Mountshannon, County Limerick, belonging to the Earls of Clare. The mansion was built circa 1790 and burnt out in the Civil War in 1922. Of the estate there is a very full account in *The Irish Gardener's and Farmer's Magazine*, Volume I (1833–34), which indicates Irish horticultural practices of the time, as well as showing prevailing tastes and describing the site:

It is situated . . . on the eastern bank of the Shannon, about three miles above Limerick, nearly a mile of the western boundary of the demesne being formed by that noble river. The demesne contains about nine hundred acres of land, nearly one half of which is occupied in plantations, pleasure grounds, &c. &c. The ground is rather flat, declining however towards the river, from which the mansion is distant nearly a mile, and of which, in consequence of the intervening trees, no view, or at most a mere glimpse, is obtained from the lower story; but the views from various parts of the grounds of the Shannon and of the distant mountains, as well as of the wooded lands on the opposite bank, are rich in the extreme . . . A large portion of the ground was originally of a very inferior description, being either bog or inundated marsh; but by banking off the Shannon, levelling, draining, and even by trenching, it has been changed into the finest pasture, meadow, and arable land.

The climate of this part of the country, as indicated by some plants which we observed, is very good indeed. The following kinds of vines, viz.: – Miller, white Muscadine, Sweet-water, black Frontignac, and Zante, are now (October 12th) loaded with ripe well flavoured and fair sized bunches of grapes, without any artificial heat but merely trained against a south brick wall.

The kitchen garden is extensive, and the pleasure grounds, considering the remoteness of the place, contain a considerable collection of flowering shrubs and plants. Amongst them the *Magnolia grandiflora*, and the Scarlet Arbutus were very conspicuous; both were in full flower, and have attained a large size.

. . . there are, nevertheless, a few things in which, in our opinion, an improvement might be made.

The approach from Castleconnell, for instance, is carried almost for its whole extent, which is very considerable, through a plantation which partly already and in a few years will effectually exclude every distant object, whether they be mountains, wooded lands, ruined castles, or stretches of the Shannon, one or other of which, were this screen judiciously opened, would present itself at every step. The absence of single trees, groups and masses of them, gives a baldness of appearance to the lawn which might be at once remedied by transplanting some large trees, of which there are abundance well adapted to this purpose, and in this way also the lines of large trees (former hedge rows) which intersect the grounds, being first judiciously opened, might be massed. Much has already been effected in this way by Mr. Abraham, the experienced and very respectable gardener, &c. who has been most successful in the removal of trees and shrubs of a large size . . . These trifling matters being attended to, and the intended approach from Limerick, as designed by the late Mr. Sutherland, being formed.

Six years after this account was written a metallic curvilinear-roofed conservatory had been erected and stocked with new and choice exotics.[3] Horticulturally the estate was equal to many which were older. But the writer of the article in the first *Irish Gardener's and Farmer's Magazine* was rightly critical of certain imperfections in the planting, which would eventually shut out distant objects, particularly the river.

By the end of the eighteenth century, the most famous landscape with water as its main feature in the vicinity of Dublin was Woodlands, or Luttrellstown as it was called after its original owner (Simon Luttrell, first Lord Carhampton): four hundred acres within a wall, extensive Brownian lawn in front of the house and fourteen-mile rides through woods through which the Liffey flowed. The high river banks are punctuated by wild narrow ravines up one of which an approach road runs alongside a brook dropping over cascades and fed from a lake created on the high ground. The romantic, artificially-ruined arch is perhaps the finest of its kind in Ireland, the tufa dripping with ivy and ferns (Plate 77).

Successive generations of famous visitors were duly impressed – Arthur Young in 1776: 'a stream falling over a rocky bed, through the dark woods, with great variety on the sides of steep slopes, at the bottom of which the Liffy is either heard or seen indistinctly; these woods are of great extent, and so near the capital, for a retirement exceedingly beautiful.'[4] Samuel Hayes, in 1794,[5] thought the demesne possessed the finest forest trees in the county, and especially noted a Scotch fir of eighty-five years' growth with a circumference of eleven feet six inches.

Hely Dutton (1802),[6] as well as describing the terrain, extols the agricultural and charitable actions of the owner at that time:

Mr. White is annually adding to the plantations, and improving the soil; for this purpose the fine lake near the castle was laid dry in the summer of 1800, and upwards of 60,000 loads of choice manure raised from the bottom, which, after having been mixed with a large proportion of lime, was laid on the land, and has produced, as might be expected, the best effects. Some opinion may be formed of the spirit, with which improvements are carried on in this demesne,

77 LUTTRELLSTOWN, CO. DUBLIN. *The rustic arch.*

74

when it is known, that upwards of seventy people are employed through the year, beside many additional hands in harvest: this is the true method of relieving the poor . . .

The castle [Plate 78] has the appearance of antiquity; although the chief part of the building has been erected within these twenty years, yet uniformity as to its gothic appearance is preserved; and although a part of it is near six hundred years standing, the additions are so appropriately attached, that the whole has the appearance of having been built at the same time . . .

The noble elm-tree near the old-mills, so long the glory of Luttrell's-town, and the admiration of every person of taste, was unfortunately broken off within about ten feet of the ground, by the great storm in January 1802. I have been favoured with the dimensions of this father of the forest, as taken by Reverend Gilbert Austin.

	Feet.	In.	
4 feet from the ground;	14	9	circumference
15 ——————;	4	9	diameter
79 ——————;	1	0	ditto.

Much to the honour of Mr. White, he intends to preserve this previous stump, which, it is probable, will shoot out again, and continue for many years to add to the picturesque beauties of its native spot.

Pückler-Muskau, writing during his tour of Ireland (1831), having eulogized the glen, was disenchanted by the rest of the demesne: 'scanty grass, stunted trees and thick stagnant water surround a small Gothic castle, which looks like a poor scene in a play . . .' But he liked a 'pavillon rustique' which was in the pleasure ground. These woodhouses were more common in Irish estates than English at this time; and were one of the many examples of picturesque work which will be discussed in Chapters 8 and 9. This one at Woodlands, according to the German prince, was 'hexagonal, three sides solid, and fashioned of pieces of rough branches of trees very prettily arranged in various patterns; the other three consist of two windows and a door. The floor is covered with a mosaic of little pebbles from the brook, the ceiling with shells, and the roof is thatched with wheat straw on which the full ears are left.' He evidently did not notice the charming classical temple (Plate 79) reminiscent of the Temple of Flora at Stourhead which stands in a similar position at the lakeside; but which was a cold bath, and may well be the same as the cold bath where Mrs Delany dined 'very agreeably' in July 1750.[7] Luttrellstown, in contrast with the devastated Mount Shannon demesne, still survives in all its wooded splendour.

In the rest of the country, more than in County Dublin, the wooded hills and deep glens around loughs or near sea showed nature wildly and romantically dressed, which would never have suited Brown's pedantic approach. Very typical is Sir James Caldwell's account of Castle Blayney, County Monaghan in October 1772, showing how natural features such as Lough Muckno were incorporated with much sensitivity

78 LUTTRELLSTOWN. *Lithograph by C. Hullmandel after William Brocas, 1824.*

79 LUTTRELLSTOWN.
The cold bath.

into the landscape. In southern England there are no comparable ornamental waters like these Irish lakes:

There is a lake of about fourteen miles round, in which there are sixteen islands; one of 100 acres, just before the house, is laid out in wood, corn, pasture, gardens, and everything that can make it beautiful. It has also a great variety of rising and falling ground in it, and is inhabited by wild turkeys, deer, different kinds of sheep, rabbits and wild-fowl . . . We drove by very fine roads through very extensive shrubberies and woods, from which many different views of the lake appeared.[8]

Belleisle, the Gore family's estate,[9] on Upper Lough Erne, County Fermanagh was another such landscape which, however, started with a formal setting. In 1739 a parterre descended in 'an hanging level to the Lough . . . enclosed on the East and West sides with High Walls covered with Fruit Trees, and having at the Extremitys on each side, square Turretts which hang over the Lough'.[10] By the time Arthur Young arrived there the improvements had become typically Irish in their use of the superb natural features.

It is an island in Loch Earne of 200 Irish acres, every part of it hill, dale, and gentle declivities;

it has a great deal of wood, much of which is old, and forms both deep shades, and open chearful groves . . . a reach of the lake passes before the house, which is situated near the banks among some fine woods, which give both beauty and shelter. This sheet of water, which is three miles over, is bounded in front by an island of thick wood; and by a bold circular hill, which is his Lordship's deer park, this hill is backed by a considerable mountain. To the right are four or five fine clumps of dark wood; so many islands which rise boldly from the lake, the water breaks in straits between them, and forms a scene extremely picturesque . . . Lord Ross has made walks round the island, from which there is a considerable variety of prospect. A temple is built on a gentle hill, commanding the view of the wooded islands abovementioned; but the most pleasing prospect of them is coming out from the grotto; they appear in an uncommon beauty; two seem to join and the water which flows between takes the appearance of a fine bay, projecting deep into a dark wood: nothing can be more beautiful.[11]

Jonathan Fisher in his *Scenery of Ireland* (1795) shows a late eighteenth-century love of shade when mentioning 'a handsome cottage at Bellisle with a kitchen and other conveniences, in a sweet retired part, secluded from the powerful influence of the sun in the summer months' (Plate 80).

In August 1808 Edward Wakefield, after a visit, described the especial qualities of water in such a landscape:

The views on the lake are indeed delightful, and very different from those which you enjoy during a ride on land. The eye being very little elevated above the surface of the lake, the shores appear as if emerging from the water . . . a blue mist, rising . . . gave a romantic and picturesque cast to the whole scene; and suggested to my mind some of those sublime passages which occur in the works of a northern poet.[12]

He evidently refers here to James MacPherson's *Ossian* in such passages as 'The sun looked forth from his cloud. The hundred streams of Moilena shone. Slow rose the blue columns of mist against the glittering hill.'[13] And 'My hair is the mist of Cromla, when it curls on the hill; when it shines to the beam of the west.'[14]

Although by 1818 the estate had changed hands, it continued to bring forth eulogies from the guide books for tourists: *The Scientific Tourist through Ireland* praises 'the lofty mountain which gives an almost magic relief to the whole', and 'the prospect from the handsome temple which commands the whole of this scenery'. *The Post Chaise Companion* (1820) copies Arthur Young's account almost word for word except for changing the ownership of the estate from Lord Ross to Mr Hannington.

Castle Hume on the west side of Lower Lough Erne was Richard Castle's first house in Ireland, of which but a dovecote and some of the stable block remain. Like Castle Caldwell it was on a peninsula which pierced the lough for about a mile.

81 CASTLE CALDWELL,
CO. FERMANAGH. *Line
engraving, 1780.*

Thanks to the Reverend William Henry we have a clear description of it before the
formal features had been entirely superseded by the more free landscaping:

The house is Built of a Beautiful light coloured Freestone cut off Shaen Mountain . . . It fronts
southwards toward a pretty steep Hill from which the approach is carryed on to the house by a
spacious Avenue . . . The Chambers on the North Side look over the Main Bay of the Lough . . .
Adjoining the East End of the House are pleasant Gardens, which are continued along the side
of the Lough to a Woody Hill that forms the Eastern Coast of the Bay that runs up to the
Castle . . .

Then he describes the formal distribution of avenues on an island which

nearest to Castle Hume has cut out on its summit a spacious Circle, from which are cut thro the
thick Woods 15 (as near as I remember) vistos which descend to different parts of the Lough,
each of them presenting to the eye a vast piece of Water and some agreeable object beyond it.[15]

The woods remained until Arthur Young's time; but by 1812 the house had been
pulled down and all the timber felled.[16]

In a later piece of landscaping, Sir James Caldwell improved the demesne named
after him on the north-east side of Lower Lough Erne (Plate 81). He was inordinately
proud of his work and wrote to his eldest son in Canada in October 1778:

laid out above sixteen thousand pounds upon a most comfortable good house, a very large
court of excellent offices, where every convenience of every sort is placed, two very large
walled gardens with fish ponds, a most beautiful temple built on the Black Rock glazed with
painted glass, and a vast expenditure on the demesne of 700 acres, making it worth three times
as much as what it was, so that I may say you will have a place universally allowed to be the
most beautiful in England or Ireland, I have preserved for you most valuable ornamental
woods, and managed the estate to the best advantage.

Arthur Young describes it at some length,[17] the chief features being the headlands
of thick wood which shot out into the lake, the high ridge of mountains at the back,
the promontory extending into the lake on which the house and gardens lay, the
octagon temple on the point, and the many and various islands of the lake.

Castle Coole, although only a mile and a half from Enniskillen, which is on an
island in the River Erne between the Lower and Upper Loughs Erne, suffers from
having hardly any views of the lough, although it has its own small Lough Coole in
the grounds. It is a chaste classical house designed by James Wyatt for the first Earl
of Belmore, and built, it is said, at a cost of about £90,000. The landscape is Brownian
with its open and extensive lawn on gently sloping ground, and its distant views of the

mountains to the south and south-west. It is one of the few great landscapes in this county not to include the Loughs Erne, which stretch the whole length of the county, and it is a notable omission. However, by 1836 the planting was evidently impressive:

On the lawn, in front of the mansion, are some magnificent old trees; and, among others, an ash which measures 65 ft. in height, and 23 ft. in girt; the tree has a fine straight bole, and its branches extend over a space 270 ft. in circumference. There are, also, a noble beech, which, at a distance, resembles a group, more than a single tree, and which is 123 ft. high, and 13 ft. 10 in. in girt, circumference of the top 885 ft., forming a beautiful, close, regular column, crowning a fine clear bole, 25 ft. high; a sweet chestnut, 80 ft. high, 10 ft. in girt, 20 ft. of a clear bole; a horse-chestnut, 50 years old, 60 ft. high, girt of the trunk 7 ft. 7 in., and diameter of the head 60 ft. This is a very superb specimen; and Lord Belmore told us that it increases one inch every year in solid timber. We measured another very fine beech, which was planted by Lord Belmore about thirty years since, and found it to be 80 ft. high, 10 ft. in girt, with a head 18 ft. in diameter, and a straight bole of 20 ft. We saw, also, some other fine specimens, which we noted down for the *Arboretum Britannicum*. In a noble avenue of oaks, we measured several, one of which was 90 ft. high, girt 10 ft. 5 in., bole to the branches 30 ft. Here we were shown an old oak, taken out of the wood when it was 70 years old, and planted in the lawn, in a very exposed situation, by His Lordship, after some peculiar method of his own, differing from Sir H. Steuart's plan.[18] This oak has now been planted 25 years; and, it having thrown out some small spray, and proved strong enough to weather the Atlantic blast, we need not say that such planting will answer the purpose, particularly where there is little shelter.[19]

Florence Court,[20] eight-and-a-half miles south west of Enniskillen uses the view to Upper Lough Erne a little better than at Castle Coole; but only from the side (east front) of the house which is of lesser importance. It also has extensive lawn and sloping ground, but with more wood than Castle Coole. We illustrate a cottage and a rustic arbour (Plates 82 and 83) which, though built in the nineteenth century at Florence Court, typically carry on eighteenth-century traditions. Neither of these houses can compare with Belleisle or Castle Hume which were on the banks of the lough; although in both there are fine prospects of mountains.

Shane's Castle, the ancient seat of the O'Neills, in the years between the painting of the picture (Plate 84) by an unknown artist in the 1770s and William Ashford's painting (Plate 85), had been modernized. In the place of the old castle was a three-storied Georgian house which, however, still preserved one of the large semi-circular bays formed by a tower of the original. Thomas Milton says 'the water formerly washed the Walls of the Castle, but within these years an Embankment was made, on which is built a Green House, the Castle Wall forming one side, and the Glass projecting into the lake on the other.' Lough Neagh, seventeen miles long, is the largest lake in the British Isles, yet its dead flat banks make most of it a dull piece of scenery,

82 FLORENCE COURT, CO. FERMANAGH. *Rustic cottage: photograph, 1860.*
83 FLORENCE COURT. *Rustic arbour: photograph, 1860.*

84 SHANE'S CASTLE, CO. ANTRIM. *Oil on canvas by unknown artist.*

85 SHANE'S CASTLE. *Oil on canvas by William Ashford.*

especially since the present water level is much lower than in previous centuries.

Sarah Siddons, when appearing in 1783 at the Smock Alley theatre in Dublin, spent a weekend with her friend, Mrs John O'Neill, at Shane's, and was duly impressed.

It is scarce possible to conceive the splendour of this almost Royal Establishment, except by recollecting the circumstances of an Arabian Night's entertainment. Six or eight carriages with a numerous throng of Lords and Ladies and gentlemen on Horseback began the day by making excursions about this terrestrial paradise, returning home but just in time to dress for dinner . . . A fine band of musicians played during the repast. They were stationed in the Corridor, which lead from the dining room into a fine Conservatory, where we plucked our dessert from numerous trees of the most exquisite fruits, and where the waves of the superb Lake wash'd its feet while its cool delicious murmurs were accompanied with strains of celestial harmony from the Corridor.[21]

Sir Richard Colt Hoare, as he relates in his *Journal of a tour in Ireland*, was unimpressed. When he went to Shane's Castle in 1806 he disapproved of it architecturally for he favoured Gothic; it was 'placed' he said:

immediately on the shores of the lake, whose waves beat against its walls; it is an old castle modernized, or rather a modern mansion attached to an old fort; its situation is bold; but its

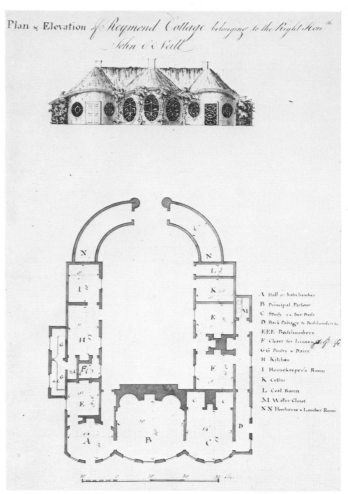

architectural design far from picturesque or appropriate. Improvements, both in gardening and farming, are advancing here most rapidly; a fine kitchen garden, with all its luxurious and glassy appendages, and very extensive and commodious offices have lately been erected.

William Beckford described Colt Hoare's book as 'the meagre notes of this dry, husky traveller whose mind is as dull and vacant as the dignified Coal-hole he has selected as a frontispiece'.

Mr John Sutherland,[22] gardener and landscaper (Plate 86), who was the subject of the portrait dated 1822, must have worked on the planting and layout at Shane's prior to 1814. A contract of 28 January between John Connor, carpenter, and Lord O'Neill states:

Notice to be given in writing, and stuff found at a convenient time by stewards, gardeners etc; and then the work to be begun by as many hands as can be employed at it. To prevent any complaints, the accounts of whatever work is done for each department to be furnished every month; and when any stuff is found for any one jobb, not to be used for another, as it always causes waste of time and timber. The rest of the work and building done according to the prices left by Mr. Sutherland in the office.[23]

In 1814 the improvements were still going on and 'a grand eating room was to be joined' to the conservatory on the lakeside.[24] In 1815 in the interests of improvement, the village of Edenduffcarrick, which is near the castle in the picture, was swept away by Lord O'Neill. But in May 1816 the uncompleted castle was burnt down as the result of a chimney fire. In the middle distance of the portrait of Mr Sutherland can be seen a tower which survived the fire. The vast and decaying demesne, with a long winding drive along the wooded banks of the river to ruined Lower Clannaboy Castle must be little changed from when Arthur Young went there, though another building by Lanyon was burnt down in 1922 during the Civil War. The conservatory and loggia, probably designed by Nash, still stand on the terrace overlooking the

86   JOHN SUTHERLAND. *Oil on canvas by Martin Cregan, 1822.*
87   SHANE'S CASTLE. *Reymond Cottage: water-colour by John Johnstone, c. 1810.*

lake, and the old cedars of Lebanon shade the picturesque ruins of the towers and rooms of the Gothic castle. Lord O'Neill had built a series of rustic seats and thatched cottages over this demesne and on Ram's Island in Lough Neagh. All of these have regrettably been destroyed, though the plan and elevation of one of them, Reymond Cottage, can be seen in John Johnstone's charming early nineteenth-century drawing (Plate 87). O'Neill housed his mistresses in these romantic retreats. He also fitted up an elaborate dairy with ornamental Wedgwood cows and utensils in the stable yard.

A more interesting view of the southern end of Lough Neagh was to be had from the demesne of Lurgan Castle, formerly the home of the Brownlows. According to *The Post Chaise Companion* (1820), there were walks for many miles, some with views of the lough: 'the most beautiful scene is from a bench on a gently swelling hill, which rises almost on every side from the water.'

Very different from Lough Neagh is Lough Gill, County Sligo, flanked by mountains and the river Garavogue, and as unspoiled today as it was two hundred years ago. On a dramatic emerald isthmus clothed in arbutus, hollies and bays stands Hazelwood, one of the first and most Palladian of Richard Castle's houses. To the northwest on the skyline rises the steep side of Ben Bulben, to the south and east lies Lough Gill, studded with its many wooded islands, the largest of which, Church Island (Inís Mor) with its sixth-century remains, is clearly visible from Hazelwood. When General Owen Wynne built the house in the 1730s, it immediately excelled all others in the county on account of its superb setting embracing the whole length of Lough Gill, the mountains and river. The Reverend William Henry describes the scene in 1739 at unusual length for him;[25] yet he hopes he may

be Excused being led into this Error if it be one, out of a Desire to drop some useful Hints in the way of Gentlemen who have a spirit for Building: and to do justice to the fine taste of the late General Wynne; who by pitching on this situation, and Executing this plan, has escaped the Censure too justly cast on us by Foreigners; that 'though no Country affords more fine Situations than Ireland it is rare to see gentlemen's Houses either properly placed, or well executed'.

Dr Daniel Beaufort, when he went there in October 1787, thought the house was 'rather heavy having too few windows, but altogether a handsome building . . . yet the grounds were laid out with great taste'.[26] Only one of the many open vistas cut between woods to the lake, and also the eighteenth-century brick walls of a large hexagonal kitchen garden still remain intact. The rock house is ruined, gone are the parterres, the gardens, the cane house, the shell house, and the Chair of State constructed from the bones of a whale. Although the demesne is uncared for, the house but a ghost of its former self, and a factory sited on the south vista, the changing clouds and the soft pellucid lights, caused by reflections from lake and river, enable one to imagine the setting as it once was – the house of grey local stone looking on to the bright lake where 'peace comes dropping slow'.

Not far off the epitome of Gothic picturesque is seen in the entrance gates, lodges and walls to Markree Castle, overlooking the Unshin (Plate 88). These are the gates which inspired Mrs Cecil Frances Alexander to write with Victorian complacency (verse 3, 'All Things Bright and Beautiful', 1848):

> The rich man in his castle,
> The poor man at his gate,
> God made them, high or lowly,
> And ordered their estate.

In the north of County Cavan, the two adjoining estates of Bellamont Forest (Coote Hill) and Dawson's Grove (now Dartrey demesne) were separated by a lake (Plate 89), the former also having another lake on the other side. The ubiquitous Mrs Delany went there in August 1732 and described the setting of the four-sided Palladian villa to be called Bellamont Forest, which had just been built to the designs of

Sir Edward Lovett Pearce, for his relations the Cootes, Earls of Bellamont. It lay 'on the top of a carpet hill, with large lakes on each side which extended four miles, and are now surrounded by fine groves of well-grown forest trees. Below the house and between the lakes is a little copsewood which is cut into vistas and serpentine walks that have the softest sods imaginable.'[27] Forty years later James FitzMaurice Caldwell had less luck as there was so dense a fog he could see nothing; but he noted that Lord Bellamont kept 'vast numbers of workmen at 10d a day, winter and summer, and by all accounts it is a magnificent place. The very fine lake between it and Lord Dartrey's [Dawson's Grove] causes a communication of beauty between one demesne to the other.'[28]

Plate 90 shows the building of the mausoleum at Dawson's Grove, with Bellamont Forest surmounting one of the small hills in the background. The mausoleum, a square building (Plate 91), with a single window in the pyramidal roof, in memory of Lady Anne Dawson (1733–69), contains one of the finest monuments in Ireland, placed in an alcove of the wall (Plate 92). It is of white marble and the figures are life-size: on the left, an angel on a cloud; on the right, the draped figure of Mr Dawson, the mourning husband 'stands before the altar looking towards her, with an arm uplifted in a supplicating attitude, while his infant son stands clutching him as if

88 MARKREE CASTLE, CO. SLIGO. *The gates: engraving by C. Rosenburg after Francis Goodwin, 1832.*
89 DAWSON'S GROVE, CO. MONAGHAN. *Engraving after William Ashford.*

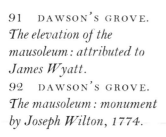

90 DAWSON'S GROVE.
The building of the mausoleum: oil painting by Gabriele Ricciardelli, c. 1772.

91 DAWSON'S GROVE.
The elevation of the mausoleum: attributed to James Wyatt.

92 DAWSON'S GROVE.
The mausoleum: monument by Joseph Wilton, 1774.

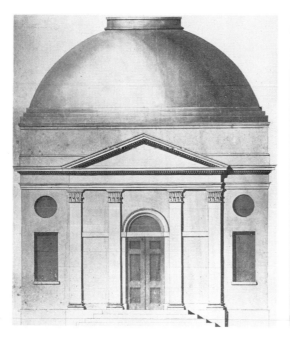

in alarm'.[29] The designer and sculptor was Joseph Wilton, who carved the lions and urns for the Marino Casino of Lord Charlemont. Sir Charles Coote in his *Statistical Survey of the County of Monaghan* (Dublin 1801) thought 'the view of the ancient mausoleum, which peeps through the adjacent wood, has all that venerable and grand effect, which it was designed to convey, and creates a melancholy satisfaction in contemplating the virtue of that admirable character to whose memory it is sacred.'[30] Also in the same county, two miles north-north-west of Cavan, is the demesne of Farnham with similar natural features to Dartrey and Bellamont Forest. Visitors in the late eighteenth and early nineteenth centuries report romantic wooded scenery to the shores of natural lakes, with drives through the woods, one of which led to a pretty eighteenth-century cottage, designed by Lady Farnham.

Belvedere, on the north-east shore of Lough Ennell, County Westmeath, from which Robert Rochfort, the son of Swift's friend (1708–74), took his title of Earl of Belvedere, inspired John Wesley after a visit in July 1767 to comment prophetically: 'One would scarce think it possible to have such variety of beauties in so small a compass.

> How soon, alas! will these upbraid
> Their transitory master dead!'

Samuel Whyte was also inspired to write some inferior though topographically accurate verse 'in the absence of some ladies there Sat Sept Vth MDCCLXXII':

> Here every view, hill, vale and grove
> With various wonders grac'd
> The noble owner's judgement prove
> His genius, and his taste.
>
> . . . .
>
> Bright precedents! – first, sweet retreat
> That airy crescent stands,
> And shielding off the noontide heat,
> That region round commands.[31]
>
> That pillar'd dome, in rustic style
> And sylvan pomp profuse,
> How rich to sight! a cavern'd pile,
> For ornament and use.[32]

Arthur Young saw

spreading to the eye a beautiful lawn of undulating ground margined with wood . . . Lake Ennel, many miles in length, and two or three broad, flows beneath the windows. It is spotted with islets; a promontory of rock, fringed with trees, shoots into it, and the whole is bounded by distant hills. Greater and more magnificent scenes are often met with, but nowhere a more beautiful or a more singular one.[33]

Jonathan Fisher[34] remarks on the smallness of the demesne – only a mile and a half – with many temples and rural seats on its most conspicuous points. In fact, neither house nor grounds were for show, as some larger settings often were, but for comfort, and constructed with quiet taste, except for the one remarkable feature which none of the visitors seems to have commented upon. This was a huge wall (Plate 93)[35] like the shattered wing of a Gothic house, built in about 1760 by the Earl to shut out the sight of his brother's larger Rochfort house only a quarter of a mile away. At the other end of the park stands a Gothic arch with tattered top, a progeny of the wall closing a vista to the west (Plate 95), a Gothic octagonal summer house, now ruined, on a hill overlooking the lake, and a grotto (Plate 96).

John Wesley's prophecy has come true, as the present eighteenth-century house was but the Earl's fishing lodge; Gaulstown, his large mansion five miles off, has disappeared, and his brother's house is a picturesque ruin in a deserted park. The visual obstruction between the demesnes is no longer necessary; yet it has survived, and is the largest constructed ruin of its kind in Ireland.

93 BELVEDERE, CO. WESTMEATH. *The Gothic wall.*

94 BELVEDERE. *Plate 6 from* Universal Architecture, *Part II, by Thomas Wright.*

Charleville Forest, about twenty miles south of Belvedere, has a stream in the grounds, but the country round is dull and uninterestingly flat. In June 1798 Lord Charleville (then Lord Tullamore) brought his bride to an old-fashioned and inconvenient house about two miles south west of Tullamore, King's County (County Offaly). Soon he set about building a castle with Francis Johnston as his architect. In November 1800, Louisa Conolly wrote she was glad to hear he had begun, for there were 'few occupations more entertaining than Building'. But like many building operations in Ireland, the work ambled along in leisurely fashion. In the summer of 1805 he hoped he might be able to inhabit part of the building in the following summer, but it was not finished until the autumn of 1808. Perhaps it is not surprising it took so long as the castle is a massive structure in the form of a rectangle, with a vast octagon tower, resembling Guy's Tower at Warwick Castle, at one corner, and a more graceful 150-foot tower at another. The terrace, on which are walks and lawns, built on a stone wall above a sunk fence, was not completed until 1813. Yet the artificial lake of eight acres was only visible from the first floor windows, and the Clodiagh stream winding through broken ground to the west played only a small part in the scene from the house. But the grotto, rustic bridges, the cascades and Gothic dairy (Plates 97, 98 and 99) compensated for this. Sir Charles Coote was full of praise:

1500 acres delightfully wooded with fine full-grown timber . . . Clodiagh river runs with rapidity through the demesne, which is well supplied with several mountain streams, and with several rustic bridges, which with cascades have altogether the most charming effect. The grotto, which commands a principal fall, is finished in true rustic style, the tumbling rocks, the hermit's bed, and the well are most happily situated, and the incrustations and petrifactions . . . give it all the venerable appearance of antiquity. When lights are introduced they give the grandest illumination to the reflecting spars and transparent petrifactions. This grotto was designed by the late Lady Charleville, and built at considerable expence, to give employment to the poor peasantry in a season of scarcity.[36]

Edward Wakefield saw it all differently: 'The domain is very large, and abounds with trees universally stunted by loads of ivy, which has been suffered to grow so thick as to smother them. Neither the house nor grounds command any distant views, and beyond the wall by which they are surrounded, nothing is seen but one bog succeeding another . . .'[37] Evidently his Lordship had not paid enough attention to the eminent statistician, Wakefield!

Many larger houses, with landscapes on a scale quite different from Belvedere or

97 CHARLEVILLE FOREST, CO. OFFALY. *A rustic stone bridge: oil on canvas by William Ash-ford, 1801.*

98 CHARLEVILLE FOREST. *Cascade on the Clodiagh by William Ash-ford, 1801.*
99 CHARLEVILLE FOREST. *Lake and Gothic dairy: oil on canvas by William Ashford, 1801.*

Charleville, were altered and enlarged by the nobility in the second half of the eighteenth century, and nearly all of them are sited on a river or lake. Slane Castle, County Meath (Plate 100),[38] on the banks of the Boyne, was enlarged by James Wyatt for Lord Conyngham, and the landscape improved at the same time. It has all the essential features: a rising promontory on which it stands, the winding river, views to a lake with islands, plantations, distant hills, and shelter. Arthur Young comments significantly on the fact that although Lord Conyngham was an absentee, he spent large sums on its upkeep, 'while it is so common for absentees to drain the kingdom of every shilling they can, so contrary a conduct ought to be held in the estimation which it justly deserves.'

It was one of the first estates laid out (circa 1767) by Mr John Sutherland when, according to James Fraser, himself a landscape gardener, Sutherland was 'in the heyday of his youth and fancy'.[39] Sutherland worked at Caledon in 1807 (see page 44) where the final bill for the hot-houses totalled £2,024, and his name occurs in certain smaller payments.[40] We also mention his work at Ballyfin for Sir Charles Coote, post 1781 (see page 96); at Lough Cutra for Lord Gort, circa 1809 (see page 182); at Shane's Castle for Lord O'Neill in 1814 (see page 82) and at Mountshannon for the Earl of Clare in the 1820s. He was the best-known landscape gardener (to use a term later invented by Humphry Repton) in Ireland during this period. When landscaping he sometimes prejudged effects and failed to harmonize outlines with the surrounding scenery in what appears to have been the manner of a poor follower of Brown.[41]

The absenteeism at Slane, commented upon by Young, had been resumed fifty years later. Fraser's writing reveals the eye of a true landscape gardener with the knowledge of a horticulturalist:

A casual effect as to tinting has been produced by a few evergreen oaks, which have been thrown into a broken recess on this finely wooded slope. This is evidently the result of accident, as, although this and many other parts of the demesne would in every sense justify grouping, so as to produce a diversity by their various tints, no attention whatever has been paid to the subject. The gardens and plantations of this place have been long neglected . . . There are here some beautiful detached forest-trees; and the most picturesque acacia (Robinia), we remember to have seen, stands neglected in the eastern plantation. As a proof of the powers of the Canadian poplar to resist the storm, we may refer to the wood in question: on the most exposed point of which, when the oak, elm, &c. have been more or less injured, this tree bears up stoutly against the boisterous south-west blast.[42]

Blending with Slane, also commanding a fine view of river scenery from a high bank, is Beauparc, a house which Sir Richard Colt Hoare, in his Gothic bias, found to be an 'inappropriate and discordant building', as it was plain, square and Palladian (Plate 101). His reaction was customary at that time when eyes were sensitive to the picturesque, and here was a setting in that genre. The Boyne was grand, sombre, of considerable breadth, and its waters were gloomy through the masses of spruce which overshadowed them, a place suited to *Il Penseroso*. James Fraser associated a bright, cheerful scene with neo-classical building, thus his unfavourable comment:

Had a castellated structure, with its towers and battlements, stood frowning over the precipice, instead of the tame city-looking building which here commands the whole of the scenery we have hastily glanced over, how different would have been the effect! In nine tenths of the modern country residences, we find buildings wholly unsuited to the localities of the place: castles where there is not a single feature to warrant such erections; and Grecian buildings amid the wildest scenery. These are serious faults; but until landscape-gardening forms a part of the education of professional architects, we may in vain look for a remedy. Along the banks of the river we observed a few trees of the ashen-leaved maple and entire-leaved ash. The singularly yellowish-green pinnated leaves of the maple and the entire dark leaves of the ash produce a striking contrast with those of the common trees around. On the borders of a plantation the former might answer well when a relief was necessary from heavy masses of oak, &c.: the latter is a robust growing tree in any situation, and the leaves are of a different shade from those usually planted. The common varieties of the pine-tribe thrive uncommonly well here, and a good many seedlings are raised from them for the Dublin market. In those departments of this demesne, to which our observations were more particularly directed, everything is in the best possible order.[43]

Near Ardbraccan, County Meath, and close to these two estates was Ballybeg, one

100 SLANE CASTLE, CO. MEATH. *Aerial view.*

101 BEAUPARC, CO. MEATH. *Engraving by Thomas Milton after Thomas Roberts.*

of the oldest and most extensive nurseries in Ireland in the late eighteenth century, owned by the O'Reilly family. It was nearly fifty acres in extent, and planting was not close, as is often the case in smaller nurseries. Rare and new hardy plants of forest and fruit trees, and also ornamental shrubs, were constantly introduced, so that the nursery gained an international reputation. It provided many fine plants for estates along the banks of the Boyne, as transplanting trees long distances (apart from the expense) often resulted in considerable damage to the roots, either from injury in carriage, or from remaining too long out of the ground. There were several smaller nurseries at this time in and round Dublin and in County Cork and County Kilkenny.[44] The best known were Ballybeg and the Honourable John Foster's at Collon where his public nursery had two hundred and fifty trees and shrubs for sale in 1797.

Another fine demesne, overlooking the site of the Battle of the Boyne (1690), some three miles up the river from Drogheda, was Townley Hall. It included, on the east side, King William's Glen, associated with the battle, and now leading down to the site of the obelisk commemorating the occasion (Plate 102); the viewpoint of the engravings being in the demesne. In 1794 Francis Johnston designed an austere house for Blaney Townley Balfour replacing an older one. Balfour became the most successful planter in the county with the exception of John Foster at Collon. Complimentary

102 BOYNE, CO. MEATH. *The Boyne Obelisk: engraving by W. Walker and W. Angus after Paul Sandby.*

yet critical of his endeavours, *The Gardener's Magazine*, Vol. 2 (1827), p. 148, lists one of his deficiencies:

A fine wooded glen runs through the demesne, on the eastern bank of which the principal approach to the house has been judiciously carried. The extensive young plantations are suffering much by want of thinning and pruning; a circumstance to be regretted in a place of this magnitude . . . Townly-Hall bids fair to be one of the most magnificent demesnes in the kingdom . . . The gardens are well kept in every department: the drest-grounds are upon a large scale, and contain an extensive collection of shrubs. In short, the whole place forms a striking contrast to those around.

Headfort House, County Meath, on the Blackwater,[45] a tributary of the Boyne, impressed Arthur Young in July 1776. However, other than some small lakes and islands, the demesne has few natural features, and has the appearance of an English park, but Young was interested in the husbandry:

His Lordship [Lord Bective] transplants oaks 20 feet high without any danger, and they appear to thrive perfectly well; but he takes a large ball of earth up with the roots . . . Besides these numerous plantations, considerable mansion, and an incredible quantity of walling [done during famine years], his lordship has walled in 26 acres for a garden and nursery, and built six or seven large pineries, 90 feet long each.

A fine hedge of Irish or Florence Court yew (*Taxus fastigiata*) antedates the present house with its Adam interior (Plate 103) and is all that remains of a formal garden designed in the 1720s by Robert Stevenson (Plate 104). Like many inland demesnes it suffers from severe frosts, and in 1849 it was suffering from the great malady of prolonged absenteeism during which the grounds were neglected.

The details of problems incurred by even temporary absenteeism at Lissanoure near Ballymoney, County Antrim, are indicated very clearly in the following letter. If read in conjunction with the estate map (Plate 105), it illustrates a very typical Irish late eighteenth-century demesne: with its house (Plate 106) on Castle Island, the main rooms facing south; surrounded by two loughs joined by a stream; its plantations on land reclaimed from the bog; its kitchen garden formally designed but distant and hidden from the house; its cabins built for workers; and above all, its optimistic planting for the future in a living landscape 'chastened and polished but not transformed', in the tradition of William Kent rather than of Lancelot Brown. The letter is

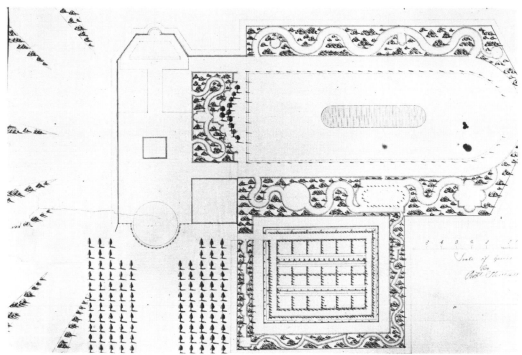

103 HEADFORT HOUSE, CO. MEATH. *House and park: watercolour possibly by George Holmes, c. 1790.*

104 HEADFORT HOUSE. *Formal gardens: plan by Robert Stevenson, c. 1720.*
105 LISSANOURE, CO. ANTRIM. *Estate map, c. 1800.*
106 LISSANOURE. *View of the house: detail from an estate map, c. 1810.*

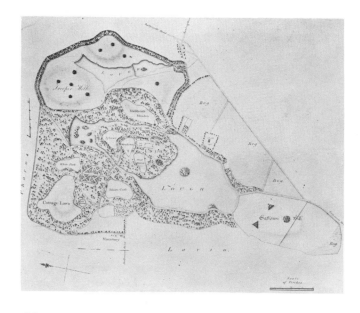

written by Richard Jackson of Coleraine, County Londonderry, agent to Earl Macartney in London, on 19 October 1789:

We got to Lissanoure before dinner. We were all very much delighted with the appearance of everything . . . the trees through the plantation are in great vigour and growing fast; the drains are kept open and correctly attended to, and the walks in good order; the two lakes in the front and back of the house, with the canal, are brim full and clean; the water is greatly increased by the Stoney Burn you have turned into it, and makes an agreeable murmuring noise.

The new wall is now completely finished from the deep drain in the bog to the gate above the old mass-house. It is exceedingly well built: it contains 160 perches, is eight feet high, and at the fairest calculation that can be made, counting the work of your horses, it stands in £1. 7s. a perch amounting to £216; the continuance of that wall, from the great drain in the bog on the west side to the new cabins at the ten acres, will be in length about one hundred perches more, which at the same estimate of £1. 7s. per perch will amount to £135, so that the whole expense of the wall will cost £351 and no more. I had the whole measured and I believe the calculation is most accurately made. I think that this wall will be a substantial improvement to your demesne. It will effectually secure the most open and exposed part of it and be a great ornament from the different views you will have of it. When the new plantation on the opposite side of the demesne is finished which is now to be proceeded upon – from Kendall's ditch through Kithcart's bog (the purchase of Kithcart's bog being finally settled), you will then have your whole farm terminated and enclosed, except the part where McCollum's land comes in, with all the advantage and beauty on every side that can possibly be had from the situation of the ground.

James Dunn will soon set about to drain, ditch and level Kithcart's bog, in order to prepare it for planting in the spring; this will finish the new plantation, and a beautiful appearance it will make, from the house across the lake, when the trees grow up; they are thriving at present extremely well.

The chief work that James will be employed in this winter will be – to prepare one-half of the ground from the great drain in the bog to the demesne ditch in order to have it planted in the spring with willows etc. – to take old rubbish of Lissanoure house, now lying in a heap on Gallows hill, and draw it to the new plantation at Kendall's and Kithcart's part of the bog; – and to draw compost to Blair's croft and the other meadows, to be spread on them, after the hay is cut next year. He also intends to begin in a few days to plant between the garden and the canal, the spruce and larch firs; – the land within the new wall, got from the four tenants below the mass-house, about five acres, has been limed with 80 barrels to the acre. James intends to level and plough it as soon as horses can be spared and sow it with oats and grass seed.

You have this season a remarkably fine crop of hay and oats. You will need none to buy. All was in the fields when I left Lissanoure last Saturday but may be in in a few days if the present dry weather stands. The garden and nursery are in good order . . .[46]

Curraghmore, County Waterford has always been cared for by the Beresfords who have lived with a magnificence which the estate still shows. In 1794 they were reputed to be in residence for nine months of the year which thereby set 'a laudable example to the neighbouring gentlemen'.[47] This had been going on since Sir Marcus Beresford, Bt. acquired the property in 1717 by marriage with Lady Catherine Power (Cáitlin Paor), the heiress of the last Earl of Tyrone. It was she who made the shell house (see page 41), and it was her son's death which caused the erection of the de la Poer tower on a nearby hill. Richard Pococke in 1752 was most impressed by the primeval trees, which one still sees on following the drive alongside the small river Clodiagh. Samuel Hayes[48] called them 'unrivalled' trees, counting six each of hugh ash, beech and oak of up to ten to fourteen feet round, and two hundred more of the same dimensions. Edward Willes in 1759 was similarly impressed:[49]

I received an invitation to breakfast at Lord Tyrones at Curraghmor which is a most magnificent place: the house itself is a large and good one tho nothing particular in it but the situation is grand, we drive for near two miles thro the only Wood I had then seen in Ireland and the woods extend like Stoken Church for several miles, a fine river runs thro them, his house is situated very oddly, Tis on a rising Ground surrounded by mountains covered with wood and the river is brought into the garden and forms 6 fine Cascades, one below another, in the Front of his house and at the back of the house forms 4 fine cascades likewise; and then tumbles over Rocks into its natural course again. In the Garden is the largest and finest grotto covered with shells I ever saw . . .

Louisa Conolly, during a visit in 1777, thought the terrain resembled Goodwood where she had been brought up.[50] There were similarities certainly: both houses were comfortable but not magnificent, with miles of park wall, surrounded by hills not too near, with views to the south; both estates were finely planted and had distinguished shell rooms; yet at Curraghmore the serpentining river and the view across the artificial lake exceeds any such view from Goodwood House. John Barrow (1835) says the Beresfords were as absentee as the Devonshires or the Bessboroughs.[51] Yet the family must have spent some time there as the large formal terraces and gardens were laid out as late as 1843 by Louisa, Lady Waterford. In the house there are designs by Alexander Robertson for Gothicizing the whole mansion so it is more than likely he designed these terraces, which do not really fit into the woodland and mountainous Irish scene. Yet Curraghmore and Powerscourt are indications that certain of the nobility, who were rich and wished to appear exceptionally grand, looked longingly back to Versailles and Le Nôtre rather than to Blenheim and Brown.

A less grand but more elegant estate was Heywood, Queen's County (County Leix). The first mention of this estate, which belonged to the Trench family, is in a letter written in the summer of 1763:

Near this [Lord Shelbourne's estate] is a town called Ballynakeil, a very pretty one, where a Parson the Rev. Frederick Trench has a sweet Habitation. He has 24 Acres Walld round 10 feet high. The ground naturally in fine Slopes and Rising, large trees properly disperst, a River of very clear Water running through it. Pouring Cascades, upon which I counted near 100 Couple of rabbits & of 100 Brace of Hares which are in these Grounds . . . very extensive Views.[52]

The builder of a new house in 1773 was Michael Frederick Trench, who later had experience architecturally with Richard Johnston in the New Assembly Rooms next to the Rotunda, Dublin, and obviously designed and laid out Heywood himself. It stood in grey local stone, on the side of a hill facing south-west and sloping to a lake, out of which ran a stream which fell into two more lakes for a mile to Ballinakill. The whole landscape was designed to be seen from the drive, and from the windows of the drawing room (Plate 107). In the far distance through the trees was the Gothic entrance gate (Plate 108) from the Dublin road, with a small octagonal tower similar to that of the entrance front at Charleville Castle, County Offaly, by Francis Johnston (1801). The drive then wound along the stream and lakes, passing first a motte and a stone cross (Plate 109), which could be seen through the trees from the drawing room; indeed, the end of the house can be seen on the skyline in this picture. The *chef d'oeuvre* of the landscape was the Gothic ruin on the hill to the left as one drove in. This had been transported some twelve miles by Frederick Trench from the ruined Dominican

107 HEYWOOD, CO. LEIX. *Gothic landscape: lithograph after F. W. Trench, 1818.*

108 HEYWOOD. *The Gothic entrance gate: lithograph after F. W. Trench, 1821.*

109 HEYWOOD. *Entrance avenue and stone cross: watercolour by George Holmes.*
110 HEYWOOD. *Classical view: lithograph after F. W. Trench, 1818.*

friary at Aghaboe. The fifteenth-century window tracery, framing the green foliage of trees behind must have been especially effective and had 'all the appearance of Gothic antiquity'.[53] From the windows of the drawing room on the main south front one saw the classic view (Plate 110), with buildings skilfully placed. On a hill in the distance was the Ionic Temple of the Winds,[54] and at a bend in the river, a three-arched bridge: in the background, open country to the mountains. Before Frederick Trench died (1836), this landscape, in the Stourhead romantic-poetic tradition, was perfect.

A later example of the work of Mr John Sutherland was at Ballyfin, Queen's County, belonging to the Honourable William Pole (Plate 111). Its artificial lake gave it a Brownian aspect which was not especially Irish. As early as 1759 Emily Kildare spent the day with Mr Pole and his wife Lady Sarah, noting the lake: 'There is a piece of water there very like what I fancy our own will be, only broader; fine plantations, and the greatest variety of trees and flowers almost that ever I saw . . .'[55]

The house was unfinished in 1781 when the owner died; later it possessed 'agreeable walks and recesses in the wood which skirts the lake, ample gardens, extensive demesne and deerpark'.[56] Finally it was improved further by Sir Charles Coote who spent £120,000 on improvements by Mr Sutherland, rebuilding the house and building a complete medieval round castle with entrance turrets, moat and drawbridge[57] (Plate 112).

The second and third Earls of Dunraven at Adare Manor, County Limerick, were model landlords who between them rebuilt village and house, as well as laying out grounds. The demesne has much to commend it: the river Maigue flowing through the grounds, the magnificent ruins of a fifteenth-century Franciscan friary and a Geraldine castle[58] (Plate 113). Broad steps lead down to the river, and some of the trees are very noble. It is rare to find an account of an estate written by the head gardener himself, and although one has to make allowances for an understandable pride in achievement, yet the details of the planting in the period 1820–30, and the methods employed, are of interest as being typical of an estate in Munster at its best:

At the entrance into the premises stands a commodious garden-house, tastefully built, and displaying magnificence and comfort, both interiorly and exteriorly: contiguous to which are a melon-yard, with pits and frames; and mushroom, tool, and compost sheds.

The gardens, which contain more than three Irish acres, and are so highly celebrated for their fine fruit trees, particularly apricots, figs, and peaches, are surrounded, and divided into three equal parts, by lofty walls faced with brick, and communicating with each other by great double stone arches. In the middle garden stands a fig tree; a rarity indeed, for its equal would be sought for throughout this country in vain; having never been known to fail, and generally producing two yearly crops, one in June and the other in August. In the lower, or cherry, garden stands a curious chain of rocks, beautifully planted with alpine plants, rising to a great eminence, and surrounded by a pond planted with water lilies; on the banks of which are some quince trees, that are remarkable for their fine fruit. The interest of this spot is increased by the circumstance of an eagle having taken up his residence here; where he sits perched upon the tallest rock, while the small birds look upon him with terror, and depart from his presence with precipitation; so that he answers the double purpose of use and ornament.

Adjoining is the Earl of Dunraven's splendid new house . . . To the south of this noble edifice lies the pleasure-ground, containing more than twenty acres; at the end of which is a well-constructed heath-house, on the verge of the beautiful river Maig, which flows through the demesne, close to the mansion, and the falls on which are very interesting. This pleasure-ground, which is surrounded with beautiful oak and elm trees of immense magnitude, strikes the eye of the beholder with an appearance of the most pleasing undulations, heightened by its picturesque situation along the banks of the river, where a great curiosity presents itself in a grand line of thirty English elm trees, more than 150 ft. high, and girting 14 ft. on an average. These beautiful trees stand in regular order on the brink of the river, across the bed of which, their roots extend, and derive their nourishment from thence. Amongst the great trees is a renowned and venerable ash, under the roots of which the treasure of His Lordship's ancestors lay concealed during the troubles of 1688. This highly favoured tree is 15 ft. in girt. A little further on, in the pleasure-ground, stands a cock's-spur thorn, forming itself into an arbour, surrounded by an evergreen privet hedge, planted with standard roses; the intention of which was to hide the naked stems of the roses. You next behold three cast-iron bowers, which you approach, passing first under three magnificent iron rail double arches, planted with roses. A little further on appear some beautiful cedars of Lebanon, in grand style, near which are an

111 BALLYFIN, CO LEIX. *Engraving by Thomas Milton after William Ashford.*

112 BALLYFIN. *Medieval round castle.*

113 ADARE MANOR, CO. LIMERICK. *Oil on canvas by unknown artist, c. 1740.*

American border, and a Portugal laurel 35 yards in circumference. Close by are a green-house, and a grapery of exquisite beauty, surrounded by a garden of evergreens. A large yucca, above 40 ft. high, stands at the end of the green-house, and makes a noble appearance: it flowers every second year. Several acacias, in good bloom, grow hard by, one of which girts 9 ft; with some beautiful Portugal laurels and evergreen oaks. In the evergreen garden are several clumps of rockwork, planted with alpine plants. Outside the iron railing stands a beautiful specimen of the hickory tree, 6 ft. in circumference; with several huge elms and silver firs, sweet chestnut, and walnut trees, one of which is 9 ft. in girt, and the branches thereof 70 ft. in circumference; the branch circumference of the hickory being 90 ft.

A little further on appears a castellated wall, beautifully planted with magnolias, *Sophora japonica*, *Edwardsia grandiflora*, and *E. microphylla*; myrtles, camellias, *Nerium splendens*, pomegranates, with a vine at the extremity (a never-failing sweet-water grape); and a great profusion of other ornamental plants, too numerous for insertion.[59]

A lighter touch which, nevertheless, shows the admirable attitude to planting of the first Earl of Dunraven (then Sir Richard Quin), can be seen in the two inscriptions on stones at the base of some magnificent oak trees in the garden:

I came from the woods of Killarney in 1791 in the pocket of Sir Richard Quin's shooting-jacket. Dear owner of Adare, don't put me into your pocket.

Though planted in 1768,
We hope to flourish in peaceful state.
Let us live on
At any rate.

The Parsons family which acquired Birr Castle, King's County, in 1619 have also been excellent landlords. A formal seventeenth-century garden and maze with box hedges, thirty feet high, were mentioned in Chapter 1; but the eighteenth-century park landscape made by Sir William Parsons is rather flat and formlessly Brownian, the old Telescope House being the only interesting building and that for historical rather than aesthetic or architectural reasons. It still houses the case of the once largest telescope in the world, the speculum of which (now in the Science Museum, London) having been made by the astronomer, the third Earl of Rosse and finished in 1845. But the building was not used for another two years on account of works for famine relief, which included the Vaubanesque fortifications and terrace in front of the castle, a high perimeter wall and romantic crenellations (Plate 114). The most interesting feature of the landscape in its relation to the castle is the river tumbling over the rocks below the windows, and magically reflecting the dancing of white and gold light on to the vaulting and mirrors of the Gothic room. On looking out from this beautiful room

114 BIRR CASTLE, CO. OFFALY. *Pencil drawing by R. Smith, 1820.*

one sees the delicate and charming suspension foot bridge,[60] erected between 1820 and 1825, and said to be the first of its kind in Ireland.

As poverty and famines caused by failure of the potato crops required help on a large scale from landlords, few of the better ones failed to promote gardening, landscaping and building activities. Having sympathy for the appalling difficulties under which many of the poor laboured at such times, they imaginatively found work to help them, and improvements on the estate, both of workers' cottages and landlords' grounds, provided a solution. Like the Parsons at Birr, the Villiers Stuarts at Dromana, County Waterford, have an excellent record of public service.[61] Whereas Birr is a picturesque Gothic building looking out on to a Brownian park, Dromana was a classical house in a picturesque wooded setting overlooking the Finisk which joins the Blackwater at Affane. 'The style of the house is not in character with the scene,'[62] writes James Fraser in similar terms to those he used of Beauparc (see page 89). Although he mentions the famous old sweet chestnut tree, the largest in the county, he fails to note a unique building, the Hinduesque Gothic lodge which stands by the river. This gate lodge, circa 1830 (Plate 115),[63] is the only one of its kind in the country, though predated in England by S. P. Cockerell's Sezincote (1803) and John Nash's Brighton Pavilion (1822). The Dromana Gateway and bridge were built for a

115 DROMANA GATE-
WAY, CO. WATERFORD.
Photograph, 1972.

returning honeymoon couple to whom they must have seemed like a setting for the Arabian Nights as they returned through the woods to their home.

In fifty years a demesne can disintegrate although in the ownership of the same rich family. Two different accounts of the Boyles at Castlemartyr, County Cork (see page 22), show this. In September 1776 Arthur Young[64] was full of praise for Lord Shannon's and his father's works: much well-grown wood; considerable lawns; walks along a serpentining river; an old, picturesque ruined castle; and, above all, Lord Shannon's husbandry – extra large turnips, cabbages and potatoes; special ditches; bounties to labourers (if they spoke English); land reclaimed and walled; the best barn in Ireland; and the foundation of a flourishing linen manufactory. All this was the work of Richard Boyle (1727–1807), second Earl of Shannon, who was born at Castlemartyr, matriculated at Trinity College, Dublin, was married, lived and died at Castlemartyr, as did his wife. By 1829 the estate was in a state of decay. The house was dilapidated; no one but a gardener had entered the flower garden for seven years; yet the shrubberies were being kept up; the Luccombe oaks were the finest in Ireland; *Magnolia grandiflora, Kalmia latifolia, Camellia japonica, Prunus laurocerasus* (common laurel), *Arbutus unedo*, Chinese roses, and myrtles still flourished.[65] Henry Boyle (1771–1842), third Earl of Shannon was educated in England, lived and died in

England, as did his wife. The demesne never recovered, and the house is now a Carmelite priory.

Maria Edgeworth's reports of her visits to Galway, Connemara and Mayo are invaluable as mirrors to show the conditions of living there. Edgeworthstown, County Longford, differed from the west as *foie gras* does from tripe. Ballynahinch Castle, beautifully sited over the Owenmore River, in picturesque country for Galway, was mostly built by Richard Martin, M.P., and evidently was a broken-down place in 1836:

a dilapidated mansion with nothing of a castle about it excepting four pepper box-looking towers stuck on at each corner – very badly, & whitewashed; and all that battlemented front which looks so grand, in the drawing room is more whitewashed stone or brick or mud, I cannot swear which. But altogether the house is very long and ruinous looking, not a ruin of antiquity – but with cow-house & pig stye & dunghill adjoining, & a litter indescribably in a sunk sort of backyard seen at the end of the mansion . . .[66]

In September 1787, Dr Beaufort, with his keen eye for landscaping, had given Ballynahinch an excellent mark: he was surprised at the beautiful walks Mrs Martin had created

by the lakeside which is indented & ornamented by a wooded peninsula, in which they are building a cottage. In a pretty glen there is a fine natural cascade & little thatched hermitage that have a good effect. At the other end is a bathinghouse with *necessary* buildings, & a boathouse for 2 boats. And in a very small stony Island in the middle of the lake an old Castle, which is now repairing; before it grows a very curious Elder tree of great antiquity, rooted in two places about 12 feet asunder, & very knotty.[67]

In 1803 it was agriculturally neglected, for Edward Wakefield noticed wretched or no cultivation and half-starved stock. He also estimated that Mr Martin, with seventy miles of sea coast to his name, owned the largest territory of any individual in the British Isles.[68] Twelve years later the estate needed extensive planting such as was happening in Scotland at that time; not just by hundreds of acres, but by whole mountains, and not like the 'tame thin screens or belts of the followers of Browne [*sic*] disgracing many places in this county'.[69] Maria Edgeworth expected Moore Hall, on the banks of Lough Carra, County Mayo, to be similar, but was surprised to find in 1836 'a most excellent house, beautifully furnished in the best taste'[70] by an eccentric and domineering Mrs Moore who had improved her husband's estate and built new cottages.[71]

But there were few 'magnificent great houses' in the west; almost all were poor and bare like the country in between: 'stone walls, no hedges, no trees, bogs black and interminable – rocky wastes – and wee fields seemingly covered with showers of stones'.[72] It was always a relief for Maria Edgeworth to visit her friends the Pakenhams at Pakenham Hall; although she did not take to Georgiana, the second Countess, she admired the gardens created by her. On 19 September 1832 she wrote to her friend Miss Ruxton:

We have been walking and driving all morning, and seeing all that Lady Longford has done in beautifying the place and employing the people. I never saw in England or Ireland, such beautiful gardens – the most beautiful American garden my eyes ever beheld. She took advantage of a group of superb old chestnut trees, with oak and ash for a background, which had never been noticed in that terra incognita; now it is a fairy land, embowered round with evergreens.[73]

To Lady Romilly she had written earlier: 'I take back all I have said about Lady Longford; she may want feeling . . . but taste she has.' The American garden was not without its difficulties. The amount of lime in the soil proved unsuitable for many American plants, and although Mr George, the gardener, had converted a useless swamp into a charming garden, the peat he used did not suit azaleas of which at first there was a fine collection. Nevertheless, after three or four years, they had become scrubby and overgrown with lichens. Of a hundred acacias only two, *A. dealbata* and *A. verticillata*, survived a bad winter. It was not surprising that some years later Mr George wrote to J. C. Loudon's *Gardener's Magazine* for advice.

Back at Edgeworthstown, only twelve miles from Pakenham Hall, Maria had to deal with huge family debts because of her father's death in 1817. Since 1782, when he returned to Ireland, coping with the upkeep of the house and estate had been too much of a financial burden for Richard Lovell Edgeworth. 'Damp, delapidation and waste' were far advanced, and although he did not build 'a superb mansion disproportionate to his fortune', he slowly converted the grounds from an outdated Dutch style to a naturalistic order, and slowly ran into debt. Despite Maria's acting as his agent and helper, thus avoiding middlemen, he could not survive financially. What was easy for his neighbours, Lord Longford and Lord Granard with their high rent rolls, was impossible for him. This was all the more tragic because he was a model landlord, making no distinction between Catholics and Protestants, and carrying out in every way his original dedication that he would work for 'the melioration of the inhabitants of the country from which I drew my subsistence'.

1. *The Task*, Book III, 'The Garden', lines 774–82.
2. According to Hilaire Belloc, *Sussex*, p. 104, London 1906, the small sheet of water called Knepp mill-pond near Horsham is said to be 'the largest unbroken area of water south of the Thames'.
3. *The Irish Gardener's and Farmer's Magazine*, vol. VI (1839), p. 87.
4. *A Tour in Ireland*, vol. I, p. 21.
5. *A Practical Treatise on Planting and the Management of Woods and Coppices*. Dublin 1794.
6. *Observations on Mr. Archer's Statistical Survey of the County of Dublin*, Dublin 1802, pp. 126–27.
7. Llanover, *Mrs Delany*, vol. II, p. 561.
8. W. H. G. Bagshawe, *The Bagshawes of Ford*, London 1886, pp. 323 ff.
9. Sir Ralph Gore created Earl of Ross 1772. Title extinct 1802.
10. Henry MSS.
11. Young, *Tour in Ireland*, vol. I, p. 97.
12. Edward Wakefield, *An Account of Ireland, Statistical and Political*, vol. I, p. 22.
13. 'Temora. An Epic Poem', Book VIII, *Poems of Ossian*, translated by James Macpherson. Moilena was a heath in Ulster.
14. 'Fingal. An Epic Poem'. Macpherson, *Ossian*. Cromla was a mountain in Ulster.
15. Henry MSS.
16. Wakefield, *Account of Ireland*, vol. I, p. 26.
17. *Tour in Ireland*, vol. I, pp. 188–94.
18. See Henry Steuart, *The Planter's Guide*. Edinburgh 1828. Steaurt was famous for the transplantation of mature trees on his estate at Allanton. For further details, see A. A. Tait, 'The instant landscape of Sir Henry Steuart.' *Burlington Magazine*, January 1976.
19. Loudon (ed.), *The Gardener's Magazine*, vol. XII, March 1836, pp. 109–10.
20. Florence Court was named after the wife of John Cole, who died in 1718 having built the house which stood on the site before the present one was completed about 1764. Other houses named after wives are Bettyville, Bessborough and Rosanna, and Heywood is after a mother-in-law's maiden name. In his 'Essay on Barbarous Denominations in Ireland' Jonathan Swift ridicules such names and others:

    I would readily assist nomenclators of this costive imagination, and therefore I propose to others of the size of thinking that, when they are at a loss about Christening a country seat, instead of straining their invention they would call it Booby-borough, Fool-brook, Puppy-ford, Coxcomb-hall, Mount Logger-head, Dunce-hill, which are innocent appellations, proper to express the talents of the owners.

    Herbert Davis (ed.), *Prose Works of Jonathan Swift*, Oxford 1957, vol. IV, Appendix H. Dr Maurice Craig has pointed out to us that Snugborough, Tankardstown, Castle Comfort, Whigsborough and Whiskey Hall exist in real life.
21. *The Reminiscences of Sarah Siddons 1773–1785*, edited by William nav Lennep. Cambridge, Mass. 1942, p. 27.
22. He evidently had an office in Dublin at this time, because in the *Irish Farmers' Journal*, Saturday 20 January 1816, vol. IV, no. XXI, p. 167, he is advertising for an assistant:

    Wants a situation
    As Gardener and Planter, or Steward and Gardener, A Single young Man of the Established Church – for Character and Abilities will be found undeniable by applying to Mr. JOHN SUTHERLAND, 24 Brunswick-Street . . .

23. MS Bundle D 1470/3 PRONI (Belfast). We are indebted to Mr C. E. B. Brett for this information.
24. Anne Plumptre, *Narrative of a Residence in Ireland*. London 1817, p. 161.
25. Henry MSS, 1739, pp. 31–34.
26. 'Journal of a Tour through part of Ireland . . . in 1787', part 2, p. 55, Trinity College, Dublin MS K6, 57 (4027). Dr Beaufort (1739–1821) was a geographer famous for his Map of Ireland, 1792 (six miles to an inch). His tours also show his architectural and horticultural knowledge. He was vicar of Collon, County Louth, 1790–1821, his patron being the Right Honourable John Foster (see p. 108).
27. Llanover, *Mrs Delany*, vol. I, p. 376.
28. Bagshawe, *The Bagshawes*, p. 323.
29. *Association for the Preservation of the Memorials of the Dead, Ireland*, vol. x, 1917.
30. For years the mausoleum was neglected, the roof had fallen in and vandals had broken limbs from the figures; but the Irish Georgian Society has made it waterproof and secured the door. The view mentioned by Sir Charles Coote is now blocked by extensive planting of the Forestry Commission.
31. 'A building in the Turkish style, commanding a beautiful and extensive prospect to the north.'
32. 'The Ice house; a temple delightfully fancied in the rustic taste, elevated on a pleasure mount, the excavation of which is converted into a repository for ice; the upper apartments serving the purpose of elegant perception and social entertainment.' Samuel Whyte.
33. *Tour in Ireland*, vol. I, p. 61.
34. *Scenery in Ireland*.
35. This wall and the Gothic arch are obviously derived from Thomas Wright, *Universal Architecture*, part II, plate 6·(see Plate 94 of the present volume). Wright passed Belvedere during his Irish tour. See p. 119 for further details.
36. *Statistical Survey of the King's County*, pp. 179–80.
37. *Account of Ireland*, vol. I, p. 44.
38. Plate 100, being an aerial photo, flattens the terrain.
39. 'On the present State of Gardening in Ireland, with Hints for its future Improvement', *Gardener's Magazine*, vol. II, p. 149.
40. Caledon Estate Ledger 1790–1809, PRONI (Belfast) D 2433/34/3, and Caledon Journal 1790–1809, PRONI (Belfast) D 2433/35/3. We are indebted to Mr C. E. B. Brett for this information.
41. Brown designed the stable block, his only building in Ireland.
42. *Handbook for Travellers*, p. 150.
43. *Handbook for Travellers*. He also criticizes Dromana, County Waterford, on this account.
44. Mrs Eileen McCracken, 'Notes on Eighteenth Century Irish Nurserymen', *Irish Forestry*, vol. 24, no. 1, Spring 1967, lists about thirty-five doing business in Dublin between 1780 and the end of the century, six in County Cork and three in County Kilkenny including the long-established firm of Robertson, which sold a hundred thousand seedlings in 1800.
45. A certain confusion may arise for non-Irish readers in the number of rivers named Black-water. Besides this one (1) which issues from Lough Ramor, County Cavan, to join the Boyne at Navan (An Uaimh), there are: (2) the Blackwater, Ulster, which falls into Lough Neagh at Maghery, after passing through Caledon; (3) the Blackwater, County Kilkenny (see Lismore p. 179) which starts in the Booley Mountains to join the estuary of the Suir; (4) the small Blackwater, flowing from the Bog of Allen and joining the Boyne in what was the demesne of Castle Rickard near Clonard, County Westmeath, and (5) the Blackwater, County Kerry which flows rapidly from the Dunkerran Mountains to Kenmare Bay. There are altogether eleven listed in *Phillip's County Atlas* of which *the* Blackwater (3 above) flowing through County Waterford and County Cork is the best known.
46. Macartney MSS, PRONI (Belfast) D 572/9/44.
47. 'A journey through part of the Province of Munster', 6 August 1794, *Hibernian Magazine*, October 1794, pp. 356 ff.
48. *Treatise on Planting*.
49. Edward Willes to Lord Warwick. BM Add. MSS 29 252 p. 37.
50. Desmond Guinness MSS.
51. *Tour round Ireland*, p. 353.
52. Yorke MSS. Erddig, Clwyd. Letter from Owen Salusbury Brereton to Simon Yorke of Erddig.
53. Coote, *General View*, p. 66.
54. The capitals which may have been those from the Parliament House given to Trench when the building was converted to a bank, were taken later for a pergola by Sir Edwin Lutyens who designed terraces and gardens between the lake and the house. The wish to 'improve' the siting of a house by terraces and parterres has ruined many eighteenth-century settings.
55. FitzGerald, *Correspondence of Duchess of Leinster*, vol. I, p. 76.
56. *Anthologia Hibernica*, vol. 4, (July 1794), pp. 1–2.
57. See p. 89.
58. Plate 113 shows the early eighteenth-century house with its formal avenue and gates, with gardeners at work.
59. 'A brief Description of the gardens at Adare . . . By Mr. Andrew Coghlan, Head Gardener there', *Gardener's Magazine*, vol. XII, March 1836, pp. 450–52.
60. First mentioned in Thomas Cook's *Pictures of Parsonstown*, 1826.
61. 'Good Earl John', the last Earl Grandison, died 1766, built the village.
62. Fraser, *Handbook for Travellers*, p. 232.

63. In 1967 it was falling apart – the roof leaked, the windows were broken and pinnacles had toppled into the river. Thanks to the Irish Georgian Society the green onion dome shines again, trees and shrubs have been thinned by volunteers, three of the minarets replaced by fibre glass, and the whole magnificent oriental image glows in the Irish sky.

64. *Tour in Ireland*, vol. I, pp. 321–30.

65. See letter in *Gardener's Magazine*, vol. VI, pp. 348–49.

66. *Tour in Connemara and the Martins of Ballynahinch*, p. 44.

67. Op. cit., vol. I, p. 84.

68. Wakefield, *Account of Ireland*, vol. I, p. 259.

69. Dutton, *Survey of the County of Galway*, p. 16.

70. Christina Edgeworth Colvin, 'Maria Edgeworth's Tours in Ireland', *Studia Neophilogica*, vol. XLIII, no. 2 (1971), p. 478.

71. Moore Hall, burnt by rebels in 1922, is a shell though the proud inscription *Fortis Cadere Cedere non Potest 1795* is still visible over the front portal. George Moore, the novelist, in 1870 inherited the property on the death of his father, Member of Parliament for Mayo and one of the leaders of the Tenant-Right Movement. Although the later nineteenth century is outside our scope, we think that George Moore's evocative writing of his home timelessly epitomizes the natural beauty of Lough Carra. *The Lake* (1905) opens:

It was one of those enticing days at the beginning of May when white clouds are drawn about the earth like curtains. The lake lay like a mirror that somebody had breathed upon, brown islands showing through the mist faintly, with gray shadows falling into the water, blurred at the edges.

Further on he completes the picture:

The beautiful motion and variety of the hills delighted him, and there was as much various colour as there were many dips and curves, for the hills were not far enough away to dwindle to one blue tint; they were blue, but the pink heather showed through the blue and the clouds continued to fold and unfold, so that, neither the colour nor the lines were the same . . . He stood at ease, bewitched by the play of light and shadow among the slopes; and when he turned again, he was surprised to see a yacht by Castle Island.

Under a cairn on this island the ashes of George Moore lie buried in an urn.

72. Christina Edgeworth Colvin MS.

73. Printed in a private edition of *Maria Edgeworth. Memoir*, London 1867, vol. 3, p. 72.

5 Demesnes by the Sea

I have often thought that if heaven had given me choice of my position and calling, it should have been on a rich spot of earth, well watered, and near a good market for the productions of the garden. No occupation is so delightful to me as the culture of the earth, and no culture comparable to that of a garden.

Thomas Jefferson to Charles Willson Peale (1811)

Edmund Burke (1729–97) wrote his *Inquiry into the Origin of our Ideas of the Sublime and the Beautiful* in his last year at Trinity College, Dublin. He defined sublimity in much the same terms at Longinus, the first-century Greek philosopher who was prescribed reading for undergraduates at Trinity College. The chief quality of Longinus's sublimity was awe – inspiring thoughts of grandeur rather than of elegance. The two chief components were· a vastness of dimension (in depth, height and weight) and infinity. Of all the elements in landscaping the sea is most able to fulfil the attributes of awe and infinity. In the case of Downhill (see Chapter 7), the Earl-Bishop's placing of the house on the gale-ridden foreland was a wanton challenge to horticulture; whereas at Mount Stewart, sea and climate are wooed. In similarly sheltered inlets in Cork Harbour, or Bantry Bay, the tearing Atlantic gales do not enter, although Ireland endures more from Atlantic hurricanes than does England.

In all the landscapes previously discussed, fresh water, seen and heard in rivers, brooks and loughs, was the element which cast the strongest spell over the scene. There are fewer landscapes which include the sea in this way, and some of these are round Dublin Bay – tamer park landscapes with gentler prospects and smaller slopes which might perhaps have suited Brown's treatment had he come to Ireland. After a visit to one such, Mount Merrion, in November 1761, where Richard, sixth Viscount Fitzwilliam was further enlarging his house, George Montagu wrote to Horace Walpole that: 'Nothing near Naples can be more beautiful, with such a view of the sea and Dublin as would make even your Thames blush for Richmond Hill and Isleworth; and yet there is no wood to heat even an oven, but such ships, such mountains, such as hill of Hothe as makes one not wish for any other embellishment.'[1]

By Thackeray's time the trees had grown and he admired the open variety of the scene which had 'no fatiguing sublimity or awful beauty in it, but brisk, brilliant, sunny and enlivening' views. In 1805 William Ashford was commissioned by Richard, seventh Viscount Fitzwilliam to make some drawings of the estate. In these drawings one can see the noble avenues of elms which led from the Dublin-Stillorgan road, with its views of Dublin and the bay (Plate 116). Both these avenues had been planted early in the eighteenth century by the fifth Viscount when he enlarged the house. From a survey by Jonathan Barker, circa 1761, in the National Library of Ireland, it can be seen that the demesne in 1762 was based on straight avenues, especially in the wooded area, radially cut, leading to the temple. Also, despite the straight terraces, there is no feeling of formality in any of the William Ashford drawings which we reproduce. It was a comparatively small estate (of about 259 English acres), neighbouring Stillorgan Park,[2] with a modest, 'quaint, old-fashioned house'[3] with a front of only five bays of two stories. The wood house (Plate 117) was on the north avenue and at the end of the north terrace was the Gothic building (Plate 118). From the other side of the house there were views of the Wicklow Mountains and the Sugar Loaf on the horizon. The different views of mountain and sea from open parkland, the variety of building – a classical temple, Gothic lodge, wood house and columns, the contrasting planting in ash and fir groves, the two avenues of aged elms, and the undulating ground with wood and open lawn were characteristic of this type of estate. Like many others in Ireland it developed without any one strong hand like Brown's to influence it: the sixth Viscount (1711–76) having never swept away the older avenues, it still re-

116 MOUNT MERRION,
CO. DUBLIN. *View of
Dublin Bay: oil on canvas
by William Ashford.*

117 MOUNT MERRION.
*The wood house: water-
colour by William Ashford.*

118 MOUNT MERRION.
*The Gothic summerhouse:
watercolour by William
Ashford.*

tained many of the features of his father's work at the turn of the century.

Near the sea, the difficulties of planting for shelter are hard to overcome, and the result may be like the Earl of Annesley's seat, Donard Lodge, at Newcastle, Dundrum Bay where Mrs Delany saw few trees or plants, and found that the salt spray drenched people on the doorstep. But those estates where the planting has survived have a sublimity and natural grandeur which the sea confers, and which is almost unknown in England or Wales.

One of Richard Castle's houses, surrounded by a splendid natural landscape is Westport House, County Mayo. It stands on the site of a seventeenth-century house (built by Colonel John Browne, a Jacobite) where the tide rose and fell against the walls, as there was then no lake or dam. By 1752 when Richard Pococke went there John Browne (later Earl of Altamont) had built 'two handsome bridges and had formed Cascades in the river which are seen from the front of the house', and had planted and improved 'the fine hills every way'. The tide still came up to the house, though it was now controlled, and the cascades were salmon leaps. An early topographical painting of 1761 (Plate 119), still in the house, shows Croagh Patrick and Clew Bay, the bridges and falls, formal planting, as well as Richard Castle's west front to the house, and its pair shows the scene in reverse. Arthur Young was impressed by this view and the hanging woods on either side. It has been a remarkable achievement on the part of the marquesses of Sligo to have been horticulturally successful in this landscape which is seared by salt winds from the Atlantic; but extensive shelter planting of beech and oak has made it possible. The landscape centres on the river which passes under a bridge near the house, and resembles Heyford Bridge over the Cherwell at Rousham, Oxfordshire. A church makes an excellent eye-catcher from the front door of the house.[4]

A year or two after Young's visit, James Wyatt was employed to enlarge the house and is said – though no documentary evidence can be found – to have planned the town of Westport which was to be moved further away. The cruciform or circus plan, with its tree-lined mall and hexagonal market place is a most interesting example of town planning after a forcible removal of the population from its medieval site. Villages and towns in England were sometimes removed in the eighteenth century in the interests of landscape gardening, as at Stowe, Chatsworth, Harewood, Kedleston, Ickworth, Milton Abbas and Nuneham Courtenay, producing what Oliver Goldsmith so vividly described in 'The Deserted Village':

> Have we not seen at pleasure's lordly call
> The smiling long-frequented village fall?

It was not a difficult matter for the Marquess of Sligo[5] to move Westport town away, for no blocking of local roads or removal of bridges was required and, doubtless, ecclesiastical permission was easy to obtain. However, the inhabitants managed to hold right of way through the park. Oliver Goldsmith took his stand against such destruction in 'The Deserted Village', and 'sweet Auburn' is thought to be his native village of Lissoy, County Westmeath. But it is far more likely he drew a composite picture of forcible removal of village people in England and Ireland in order that the landlords could make pleasure grounds:

> Thus fares the land by luxury betrayed
>   In Nature's simplest charms at first arrayed,
> But verging to decline, its splendours rise,
>   Its vistas strike, its palaces surprise.

Many of the details of Goldsmith's poem are un-Irish. No Irish alehouse in the eighteenth century had nicely sanded floors, varnished clocks, hearths or 'flowers and fennel gay'. Nor is it likely that the 'honest rustic' would have run after the Protestant minister, or been 'cheered by health and plenty'. Mavis Batey makes an excellent case for Goldsmith's 'Deserted Village' being based on Nuneham Courtenay in Oxfordshire, where he had witnessed the start of a classical landscape by Brown commissioned by Earl Harcourt who had pushed the village further off.[6] Westport was certainly more than a village; but the new town, like Milton Abbas in Dorset, seems to have been well planned and built, so perhaps it was not too high a price to pay for a landscape garden of such classical composition. Nevertheless, one should read two disparate accounts of the Westport scene written in the same year (1836) in order to judge fairly: Maria Edgeworth, on a tour of the West writes that 'the present and living wonders are the town and bay and prosperous country and people made at Westport by the exertions chiefly of one individual – the late Lord Sligo'[7] – and no one was more sensitive to poverty and squalor than she. Yet John Barrow saw Lord Sligo's tenants clothed in rags, living in cabins 'more fit for cattle than people', built with loose stones, 'sodded' roofs and windowless. Both are reliable witnesses, and usually Barrow is full of praise for the rural scene.[8]

In 1842 Thackeray bore out Maria Edgeworth's opinion that no one could have done more for Westport than Lord Sligo. It is one of the few places he visited where he describes the scene with much pleasure. Like Charles Lamb, he preferred the city gas lamps to the lakes and mountains. But on seeing Westport when he arrived at sunset he described it with unusual delight: 'the Bay, the Reek [Croagh Patrick], which sweeps down to the sea – and a hundred islands in it, were dressed up in gold and purple and crimson, with the whole cloudy west in a flame.'[9]

A most interesting landscape, with a very distant view of the sea, was at Oriel Temple (Mount Oriel), County Louth. On rising ground round the house were extensive plantations, walks through woods to a classical temple, from which were fine views over the lawns, as well as a splendid sheet of water in a crescent shape, ringed with woods and a grotto (see page 41). In the distance, Dundalk Bay up to the Mourne Mountains:

The blue colour of the bay, contrasted with the yellow tint of the sandy beach by which it is bordered, the Carlingford mountains in the neighbourhood, and the more elevated dusky ones of Mourne, stretching inland in the form of an immense amphitheatre, and to the eastward the

119 WESTPORT, CO. MAYO. *Perspective view by George Moore, 1761.*

sea terminating the view, form together a spectacle grand and magnificent . . . No place in the island is more worthy of notice.[10]

After 1770, the Honourable John Foster, 1740–1828, the last Speaker of the Irish House of Commons, had established a thriving cotton industry in the neighbourhood, and was a model landlord. The extraordinary horticultural interest of the Oriel Temple gardens was on account of the work of John Foster himself, who was an expert in the propagation, growth and management of trees of all possible varieties for the Irish climate. Twenty-two years before Young's visit, Collon had been a sheep-walk; by John Foster's death, Collon 'possessed 1700 sorts of American trees and shrubs',[11] five hundred acres of arboretum famous for the quality of its rhododendrons, Portugal laurel (*Prunus lusitanica*), laurustinus and myrtle. Foster had also been primarily responsible for the foundation of the Dublin Botanic Garden at Glasnevin in the 1790s by the Dublin Society. When Dr Beaufort visited Collon on 3 July 1788 he met the Speaker who showed him round: 'walked a mile thro his grounds to the Temple, a beautiful room, where De Gree is painting. Poor man seems in a bad state of health. The prospect near this of Dundalk Bay is exc. fine & the whole ground finely planted & very thriving.'[12]

In *Recollections of a Beloved Mother* (1824) Anna Dorothea, Lady Dufferin, the Speaker's daughter, describes the exact relationship of the temple to Collon House; and also the building of a cottage and grotto, both supervised by her mother:

About the year 1780 or '81 my Father made some additions to a garden house built in the Plantations at Oriel, to make it capable of receiving us to lodge there in the Summer months. The Drawingroom he built in the form of a Temple, dedicating it to my Mother. In that building were spent some of the happiest of my childish days, tho' when grown up, I hailed the day that brought us back to Collon House, where we had accommodation for friends which the Temple was too small to admit of. From being at first but the Summer Villa, it became our sole residence, leaving the house for visitors who passed to and fro in an old coach, passing their days at Oriel, their nights at Collon. This was so uncomfortable as soon to banish all visitors, even of our own family, yet for some years I thought no enjoyment greater than living in the grounds, following my Father on foot, and on horseback, when my lessons were over, (and sometimes when they were not) and sitting by my Mother at her work frame drawing, or at music, dancing in the evenings to Andrew Branigan's eternal fiddle, and enlisting such of the neighbourhood, or of our cousins in the same, as would be accommodated with Mother in the Temple, or were near enough to return home at night. The desire of increasing the accommodation – I believe it was – that first suggested to my Mother the thought of building that dear Cottage, that proved such a source of amusement to her for many years, and remains such a beautiful monument of the elegance and simplicity of her taste. She wished it to be of mud, to be built in one season, and made use of immediately as a Tea-rooms to the Temple. My Father, who was always desirous to make his work permanent, and was perhaps particularly so in an object that was to be exclusively hers, and on which she was to display her taste without any interference (for that was the agreement she made) persuaded her to let him build it of stone and mortar, with a strong projecting thatched roof. Whilst the building was going on she directed the furnishing of the walls, the recesses all to suit the plans she made from the first in her own mind, of what she wished it should be when finished. The very model of what a real cottage should be, – in the furniture the same plan was pursued. All was useful, simple, and well adapted. She composed some pretty lines for it, and selected others equally suitable. The prints with which the walls were hung she had been for some time collecting – and many friends, when they knew what she was about, contributed little decorations that they thought would gratify her. In this dear Cottage many happy hours were spent. We used often to drink tea there from the Temple and have dances in the evening, or stroll about the grounds surrounding it, till the close of evening sent us home. Sometimes with some of my cousins who were often with us, we used to dress in stuff gowns, and dear Mother in a stuff gown, used to call herself Madge of the Cottage, and tell how her old Master, the Speaker, had settled her and her daughters in that happy spot.

In the course of a few years she wanted something new to excite her to be as much in the open air as my Father thought would be good for her health. She took a fancy to a little stream, and some rocky ground, which he called Margate from her name. She proposed building a Grotto there, but soon found that it was too distant from the Temple for her to superintend it with any satisfaction. (The reversion of this was given to me).

I built a seat there and laid out walks – a boy was given to me to carry on the work, the same, who has ever since been attached to Margate, and known to those who frequent it by the name of James Murphy.

A spot near the Cottage, an old gravel quarry, was then fixed on for the Grotto, and there my Mother converted the most incongruous materials into one of the most beautiful pieces of

Grotto-work that could be imagined. Broken china, beads, lobster shells, coloured parchment, sealing wax, everything that had either colour or substance to suit the purpose were all combined, with specimens of spars and shells, and various descriptions of stones, and coloured glass and pieces of looking glass, and pebbles, and fish bones, and many more such materials, to cover the walls, which were broken across by diagonal arched partitions, which she still added, as she still wanted a fresh surface on which to display any newly acquired treasures. To the last years of her life, the working at this Grotto afforded her both health and pleasure. Latterly, by inducing her to go out, when merely taking the air would have been a dull pursuit, and previously, by dividing her leisure time with the embroidery frame, at which she was inclined to sit for hours together, without air or exercise.

Another spectacular setting nearer the sea is at Glenarm Castle, County Antrim. In 1793, at the time of the Thomas Milton engraving after a painting by J. J. Barralet (Plate 120), it was a seventeenth-century house dressed up in the second half of the eighteenth century with wings and a circular parterre, in the centre of which was a large statue of Hercules, the work of Christopher Myers.[13] The steeply rising ground is vividly described by Dr Richard Pococke, when on a visit in 1752, in his *Irish Tour* (p. 25):

Ld Antrim's 'little park', which is the most beautiful and romantic ground I ever beheld; it is the very point which makes the bay to the north and is a hanging ground over the sea, from which there is a steep ascent, it may be of fifty yards, on which there is a wood, then there is an uneven lawn with some wood in several parts and rocks rising up so as that at a distance, some of them appear like ruins of Castles . . .

He also mentions Lady Antrim's grotto with fine and curious shells and many of the pinna (molluscs) found off the north-east point of Ireland. There was also Lord Antrim's Great Park in the glen extending from the bottom left of the engraving through which ran two rivers, one of which can be seen as it passes under a bridge to enter the sea near to the parish church. The soft falls and deep folds of this green glen gently slice through the rough basaltic coastland. According to Thomas Milton, the Great Park in the glen was

120 GLENARM, CO. ANTRIM. *Engraving by Thomas Milton after J. J. Barralet.*

thirteen miles in Circuit, extremely romantic and beautiful; consisting of Woods, and broken Rock; with several Waterfalls and Salmon Leaps, formed by a large Serpentine River, winding through the Grounds; its Banks adorned with various Evergreen, Myrtles, and the Arbutus, or Strawberry Tree, almost continually in Blossom. From the Park are Views of the Sea, a distant Prospect of a ruinated Abbey, and the Scenery is considerably enriched by the singular Appearance of the adjacent Mountains, producing Corn upon their Summits.

In one of the belvederes was a banqueting room, from which the cascades could also be seen. Across the sea, in the engraving is the Scottish coast – the Mull of Kintyre, and fifty miles north, the Paps of Jura, distantly silhouetted in the early morning light.

On the shores of Strangford Lough, into which the tides rush daily, is Mount Stewart, facing south on the possessive arm of the Ards Peninsula. Such is the growth of beech and *Griselinia littoralis* in this frostless climate washed by the Gulf Stream, that trees planted as late as 1921 have completely obscured the view of the lough from the house.[14] On the other side is a seven-acre freshwater lake of some natural beauty. The grounds are extensive, and on a rise at about half a mile from the house is one of the finest belvederes in Ireland, the Temple of the Winds (Plate 121) looking out over Strangford Lough to the Mourne Mountains. It can be seen that it is based on the Tower of the Winds, Athens (100–35 B.C.), an octagon, on a stylobate of three steps, but with fenestration and balustraded balconies instead of pediments over the porticos – a more felicitous idea for taking in the magnificent view across the lough. Its architect was James 'Athenian' Stuart, whose Tower of the Winds at Shugborough in Staffordshire is similar but not so correct as the Mount Stewart temple. Lewis's *Topographical Dictionary* (1837) describes it:

On the summit of an eminence in the grounds . . . a model of the Temple of the Winds at Athens, erected under the personal superintendence of J. Stewart [*sic*] Esq.' whose skill and taste in Grecian architecture have procured for him the appellation of Athenian Stewart; it is built of stone from the Quarries of Scrabo, and the floors, which are of bog fir, found in the

121 MOUNT STEWART, CO. DOWN. *The Temple of the Winds.*

peat moss on the estate, are, for beauty of material and elegance of design, unequalled by anything in the country.

The earliest published mention of the temple appears in the first edition of *The Post Chaise Companion* (1786) where Mount Stewart is described as 'a very magnificent seat' being built by the Honourable Robert Stewart, who 'has erected on a hill near the lough, a temple of the winds, designed after the celebrated model at Athens'.[15] But the house itself had evidently not been completed by 1793 as Robert Stewart (by then a baron) had spent £60,000 on his son's election to Parliament, so had not enough money for the house.[16] The temple must predate the house by some years, for we know that when the future Lord Castlereagh, at the age of seventeen in 1786, was nearly drowned in the lough as a result of his boat overturning in a storm, his companion's and his distress was seen from the temple, and they were rescued just in time. It was designed as a banqueting house – a usual practice with belvederes; from the vaulted basement runs a passage connecting wine cellar and scullery, leading to a few small offices hidden from view by the contours of the hill. 'By day members of the family and their guests would repair to it for rest and contemplation, and by night for dessert and post-prandial conversation.'[17] As well as the excellent condition of the exterior ashlar of local Scrabo stone, the interior plaster work, the bog fir floor, the spiral staircase with cast iron balusters and coffered dome above make this temple one of the most elegant garden buildings in Ireland,[18] a direct link of over two thousand years with ancient Athens.

Much of Castleward, also overlooking Strangford Lough, might have been landscaped by Capability Brown – the house on a hill in late eighteenth-century fashion, wide and open lawns on three sides, a small garden on the fourth, clumps and perimeter planting of oak, beech and Spanish chestnut for shelter. Yet once again the chief feature of the landscape is water, the ruined tower of Audley Castle standing on a bluff overlooking the lough. In 1763 Mrs Delany thought the site was 'uncommonly fine' yet it was not 'judiciously laid out. He [Mr. Ward] wants taste and *Lady Anne* [his wife] is so whimsical that I doubt her judgment.'[19] It was then too formal for Mrs Delany, as Richard Pococke remarks on the 'rows of trees' when he went there in 1752.[20] But Mrs Delany was certainly correct in suspecting Lady Anne Ward's eccentricity, for the house of Bath stone, which was finished about nine years later, has the south-west front Palladian with pediment supported by Roman Ionic pillars, while the north-east front, at the insistence of Lady Anne, is neo-Gothic with machicolation and pinnacles.[21] Sir James Caldwell stayed there in October 1772 and found it 'the finest place in this kingdom', excluding, no doubt, Castle Caldwell: 'The view from the windows very fine. A great extensive lawn sloping down from the house; beyond that, through vistas of trees, an area of the sea forming itself into a river or ferry, and numbers of ships passing backwards and forwards, and the town of Portaferry in view.'

There is a painting by William Ashford from the Doric Temple (1770s) to the Gothic front of the house, the top of the tower of Audley's Castle just visible at the head of the lake. The Doric Temple with flanking demi-pediments (which do not show in the painting), seems to be an adaptation of a design by Robert Morris who has taken it from Palladio's Il Redentore on the Giudecca, Venice. Mrs Delany's drawing (Plate 122) shows this, as well as a grotto entrance below it.

In the extreme south-west of Ireland the Gulf Stream brings a mildness of climate equal to that at Mount Stewart. Edward Wakefield in 1808 noticed the lack of frosts there, allowing myrtles and geraniums to grow out of doors if sheltered by a wall, and enabling deciduous trees to retain their leaves for all but a small portion of the year. A traveller with a distinguished eye for landscape, Prince Pückler-Muskau of Prussia, went to the south-west in the course of his tour in 1828–29. He wrote well, showed international standards of landscaping criticism, had read the major English and French works on the aesthetics of landscaping and had horticultural knowledge. He visited many houses and gardens in Ireland and, perhaps because he came from the cold north of Germany, was most excited by the possibilities of the sub-tropical climate in the south-west, particularly of the beauties of Bantry House, County Cork.

The site overwhelmed him, with its torrents, rocks and eagles. As can be seen (Plate 123) it is enclosed on one side by high mountains, but with a view of nine miles across Bantry Bay to the mountains and lesser bay of Glengariff. The harmony of the park, the lay-out of the plantations with paths cut through them especially pleased him, for every path seemed to be cut in the right direction and each wood and plantation had contrasting masses of texture and tone so that 'the eye is attracted first in, then above and below the boughs'. In the midst of this variety the house appeared as a surprise. But above all, it was the abundance of growth induced by the warm, moist climate which impressed him – pomegranates, magnolias, liriodendrons in profusion, as well as walls 'garlanded with ivy and roses antiquely picturesque'. It had all been achieved, says Pückler-Muskau, in forty years by the White family, the Earls of Bantry. But although this was possible, for one only has to look at the plant growth at Mount Stewart since 1921, it seems likely that the planting was started when the house was built for Simon White, father of the first Earl of Bantry, in the 1750s.[22] The path, flanked by statuary and urns leading to a terrace overlooking the bay, was worthy of the Prince's superlatives in 1828, for the view over the water to the Sugar Loaf Mountain is one of the finest in Ireland. Today the lawns are rough and the flower beds wild; it deserves restoration.

122   CASTLEWARD, CO. DOWN. *Anne Ward's Temple: watercolour by Mrs Delany, 1762.*

123   BANTRY HOUSE, CO. CORK. *View from the house.*

The shores of landlocked Cork Harbour were ideal for siting eighteenth-century houses and grounds – sunny, sheltered, on high ground and frostless. Rostellan Castle was splendidly placed on the eastern shore with magnificent views across the water and Great Island. Further west, Dunkettle and Lota were also set above the harbour, their fine woods united by rising lawns in which lay the houses. Arthur Young is unusually enthusiastic in his description of these. Dunkettle 'surrounded on one side by a reach of Cork harbour, over which it looks in the most advantageous manner; and on the other side by an iriguous vale, through which flows the river Glanmire: the opposite shore of that river has every variety that can unite to form pleasing landscapes for the views from Dunkettle grounds . . .' And Lota, similarly placed in a scene 'alive with the cheerfulness of ships and boats perpetually moving'.[23]

Tivoli is on the Glanmire road outside Cork City and was one of the most interesting folly-studded gardens in southern Ireland. Plate 124 shows the now very much altered Gothic temple and the view towards Cork. The temple appears to be late eighteenth century and more in the Gothic style of Capability Brown than Batty Langley.[24] With its balconies supported by exterior vaulting, the whole surmounted by ogees and crockets, it was, with the Batty Langley Lodge at Castletown (see Plate 68), one of the most fascinating buildings in the eighteenth-century Gothic

124 TIVOLI, CO. CORK. *Gothic temple: oil on canvas by Nathaniel Grogan.*

125 BLACKROCK CASTLE, CO. CORK. *View towards Woodhill, Tivoli and Lota Beg: oil on canvas by Nathaniel Grogan.*

taste in Ireland. It still partially stands surrounded by houses looking down on the river Lee. Tivoli House, recently demolished, was higher up and the whole layout can be clearly seen in a recently discovered huge canvas by Nathaniel Grogan now in the National Gallery of Ireland. Grogan was also responsible for a view of the Temple of Vesta; hence the name 'Tivoli' for the estate. Another of his views shows Tivoli and its neighbouring properties, Palladian Woodhill, now in ruins, and Lota, taken from the domed old Blackrock Castle on the other side of the Lee estuary (Plate 125). The Castle was reconstructed in the baronial style in the early nineteenth century (Plate 126) by James and George Richard Paine. Also on the other side of the river, at Vernon Mount, ruins and cascade, and a shepherd drinking from his hat form a romantic-poetic scene also painted by Nathaniel Grogan (Plate 127).

Many County Kerry estates within easy reach of the sea had the agricultural advantage for their land of seaweed and composted sand, exclusive of manure from farmyard and stables. So at Ballyheigue (Plate 128),[25] the demesne of Colonel Crosbie, a rich 'front lawn' of fifteen acres surprisingly supported fourteen cows, sixty-two sheep, three horses and some deer. Nearby, Ardfert Abbey (see page 17), the estate of Lord Glandore, the head of the Crosbie family, in 1814 suffered from agricultural neglect,[26] though in Charles Smith's time there had been extensive well-kept gardens with a spacious lawn bounded by trees cut into an arcade on the south side. It was within a mile of the sea, 'the prospect of which, in some measure, supplies the want of water, which nature has not afforded to embellish it, although it is the best improved place in the county at present; other places which I have described being more indebted to the beauties of nature than of art.'[27] The adjacent ruined Franciscan friary with its spacious windows, noble arches and Gothic pillars, added a 'solemnity to the lofty avenues of elms' and was obviously the main feature of the landscape. In August 1788 Dr Beaufort was not impressed by either house, or gardens: the former 'extremely low, ill-contrived and ugly', the latter's 'shady walks, clipt arcades, weeping willows in abundance & everything *pour inspirer la melancholia*: to

126 BLACKROCK CASTLE. *As reconstructed in the early nineteenth century.*

114

127 VERNON MOUNT, CO. CORK. *Oil on canvas by Nathaniel Grogan.*

128 BALLYHEIGUE CASTLE, CO. CORK. *Engraving by W. Radcliffe after J. P. Neale.*

which the ruin of a large fine Abbey contributes its share'.[28] But Sir Richard Colt Hoare was much attracted to this as the walls of the thirteenth- to fifteenth-century nave, chancel, tower and transepts were almost fully standing when he went there. Lady Portarlington, on a visit in September 1785, agreed with Dr Beaufort in thinking it 'an old-fashioned place in a very bleak country, with a bowling green surrounded with clipped hedges to look out on; there are a few trees about the house, but I must confess a dismall place and he is so partial to everything that is old that he is determined not to alter it.'[29]

A more modest demesne by the noble estuary of the Shannon is at Glin Castle, County Limerick (Plate 129), where a 'cardboard' embattled house is surrounded by a series of towered lodges (Plate 130) and, on the hill opposite, the village is decorated with an eye-catcher. In a wood behind the house stands a little hermitage made of tufa (Plate 131). These improvements all date from between 1790 and 1836.

Three miles further down the river is Tarbert, the house of the Leslie family. Plate 132 shows a view[30] of the demesne from the river and across the river in 1795. The fort was replaced in the early nineteenth century.

Descriptions written in diaries or letters by friends of the family are more reliable

129 GLIN CASTLE, CO. LIMERICK. *View: oil on canvas by J. H. Mulcahy, 1839.*

130 GLIN CASTLE. *A Gothic lodge.*

than the professional praises of the tourist guides of the nineteenth century. One suspects these were used either as propaganda, especially if illustrated by firms of architects responsible for rebuilding the houses and laying out the landscape,[31] or written with the object of reimbursing the author for the expenses of travelling. Maria Edgeworth's letter to her mother, 21 March 1806, describing Fort Hamilton,[32] her aunt's house two-and-a-half miles from Rostrevor, County Down, shows with sincerity how the smaller setting by the sea was tackled, especially when it had been previously laid out:

Sublime mountains [of Mourne] and sea with which you would be delighted I am sure and I think my father would – road, a flat gravel walk walled on the precipice side. You see a slated English or Welch farm house amongst some stunted trees apparently almost in the sea. You turn down a long avenue of three foot high but old looking fir trees 6 rows deep on each side. The two former proprietors of this mansion had opposite tastes, one all for straight and the other for serpentine lines and there was war between Snug and Picturesque of which traces appear every step you proceed – you seem driving down to the sea to which this avenue leads, but suddenly turn and go back from the shore through some stunted trees of various sorts scattered on a wild Common – then a dwarf mixture of shrubbery and orchard and you are at the *end* of the house which is pretty . . . before the door a semicircular terrass of gravel – from that a slope of very green lawn, then two wildish fields with loose stones sloping more

131 GLIN CASTLE. *The hermitage, 1790.*

132 TARBERT, CO. KERRY. *View of the house: watercolour by John Barrow, 1795.*

and more to the sea shore – the bay of Carlingford – Carlingford head rock opposite to you, the summit in the clouds, a mist thin at the edge spreading half way down – vessels under sail – near and distant – little islands, seabirds – and landmarks standing up in the sea. Behind the house immediately sheltering its back the mountains of Morne. Sublime!

Also overlooking Dundrum Bay, with a full view of the Isle of Man from the highest points of the park (Plate 133), at the base of Slieve Donard, is Tollymore Park. Sir Richard Colt Hoare, who rarely praised the seats of the Irish nobility, remarked: 'Few, if any, nobleman, either in Ireland, or in the sister kingdom, can boast of a residence placed in so singular and romantic situation. The approach to it, under a Gothic gateway, is truly prepossessing.'[33] This gateway, called the Bryansford Gate, is dated 1786 (Plate 134). The demesne is eccentrically bounded by curious Gothic pinnacled gate piers and a little dummy Gothic postern with a pyramidal roof decorated with large round stones. Elsewhere stand an octagonal, battlemented and spired folly, complete with arrow loops, called the Clanbrassil Barn (Plate 135), other follies (Plates 136 and 137), and a small Gothic bridge.[34] The park was originally laid out by James Hamilton, Lord Limerick (who became first Earl of Clanbrassil in 1756) as a summer retreat, before the mid-eighteenth century.[35] Lord Limerick is chiefly important as being the Irish patron of the mathematician, astronomer, architect and

133 TOLLYMORE, CO. DOWN. *Engraving by Thomas Milton after J. J. Barralet.*

134 TOLLYMORE. *Bryansford Gate.*

landscape gardener, Thomas Wright of Durham.[36] Wright specialized in grottoes, follies, root-houses and the like, and some of his curious creations still remain at Badminton, Gloucestershire. He visited Ireland at the invitation of Lord Limerick and made a survey of the antiquities of County Louth in 1746, Lord Limerick's main residence and property being situated at the edge of its county town, Dundalk. The fruit of his researches into dolmens, Danish ring forts and the tower houses of the area was published two years later and entitled *Louthiana*.[37] Wright also travelled all over Ireland and kept brief notes of his various itineraries. These have been published, and in the introduction to them it suggests that Wright worked as landscape gardener for Lord Limerick at his Dundalk property.[38] Bishop Pococke describes the garden at Dundalk (in 1752) as having 'walks with Elm hedges on each side, an artificial serpentine river, a Chinese bridge, a thatch'd open house supported by the bodies of fir trees etc . . .'[39] This rustic building obviously resembled one of those beautiful engravings of arbours (Plate 138), which Wright published in 1755 as the first part of his set of plates optimistically entitled *Universal Architecture*, so the tradition may well be correct. Bernard Scalé's highly decorative miniature estate map of Dundalk of 1777 (Plate 139) shows us something of the layout there: serpentine walks weave around the inside of the planted clumps, the pheasantry and wall garden being hidden by woodland.

Pococke[40] also visited Tollymore, noting the highly romantic mountain situation and mentioning that the park was cut in two by a 'rivulet' running through rocks and trees, spanned by a handsome bridge. The woods were cut into vistas up the side of the hill and, most significantly, 'just over the rivlet Lord Limerick has built a thatch'd open place to dine in, which is very Romantick, with a stove near to prepare the Entertainment' – a site very reminiscent of the Dargle. Wright may well have helped Lord Limerick with his rustic building, as he spent eight days there in the summer of 1746.[41] Pococke further described Lord Limerick's activities: 'He has begun to build a pretty lodge, two rooms of which are finished, designing to spend the Summer months here,' and charmingly goes on: 'between this park and the sea, are houses for those who come to drink Goat's whey in May and June, when the milk on account of the flowers on which the goats feed is in greater perfection.' Paths and steps were laid out alongside the natural curiosities.

Scalé's estate map gives a good idea of the terrain in 1777, by which time Lord Limerick was dead and his son had inherited. The second Earl continued to beautify the estate, planting many trees and building a grotto deep down by the 'rivlet', possibly on the site of the thatched banqueting house. This grotto or hermitage recorded the friendship between Lord Clanbrassil and the Marquis de Monthermer, son of George, Duke of Montagu.[42] Clanbrassil considerably enlarged the mansion house, round a courtyard, all on one floor, part of which is shown in Milton's romantic view.

Wright may have done other work in Ireland, and the influence of the second section of *Universal Architecture*, called 'Seven Designs for Grottoes', is graphically shown by comparing the artificial ruin of Belvedere, County Westmeath with Plates 94 and 95.

But though he went by Lough Ennell in May 1747,[43] he does not mention meeting Lord Belvedere. However, he did stay at the much admired Belleisle[44] on Lough Erne, twice in August of the previous year, and one therefore must associate the thatched rustic cottage (hermitage), shown in Fisher's view, with him (see page 78). While at Belleisle, Wright went 'to see ye marble arch near the head of the Shannon, and din'd with the proprietor Mr Cole', who later became the first Lord Mountflorence and built Florence Court near Enniskillen. It seems no coincidence that a very Wrightian arbour (Plate 83) existed there in the nineteenth century, and a small cottage, though without its thatch, still stands in the grounds (Plate 82). The way in which ivy and roses were trained to climb up the arbour's tree trunk columns exactly illustrates a comment by George Mason that Wright's work made admirable use of 'old pollards clad with ivy', and that 'silvan spinnies were decorated with roses'.[45] The thatched cottage has a bow which is like the side of Wright's root-house at Badminton, Gloucestershire, therefore these Florence Court buildings may well have been sketched out by him when he was there. If, on the other hand, they date from the

nineteenth century, these two old photographs still show the type of building which Wright designed and which is a rarity today, for such whimsical structures are the most ephemeral of garden ornaments. These *cottages ornés* are more common in Ireland than in England, ranging from the larger Swiss cottage type with thatch or moss, like Glena Cottage on the Herberts' estate at Muckross (Plate 140), and the cottage on the La Touches' demesne of Marlay (Plate 141), and the Nash style Swiss cottages at Cahir, County Tipperary (Plate 142) and the Bantry Lodge, near Glengariff, County Cork (Plate 143). The oldest was the E-shaped cottage of Derrymore House, County Down (Plate 144), where the demesne was also laid out by John Sutherland. These could all be lived in, whereas Wright's type are obviously smaller, for visiting on a walk or for taking a light meal in. In the latter category, but used for nineteenth-century photographic experiments, is the cottage at Clonbrock House, Ahascragh (Plate 145), built by Letitia, Lady Clonbrock, circa 1820, and thatched with heather.

Tollymore passed out of the hands of the Roden family, the Clanbrassils' descendents, in the twentieth century, and now the demesne is a fine arboretum and Forest Park open to the public. The house has been pulled down, but the stables with their church-like steeple, the two Gothic gate arches, the grotto and follies are still there, perhaps pointing to the influence of that eccentric and forgotten eighteenth-century

135 TOLLYMORE. *Clanbrassil Barn with its steeple.*

136 TOLLYMORE. *A folly.*

137 TOLLYMORE. *Gateposts.*

genius Thomas Wright, who after his Irish visit published his *Original Theory . . . of the Universe* (1750).

Most of these estates by the sea overlook sheltered or landlocked areas like Strangford Lough or the Shannon estuary. Fortunately, the larger mountain ranges in Ireland lie along the coast and break the fury of Atlantic gales, but where there are no mountains to protect, the salt is carried, as at Coole Park, County Galway, many miles inland. Only the foolhardy endeavoured to landscape in such places near the sea unless extensive shelter planting or high walling had first been carried out. Although it is outside the dates of this book, it is interesting to note a superhuman effort to beat these Atlantic gales, made in the 1870s, in the Pass of Kylemore, one of the best-known beauty spots in County Galway. Mitchell Henry, Member of Parliament for Galway and a rich Liverpool merchant, tackled landscaping of over two hundred and fifty thousand acres on a 'Citizen Kane' scale, alongside Pollacappul Lough at the foot of steep Doughruagh. Surrounding his Victorian 'castle' built of Dublin granite, he conquered a bog by drainage, and laid out a six-acre garden entirely enclosed by a wall. Thanks to three miles of hot-water pipes he was able to keep twenty-one greenhouses going, containing tropical fruit, orangeries, pineries, vineries, peaches, etc.

121

138 TOLLYMORE. *Plate from 'Six Original Designs of Arbours'*, Universal Architecture *by Thomas Wright, 1755.*

139 TOLLYMORE. *Estate map by Bernard Scalé, 1777.*

140 MUCKROSS, CO. KERRY. *Glena Cottage, Killarney, c. 1860.*

141 MARLAY, CO. DUBLIN. *The cottage: pencil drawing by Anne La Touche, 1834.*

142 CAHIR, CO. TIPPERARY. *Swiss cottage.*

143 BANTRY LODGE, CO. CORK. *Swiss cottage, Glengariff,* c. 1890.

144 DERRYMORE, CO
DOWN. *The cottage-style
house.*

145 CLONBROOK
HOUSE, CO. GALWAY.
The cottage.

He was also fairly successful in his planting of three hundred thousand trees a year
in his nursery, with a view to using them as protection for his garden.[46] But it was a
constant battle with the elements. The wise sited their houses so that they looked
across the sea to other shores, as in Dublin Bay, Cork Harbour or Bantry Bay, where
they enjoyed the scenery without enduring the gales.

1. W. S. Lewis and R. S. Brown (eds.), *Horace Walpole's Correspondence with George
    Montagu*, vol. 9, p. 400.
2. See p. 7. By 1802 it had already been broken up into various villas.
3. W. M. Thackeray, *The Irish Sketchbook of 1842*, London 1895.
4. This was acknowledged by Dr Beaufort, but he thought, after his visit on 12 October 1787,
    that the walks were much too narrow, 'ill-gravelled and slobbery after rain, & the way to

the Temple absurd'. *Journal of a Tour . . . begun August 26th continued from October 1st 1787*, part 2, p. 35. Trinity College, Dublin, MS K.6.57 (4027).

5. John Dennis Browne, third Earl of Altamont and first Marquess of Sligo (1756–1809) succeeded to the estate in 1780, when he started improvements.

6. *Oxoniensia*, vol. XXXIII (1968), pp. 108–124. Mrs Batey has also pointed out to us that in a Paul Sandby drawing of Nuneham a windmill tops the hill, thus exemplifying the exact detail in 'The Deserted Village'.

7. Colvin, 'Maria Edgeworth's Tours in Ireland', *Studia Neophilogica*, vol. XLIII, No. 2 (1971), p. 482.

8. Barrow, *Tour round Ireland*, p. 179.

9. Thackeray, *Irish Sketchbook*, p. 215.

10. Wakefield, *Account of Ireland*, vol. I, p. 46 also says he measured an oak which had a diameter of four feet although only thirty-six years old.

11. Forbes, 'Tree Planting in Ireland', *R.I.A.Proc.* 41, Section C, 1932–34, p. 183.

12. Op. cit., part IV, p. 2, Trinity College, MS K.659 (4029).

13. By the time that John Barrow went there in 1835 it had become a turreted baronial castle designed by Morrison.

14. After the First World War, Ulster landlords were asked by the government to employ as many extra labourers as possible, so Lord Londonderry, following a long tradition, employed at least twenty for planting and landscaping a new garden.

15. Since this was written, the documentation for the temple has been discovered by Edward McParland in the Mount Stewart Papers PRONI (Belfast) D 654/41/1, 4 and 6. Lord Camden supplied the plan for the temple from Stuart on 30 March 1782 and Stuart was paid fifty pounds for this plan on 10 June 1783. Both Robert Oran and David McBlain were involved in the building. William FitzGerald was the stuccoman.

16. *Memoirs and Correspondence of Viscount Castlereagh*, edited by the Marquess of Londonderry, London 1848, vol. I, p. 7.

17. H. Montgomery Hyde, *The Rise of Castlereagh*, London 1933, p. 28.

18. Like the Casino at Marino (p. 138).

19. Llanover, *Mrs Delany*, vol. I (2nd series), p. 21.

20. *Pocock's Tour in Ireland in 1752*, edited by George Stokes, 1891, p. 15.

21. The marriage broke up later.

22. The fourteen-bay south front was not added until 1840.

23. Young, *Tour in Ireland*, vol. I, pp. 316–17.

24. Compare the Pulpit at Tong, Salop, and the Bath House at Corsham Court, Wiltshire. See Dorothy Stroud, *Capability Brown*, London 1957, p. 209.

25. A romanticized view. It does not stand on the cliff edge.

26. The Reverend Thomas Radcliff, *A Report on the Agriculture and Live Stock of the County of Kerry*, Dublin 1814, p. 213.

27. *The Ancient and Present State of County Kerry*, Dublin 1756.

28. Op. cit., part IV, p. 27.

29. To Lady Louisa Stuart, *Gleanings from an Old Portfolio*, edited by Mrs G. Clark, Edinburgh 1895, vol. II, pp. 36–40.

30. Today it is much disfigured by an enormous Electricity Supply Board power station.

31. Especially those houses mentioned in J. M. Brewer and J. P. Neale, *Beauties of Ireland*, 1825, which are advertisements for the firm of Sir Richard Morrison.

32. Known as Ballyedmond, and demolished in 1848. See Colvin, 'Maria Edgeworth's Tours in Ireland', *Studia Neophilogica*, vol. XIII, p. 322–23.

33. *Journal of a Tour in Ireland* 1806, p. 231.

34. For photographs, drawings and a history of Tollymore see the Ministry of Agriculture, Northern Ireland guide, *Tollymore Forest Park*.

35. For instance Walter Harris, *The Ancient and Present State of the County of Down* (1744), p. 82, talks of Limerick's two deer parks, woods, ridings, vistas, rocks, river cascade, precipices, and the Old Bridge (1726) of hewn stone.

36. We are indebted to Dr Eileen Harris for information about Wright: see *Country Life* 1971, pp. 612–15. Dr Harris suggests that the follies at Tollymore might be compared with one possibly designed by him at Rushbrook in Suffolk. See also Christie's (London) catalogue, 'Fine English Drawings and Watercolours'. November 1974, p. 889.

37. *Louthiana, or an Introduction to the Antiquities of Ireland* was dedicated to Lord Clanbrassil, and in the preface Wright states: 'As it was chiefly to the Friendship and Assistance with which your Lordship was pleased to honour me during my stay at Dundalk . . . your Lordship has an undoubted Right to this Address.'

38. James Buckley, 'The Journal of Thomas Wright, Author of Louthiana (1711–1786)', *County Louth Archaeological Journal*, vol. II, 1909, p. 165.

39. George T. Stokes (ed.), *Pococke's Tour in Ireland in 1752* (1891), pp. 3–4.

40. Stokes, *Pococke's Tour*, p. 8.

41. Buckley, *Journal of Thomas Wright*, p. 182.

42. The plaque has been removed, as has a bust of Monthermer; but a notice translates the original Greek as: 'Clanbrassil, to his very dear friend Monthermer 1770'.

43. Buckley, *Journal of Thomas Wright*, p. 184.

44. Buckley, *Journal of Thomas Wright*, p. 182. Wright describes 'the lake fronting an avenue of islands', as well as an additional '80 islands all covered with green wood'.

45. *An Essay on Design in Gardening . . . now greatly augmented* (1895), p. 127.

46. *Irish Builder*, 'Notes on Early Gardening in Ireland', 15 May 1872, p. 139.

6 Ecclesiastical Landscapes

No one feels himself easy in a garden which does not look like the open country.

Goethe, *Elective Affinities*

On 8 July 1634 at Archbishop Ussher's palace at Termonfeckin near Drogheda, County Louth, Sir William Brereton on his travels reported there was 'a prettie neat garden, and over and against the window in the gallery end, upon a bank, these words in fair letters are written, "Oh man, remember the last great day." The bank is bare, the proportion of the letters is framed and cut in grass.'[1] In the days of branch line railways the name of a station might sometimes have been seen to be laid out as ornamental gardening, perhaps in flowers, turf, shells or stones. But, as the *Irish Builder*[2] tartly remarks, the practice of lettering when used in 'religious gardening might be pardonable in a cemetery at first sight, though on reflection we think it is out of place anywhere'. As far as we know, no other Irish ecclesiastical gardening adopted this high moral tone; in fact, the Protestant prelates' gardening often rivalled the skills of laymen in taste and extent, after Dean Swift and Dr Delany had modestly led the way out of formal avenues, clipped hedges and pleached alleys.

In 1709 Samuel Molyneux wrote of an exceptional piece of ecclesiastical gardening at Blessinton where 'the late Lord Primate Boyle chose to build one of the finest seats in Ireland, it is now enjoyed and kept in good order by his son Lord Bessington [*sic*]. The house and furniture are very great and beautiful . . . a very handsome noble garden wilderness, green house, fish ponds, a noble large park and Paddocks is in short much beyond any seat in all respects that I have seen in this kingdom.'[3] By 1718 it was enough to make Lord Molesworth jealous (see page 14), and was evidently a very splendid baroque garden (Plates 146 and 147).

But very soon the more free gardening styles of Dean Swift and Dr Delany were copied by many churchmen, and often on a grand scale. Prior to 1833 there was an episcopal glut in the established Protestant Church of Ireland: four archbishoprics – Armagh, Dublin, Tuam and Cashel – and eighteen bishoprics. Many of the bishops built palaces and improved their grounds, being in an enviable financial position, for by the Statute of 10 William III, they could legally charge their successors, after archepiscopal permission, two-thirds of any sum spent on building or improving. Evidently, Josiah Hort, who succeeded to the see of Kilmore, County Cavan in 1727, was one of those who paid what he owed on his predecessor's expenditure, and passed on more to his successor:

Besides the large sum [£2,632] expended by his Predecessor on the Episcopal House of *Kilmore*, of which he paid the Statutable Proportion; to render the said improvement more compleat, he hath laid out the Sum of five hundred and ten Pounds in improving the said Episcopal Seat, with large Gardens, Plantations and other Ornaments, and hath the usual certificate of Allowance from his Metropolitans.[4]

For a description of this formal garden in 1739, see page 22. When Arthur Young visited Kilmore in August 1776, the palace was sheltered by 'very fine trees', yet still had a view of the woods of Farnham (see page 85). Similarly, Edward Synge, later Archbishop of Tuam (1716), 'laid out improvements in Castle [Episcopal House] at Raphoe, County Donegal, had an Allowance for it, and was paid two thirds of that Sum by his Successor, pursuant to the Statute of 10th William the 3rd.'[5] This work was continued by Bishop Oswald who, according to Dr Beaufort, laid out 'pretty walks', walled fifty acres and planted, 'charging every oak, laburnum, ash etc. that he planted' in his park to his successor.[6]

Edward Willes writing to Lord Warwick in 1759 gives details of the ecclesiastical hospitality of Bishop Synge at the palace at Elphin. No other family did as much during three generations:

146 BLESSINTON, CO. WICKLOW. *Detail of John Rocque's map, 1757.*

£3,500 a year a very large fortune near 100,000. [Father was Archbishop of Tuam; uncle, himself and brother were all Bishops.] He built the present palace himself, and all the offices, tis an extreem Good Gentleman's House of 6 Rooms on a Floor, with Colonnades, & offices at Each end of them, His Demesne which he has finely improved is about 300 Irish acres. He lives in great plenty & Hospitality, & Keeps an Exceeding Good and Genteel Table, the Demesne, he tells me, furnishes the House so that he Buys nothing at the market.[7]

As the century progressed, the financial rewards increased. Under a Statute of 12 George I (1726), a reimbursement of three-quarters could be made against the next successor. So John Sterne, who succeeded to the see of Clogher (Plate 148), spent three thousand pounds in building the palace dominating the town, with its basin, canal and forts as eye-catchers, which he was able to pass on financially in 1745 to Dr Clayton. This was the see which Dr Delany much desired. Through Mrs Delany we have details of Dr Clayton's landscaping at Killala in the five years he was bishop there (1730–35). By the time he went to Cork and Ross as bishop, after Killala, he had a reputation as *arbiter elegantiarum* (Plate 149). According to Lord Orrery he ate, drank and slept in taste, for after travelling 'beyond the Alps, has brought home with him, to the amazement of our mercantile Fraternity, the Arts and Sciences that are the Ornament of Italy and the Admiration of the European World'.[8] At Cork he initially had nothing to pay on his predecessors' works, for Peter Browne had 'expended £2000 on a Country House, and Improvements . . . which he built for a Summer Retreat, and left his Successors free from any Charge, as he did also on his Improvements at Bishop's Court, in Cork, of a considerable Value'.[9] Compared with Dr Clayton, Peter Browne lived very simply, and visitors said they 'trembled at a Bumper',[10] and rarely toasted. Clayton's successor at Cork, Dr Jemmett Browne, came of the same family as Peter Browne, and was equally influential on the taste of the time. Their family house, Riverstown, on the Glanmire, three-and-a-half miles north-north-east of Cork, is rightly famous for the fine stucco decoration of the Francini brothers,[11] employed by him sometime before 1750; and his grounds were worthy of the house:

The present Bishop of Corke has a house here of his own where on his Invitation we spent a day. He has a fine natural Cascade of 15 yards height opposite his house, & his road from Cork lyes partly by the river side & through a celebrated Valley calld Glanmire finely wooded & water'd the rest of the way; at a small distance from the house are all the views I before mentioned in the highest perfection, in truth it was the Grandest Scene I did ever behold.[12]

In 1826 it had aged timber in a pleasant deer park, which came up to the house, and the whole demesne wore 'an air of dignified seclusion'.[13]

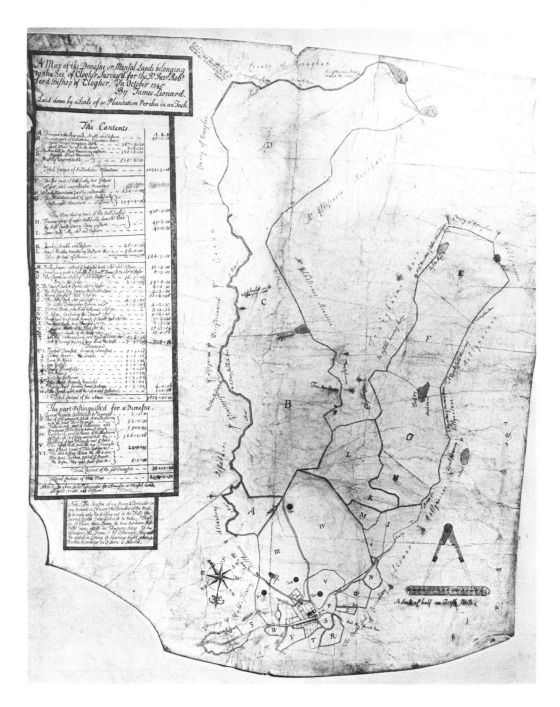

148 CLOGHER, CO. TYRONE. *Detail of the survey of the Bishop's demesne by James Leonard, 1745.*

149 BISHOP CLAYTON AND HIS WIFE. *Oil on canvas by James Latham.*

Equally famous was George Berkeley (Plate 150) who, when Bishop of Cloyne (1734–53), had a garden of about four acres, an estate of fifty and a farm of four hundred. In a rocky dell he planted shrubberies and laid out gravelled walks, one of which was lined with myrtles, whose roots he personally covered with large balls of tar, as he believed in its horticultural efficacy. This seems to have been sound practice, for in 1788 the same plants were still full of blossom and vigorous, although a few years previously they had been cut down when they became straggly, from about eight feet to between two and three feet.

In 1796, a later Bishop of Cloyne wrote of, 'at the end of the garden in what we call the Rock Shrubbery, a walk leading under young trees among sequestered crags of limestone, which hang many feet above our heads, and ending at the mouth of a cave of unknown length and depth.'[14] Dr Beaufort earlier described a visit to this cave in September 1788:

This morning after breakfast, the Cave was lighted up by the young gent with 30 or 40 Candles, & we entered it down some sod steps in the midst of a flat field, at a considerable distance from the Rocks afore mentioned. It is broken & divided into numerous chambers, high, low, broad, narrow by the most fancifully perforated rocks that imagination can conceive, full of small spars & stalactical exudations petrified in the most grotesque forms, particularly a small child near the entrance exceedingly curious. As this cave is full of water in winter, the floor is chiefly thick fine mud, & in some places one sinks, half-leg up; but the Bp. has gravelled a good deal of it.[15]

A round tower, embattled at the top, with seven lofts serving as both belfry and dove house, overlooked Berkeley's philosophical and civilized retreat. As early as 1735 he had produced *The Querist*, aiming, by pertinent and leading questions, at uncivilized ways of life in Ireland, and his estate at Cloyne was the practical exemplification of his theories. One such Query was No. 121: 'whether an expense in gardens and plantations would not be an elegant distinction for the rich, a domestic magnificence employing many hands within, and drawing nothing from abroad?'

Of equal literary influence was Dr Samuel Madden's *Reflections and Resolutions Proper to the Gentlemen of Ireland as to their Conduct for the Service of their Country*, Dublin 1738.[16] He also put his ideas into practice on the splendid estate on the shores of Lough Erne, which Delany helped to design (see p. 43). From an examination of the list of subscribers to Philip Miller's *Gardener's Dictionary* (London 1732), the practical interest in gardening of the prelates of the Church of Ireland can quickly be seen. The Bishops of Clogher, Dromore, Down and Connor, Elphin, Kilmore and Killala each contributed. Deans and lesser clergy (when not absentee) followed the example of their superiors as far as they were able in their smaller glebe houses and gardens. In the 1780s, Dean Rider, for example, at Templemichael near Longford, built an excellent house with a hewn stone front and a neat court in front of it, as well as dressing the grounds as had Delany at Mount Panther earlier in the century.

Some of the primates and archbishops lived like Renaissance prelates, being as much concerned, when privy councillors or lords justice, with secular government as with spiritual duties. George Stone, Primate 1747–65, in addition to his house in Henrietta Street in Dublin, lived at Leixlip Castle, County Kildare (see page 47). There the grounds were 'extremely pleasing, on an eminence along the side of the river, very steep to the edge of the water, and skirted from top to bottom with trees of various kinds, through which the roaring of the fall at the height of about 60 or 70 feet above it, has a very pleasing effect, with here and there a break through the wood to get a peep down upon the river and the fall',[17] though it is doubtful if he would have looked on a scene as pleasant as that in Plate 151.

His successor, Richard Robinson, later first Baron Rokeby, obtained the Primacy through the Duke of Northumberland, the Lord Lieutenant, and built a new palace at Armagh. On a nearby hill he placed a 114-foot marble obelisk (Plate 152), commemorating the Duke, thereby 'unconsciously raising a monument to his own worth',[18] as he had employed labourers in time of need. John Wesley criticized his worldly expenditure,[19] and Beaufort his lack of taste: the palace garden was 'horribly placed

150 BISHOP BERKELEY.
*Oil on canvas by James
Latham, 1737.*

in front of the house, & his farmyard close by it hides the gothick arches of an old Franciscan Abby'.[20]

However, Wesley who when he went there in June 1773 and again in June 1778 was full of praise for a demesne 'beautifully laid out in meadow-ground, sprinkled with trees; in one side of which is a long hill, covered with a shrubbery, cut into serpentine walks'. On his third visit (30 May 1785) he recorded the obelisk and a dairy house and 'many other conveniences'. Arthur Young in 1776 remarked on the view across hill and dale from the terrace, and the building of a barracks, school and new church all of which he thought improved the view. In 1785 the Archbishop employed Francis Johnston as architect. The following letter from Johnston to his friend, J. N. Brewer, later the author of *The Beauties of Ireland*, gives an account of his work for the Archbishop:

Eccles Street,[21] Dublin
Feb 29. 1820.

In the early part of the year 1784 my Master Mr. Thomas Cooley (who built the Royal Exchange here &c.) died and I was in consequence appointed by the late Lord Primate Robinson, Architect to his buildings at Armagh, where I erected the present tower to the Cathedral in that city, completed the inside of the chapel attached to His Grace's palace, and an obelisk which stands on Knox's Hill in the demesne, and a few years afterwards (1789) I designed and built the Observatory for His Grace on another hill near Armagh. I was also employed by the Primate from 1785 to 94 (when he died) in erecting a very handsome mansion house and offices . . . These buildings cost the Primate about £30,000 but if they were to be done at the present day £10,000 more would not be sufficient.[22]

Archbishop Bolton in 1730 obtained the services of Sir Edward Lovett Pearce to design his new palace at Cashel, where the palace garden (Plate 154) was beautifully sited with the Rock towering over it. Secluded walks passed through flower gardens and shrubberies with planting of holly, laburnum, lilac, laurel and copper-beech. Another archbishop in 1834 was sarcastically described by Inglis as a 'close hard man'

130

who was universally disliked, having a private door communicating with the Rock in
order that 'unobserved by his numerous flock, he may retire to this solemn spot, and
meditate on the insufficiency of earthly enjoyments'.[23] The house is now the Cashel
Palace Hotel.

It was fortunate the bishops often had money to expend on their palaces and grounds,
as repairs were frequently seen to be necessary. The palace at Killaloe (Clarisford
House), on the County Clare side of the Shannon, had a fine view of several turns in
that noble river, but the grounds in 1787 were 'in a state of nature & full of quag-
mires',[24] and Bishop Carr had cut down many of the trees in order to profit from the
sale of the timber. Criticized for a similar act was the Archbishop of Dublin who,
according to Samuel Hayes, felled, three times in twenty-four years, nearly two
hundred acres of oak, on see lands near Glendalough, County Wicklow. This was
both wanton and foolish, as each sale realized only one hundred pounds. Had he or
his successor kept the timber, he would have obtained at least six thousand pounds in
fifty years. On the other hand, the Bishop of Clogher, in Edward Wakefield's time
would allow no ash trees to be cut except for repair of houses on estates of the see.
The palace of Killala was neglected after Bishop Clayton's time. Dr Beaufort found

it 'worse than one can conceive, inconvenient, damp, ruinous', yet he acknowledged that Bishop Percy, of *Reliques* fame, had previously walled in a 'very good garden and had a fine demesne of good-looking land, well divided and planted with hedgerows'.[25]

Percy continued to landscape when translated in 1782 to Dromore, where he took as his model the landscaping at the Leasowes, Worcestershire, the seat of his friend, the poet Shenstone.[26] The essential feature of this landscaping was its variety of tone, texture and the placing of objects. Sweeps of lawn, urns, seats and groves of trees contrasted with rocks to form interesting compositions from different *points de vue*. Novelty in the walks was achieved by woods suddenly opening to reveal a prospect, or an urn or obelisk appearing as a focal point. It was all on a modest scale, as must have been Percy's landscaping at Dromore. We know little of the details. However, one feature – an avenue leading to a wooden obelisk – was not to be seen at the Leasowes. Plate 155 shows this in a drawing by Thomas Robinson,[27] the portrait painter who as a friend of the Bishop often visited Dromore. The obelisk and urns were themselves painted by Robinson in *trompe l'oeil* on a flat wooden face – a theatrical, ornamental aid practised more in France than in England or Ireland in the eighteenth century. From 1799 Percy continued to landscape until his death in 1811. The four-square palace at Dromore is today empty and falling into ruin. The urns and obelisk, like all such ephemeral garden decorations, have long since rotted in the beech groves that have been felled. The artificial lake made by Percy outside his walled garden is now choked with alder.[28]

Even with the advantage of being able to pass on their expenses to successors, some of the bishops failed to keep up their demesnes. At Elphin, Dr Beaufort in October 1787 thought the palace was large and gloomy, set in amidst three hundred acres of choice land so good 'that if the sheep live on it more than a year, they rot'. Ardbraccan, the diocesan house of Meath, a wealthy benefice in 1827, had fallen

155 DROMORE, CO.
DOWN. *The painted
wooden obelisk: water-
colour by Thomas Robinson,
1799.*

from the standards set by bishops at the end of the eighteenth century. But James Fraser noticed some distinguished trees which had survived:

In the back lawn are several beautiful American thorns, scarlet oaks, &c, the handsomest trees of Fraxinus ornus, and the most magnificent horse-chestnut we have any where seen; and in front of the green-house there are two charming cedars of Lebanon. The gardens are in the antique style, (peculiar to some of the older places about London,) being blended with the shrubbery, by which you are led imperceptibly from one compartment to another.[29]

The most elaborate example of ecclesiastical landscaping was exemplified by the labours of Frederick Hervey, Earl of Bristol, Bishop of Derry. Having examined his work in detail, we found such an extravaganza unfolding that we have discussed it separately in the next chapter.

1. Sir William Brereton, Bt., *Travels*. Chetham Society, 1844, vol. I, p. 127.
2. 15 April 1872, p. 117, 'Notes on early gardening in Ireland'.
3. Molyneux MS, Trinity College, Dublin, I.I 3, p. 86.
4. Sir James Ware, *The Whole Works*, Dublin 1764, vol. I, p. 245.
5. Ibid., p. 283.
6. Either Bishop Synge or Bishop Oswald was also ahead of his time in his architectural tastes. According to A. J. Rowan, *Quarterly Bulletin of the Irish Georgian Society*, vol. VII, no. 1, January–March 1964, Raphoe Palace was the only castle-style house, other than a few garden temples, erected for a hundred years after Killileagh Castle, 1666. He writes (footnote p. 27):

   'The house, a three-storey building of five window bays, with the centre three recessed about ten feet, is now a ruin. This makes the dating difficult. The entrance door is pedimented and has a Gibbs surround which is obviously of an early 18th century date. The third story presents a problem for it is battlemented and has angle bartizans at the external corners of the building. If this too is early 18th century then Raphoe Palace must be one of the earliest Castle Style houses in the British Isles.'

   The palace was destroyed by fire in 1839.
7. BM add. MSS 29 252, p. 112.
8. Orrery, *Orrery Papers*, vol. I, p. 206.
9. Ware, *Whole Works*, vol. I, p. 572.
10. Orrery, *Orrery Papers*, vol. I, p. 206.
11. Paul and Philip Francini were brought to Ireland by the Earl of Kildare in 1738 to decorate the ceiling of the Great Saloon at Carton.
12. Yorke MSS. Letter from Owen Salusbury Brereton to Simon Yorke of Erddig, Clwyd, September 1763.
13. Brewer and Neale, *Beauties of Ireland*.
14. Bennett, Bishop of Cloyne to Dr Parr, 16 July 1796. J. Johnstone, *The Works of Samuel Parr*, London 1828.
15. Op. cit., part IV, p. 84, Trinity College, Dublin, MS 19.6.60 (4030).
16. His *A letter to the Dublin Society on the Improving their Fund*, Dublin 1739, encourages attention to gardening and horticulture.
17. J. Bushe, *Hibernia Curiosa*. 1748, p. 64.
18. H. D. Inglis, *A Journey throughout Ireland*, London 1834, vol. II, p. 274.
19. 'In seconda marmora', Horace quoted, *Journal* XXI.
20. Op. cit., part 3, p. 74, Trinity College, Dublin, MS K.6.58 (4028).
21. Plate 153. The view of his Eccles Street garden with the wooden tower for his chime of bells.
22. MS in the Armagh Museum quoted in *Quarterly Bulletin of the Irish Georgian Society*, vol. VI, no. 1, January–March 1963, pp. 1–2.
23. *Journey throughout Ireland*, vol. I, pp. 111–12.
24. Dr Beaufort, 'Journal', vol. II, Trinity College, Dublin, MS K.6.57 (4027).
25. Beaufort, 'Journal', part II, pp. 43–44.

26. See Alice Gaussen, *Percy: Prelate and Poet* (1908), p. 204. Percy suffered a severe bereavement in 1782 in the loss of his only son. Like Henry Hoare at Stourhead, Wiltshire and Charles Lyttelton at Hagley, Worcestershire, this seems to have stimulated his wish to landscape.

27. For further information about Robinson, see J. B. Nichols, *Illustrations of the Literary History of the Eighteenth Century . . . a Sequel to the Literary Anecdotes* (1848), vol. VII, p. 168.

28. For more information on Percy, see E. R. R. Green, 'Thomas Percy in Ulster', *Ulster Folklife*, vol. 15/16, 1970, pp. 224 ff.

29. 'On the present State of Gardening in Ireland, with Hints for its future Improvement', *The Gardener's Magazine*, edited by J. C. Loudon, vol. II (1827), pp. 150–51.

7 Marino and Downhill: Romantic-Poetic and Sublime contrasted

> Proceed, my Friend, pursue thy healthful toil,
> Dispose thy ground, and meliorate thy soil;
> Range thy young plants in walks, or clumps, or bow'rs,
> Diffuse o'er sunny banks thy fragrant flow'rs;
> And, while the new creation round thee springs,
> Enjoy unchecked the guiltless bliss it brings:
> But hope no more. Though Fancy forward stray
> These scenes of distant pleasure to survey,
> T'expatiate fondly o'er the future grove,
> The happy haunt of Friendship and of Love;
> Know, each fair image form'd within thy mind,
> Far wide of truth thy sickening sight shall find.
>
> John Scott, *Moral Eclogues* (1778)

Sir Uvedale Price in his *Essays on the Picturesque* (1794) thought that: 'The study of pictures can only produce any real advantage if we use it as a school in which we may·learn to enlarge, correct and refine our view of Nature and by that route become good judges of scenery.' The romantic and poetic landscaping of Charles Hamilton at Painshill near Cobham, and Henry Hoare at Stourhead, Wiltshire had exemplified this in practice many years before Price's statement. The essence of both these landscapes was that they should form a series of pictures as one walked through or drove round them. But they were not built inside the framework of a perimeter path which looked inward primarily at farming scenes.[1] On the contrary, the walks, even at Stourhead, led through a series of surprises each of which made a picture, formed by trees, water, lawn and buildings, which changed in their relationship to each other as one moved on. So it was possible to have classical and Gothic buildings in the same landscape provided they did not jar by their close conjunction in the same vista or prospect. Certainly, for example, the *cottage orné* at Stourhead would have been completely hidden by vines and creepers so that one did not notice it on looking across the lake towards the Pantheon. At Painshill a Gothic building nestled on the edge of a slope above a lake; but the whole of the lake was never seen at once for, by presenting a series of different views of woody islands, it appeared larger than it really was. As one moved on, a river passed under different bridges towards a wood, while on another side appeared a low hermitage, covered in vines in shaded gloom. Later a tower punctuated a hilltop. There was variety in the parts, yet a unity in the slopes of the ground, in the contrasting planting, in the interaction of lawns and wood; in the reflections of sky in the water. The walks might intersect, but their relation to any one scene was always apparent, never allowing the sense of unity in the whole landscape to disappear. The banks of the lake were diversified, open here and planted there; sometimes to the brink of the water, sometimes by bringing forward the walks.

In Ireland with its abundance of lakes, rivers and sea inlets, this theory of the romantic landscape found constant expression. In the mind of Mrs Delany the idea of this landscape, as exemplified at Stourhead, Hagley and Painshill in the 1740s, never really died. For although Delville, which was Patrick Delany's creation, was initially influenced by the more formal garden such as Pope's at Twickenham, she herself had a lifelong admiration for and sensitivity in seeing the practical application of the picturesque as later expressed by Uvedale Price, and this was most similar to the gardens mentioned which were created earlier in the century. There is none of the openness in acres of lawn of Capability Brown nor the gloomy, sublime terrors inspired by Payne Knight in his poem 'The Landscape'.

Another man with these views was 'a very agreeable (ugly) man – sensible, lively and polite'[2] who dined with the Delanys in September 1759. This was James Caulfeild, first Earl of Charlemont (Plate 156), a neighbour of theirs who by then had started on his landscape at Marino, outside Dublin. He was thirty-one at the time, and Mrs Delany's assessment of his character was just, but limited, for she omitted his wide scholarship and artistic sensibility. These qualities shine through his journal which he kept as a young man during an extensive Grand Tour.[3] Accompanied by his tutor, the Reverend Edward Murphy, he went in 1746 to Holland and Germany, then spent a year in Rome and Naples and, after visiting Constantinople, Athens, Halicarnassus and Malta, remained in Italy, Spain and France three more years before arriving back in 1755.

Charlemont met travellers, dilettanti, painters, architects and distinguished churchmen in Italy. His interest in architecture was recognized by Piranesi in his dedication to Charlemont of his *Opere Varie* (1750), and he also became acquainted with Luigi Vanvitelli, the Dutch (despite his name) architect who had just completed the gigantic royal palace and gardens at Caserta, twenty miles from Naples. From him Charlemont commissioned a design for a garden temple, which was not accepted

156   JAMES CAULFEILD, FIRST LORD CHARLE-MONT. *Oil on canvas by Pompeo Batoni, c. 1750.*

because it was too expensive.[4] But while in Rome he must have met and liked Sir William Chambers from whom he commissioned and accepted a design for his garden temple[5] (Plate 157). Charlemont had bought the Marino estate in October 1756; but as early as July 1755 Edward Murphy had heard rumours of money 'laid out at Marino', not a good idea in his opinion.[6]

On his way back through France, Charlemont called on the aged but active Montesquieu at his estate near Bordeaux, which was 'cultivated and dressed in the English manner', with a wood 'cut into walks'. As Montesquieu was very much an anglophile, and had denounced straight *allées* which 'une longue uniformité rend tout insupportable' in his 'Essaie sur le Goût', the walks on his estate meandered and serpentined through the woods.

After his return to Ireland, Charlemont wrote in his *Memoirs* in 1760:

I quickly perceived, and being thoroughly sensible it was my indispensible duty to live in Ireland, determined by some means or other to attach myself to my native country: and principally with this view I began those improvements at Marino which have proved so expensive to me . . . Let it not be said that Ireland can be served in England. It never was.

J. A. Froude,[7] with reference to Edmund Burke, remarked that absenteeism of landlords mattered less than that of men of genius. If more leaders of Charlemont's calibre had stayed in Ireland at that time, much tragic Anglo-Irish history might have been avoided. The situation as it developed is vividly symbolized in a description of Rathfarnham Castle, south of Dublin, with its once magnificent grounds

all eloquently waste, the undulating hills covered with rank herbiage, the rivulet stagnant and sedgy, the walls scarce traceable, the ice-houses open to the prying sun, the fish-pond clogged with weeds, while the mouldering architecture of the castle, and the crumbling unsightly offices in its immediate vicinity, even more loudly proclaim those evils of absenteeism, which have so little application to the state of other countries, that they appear the paramount – the exclusive curse of this.[8]

Charlemont's insistence on serving the best interests of Ireland was lifelong, whether politically as commander of the Volunteers in the 1780s or on returning from Rome in 1755 as a young man and bringing the best Italian craftsmen, irrespective of cost. He did not belong to the grandest Irish nobility with their huge estates, and his income was comparatively modest. According to Milton's *Views of Seats*, 1783, the Marino estate was only about two hundred acres,[9] without perimeter walls and, like Delville which had the same prospect, easily accessible from Dublin. In fact it was the ideal of the Roman villa as exemplified by Palladio in his villas in the Veneto. The house (demolished in 1921), with a moderate front of five bays, was not large, and neither populace from Dublin nor scholar from Europe was ever barred from his grounds or his library. While Charlemont was again on his travels, this time in Germany in 1757, the estate had apparently been left in great disorder by the gardener. A year later Matthew Peters[10] was so distressed by the state of the gardens that he wrote to Thomas Adderley, Charlemont's manager, that the gardeners were poor, 'the manner most proper for the Training & advantage of the wall trees not known here, and but by verry few in England, must be Distressfull to me, & such walls after the great Expence his Lordship has been at, furnished with Ignorant management'.[11] Then he added that the hot-house 'Stove'[12] was also mismanaged, and finally he offered his superintendence gratis. But by the autumn of 1760 everything was properly organized, and planting started on a big scale, many of Lord Charlemont's friends sending him trees and plants. For example, Lord Arran wrote in August 1762 from Saunders Court, Enniscorthy, that he had 'fourty shining leav'd Laurustinuses, the Plants are well rooted, carefully taken up and well pack'd, & I hope will succeed. If your Lordship choses a greater number you may command them, for as they are among the most beautifull of the Flowering Shrubs, I had a great many lay'd.' And he also offered Gilead fir, liquid amber and cephalanthus.[13]

On 27 October 1763 the Duchess of Northumberland, the Vicereine, wrote an account of a visit during which she saw the two chief buildings – the Casino (Plate 157) and the Gothic Room (Plate 158):

157 MARINO, CO. DUBLIN. *The Casino.*

158 MARINO. *The Gothic Room: pencil drawing by Thomas Santelle Roberts.*

I went in my post chaise with Mrs Graham to Ld. Charlemonts at Marino with whom we found Lord Drogheda. We walk'd thro the Kitchen Garden wch. is 6½ Irish Acres to his Hot House it is 170 Feet long; in the *Anti Room* of which we breakfasted. The Walls were all Tapstried with Myrtle and an innumerable quantity of flowering Plants perfumed it on every side by their Fragrance. The rest of our Company were Lord and Ly. Stopford, Lord Tyrone and Lord Powerscourt. We then visited the Stables which are grand and handsome, the Farm Yard Barns &c. Then we walk'd thro a very pretty Shrubbery to a very handsome *Gothic Room* (the Windows of painted Glass.) We went to the *Temple.* The Stonework is admirably well executed all of Portland Stone, it is a beautiful Building but very ill qualified to be a Dwelling House.[14]

The estate possessed all the basic features of the best romantic-poetic landscapes: wood, water, a chain of ponds, varied ground and wide prospects of river, sea and mountains. Considering the landscaping started simultaneously with the fashion in England for 'the bare and bald' of Capability Brown, it was quite uninfluenced by current tastes. Nor was it a *ferme ornée.* As at Painshill there were at least three areas, a park, and garden and a section which was heavily planted and which could be called picturesque, with Gothic buildings. At the head of the principal lake was the Gothic Room, entitled Rosamund's Bower, with a 'highly ornamented screen, adorned with tracery and niches . . . a crocketed pinnacle conveying the idea of a spire',[15] the in-

139

terior fitted up to imitate the nave and aisles of a cathedral. On the ground floor, four quatrefoil windows of stained glass admitted light into a room with its floor in mosaic. According to John Harris,[16] it was very like the 'Gothic cathedral' at Kew designed by Johann Heinrich Muntz, the Swiss painter and architect, who worked with Horace Walpole and Sir William Chambers. Muntz's designs for Kew (1759) were used by Chambers and were therefore nearly contemporary with the Gothic Room at Marino (1762).[17] From the scale of the human figures it can be seen that it was a structure of impressive size at the head of the lake. In the grounds there were rustic hermitages, a root house (Plate 159), a moss house and a 'cane house constructed after the Eastern model'.[18] In addition, such minor features as a group of rocks forming a cascade, on the largest of which was an inscription much after the Shenstone manner at the Leasowes:

> Le penchant nous unite;
> Le destin nous sépare.

Also an elaborate Gothic seat (Plate 160) in the Muntz manner, pinnacled and crocketed, with a quatrefoil ornament in the spandrels above. On the north side was the

159 MARINO. *The root house: pencil drawing by Thomas Santelle Roberts.*

160 MARINO. *The Gothic seat: pencil drawing by Thomas Santelle Roberts.*

walled garden of nine acres, parts of which can still be traced. A visitor in 1816, after Charlemont's death, describes the layout of the grounds and some of the details of the Gothic Room and the root house very clearly:

Leaving the temple [the Casino] you enter a Close embowered walk which leads to a sheet of water at the extreamity of which is a summer-house fitted up as a Gothic nunnery with stain'd Glass windows. A little distance from this is an hermitage surrounded with shrubs. This building is most ingeniously created with small bits of stems & roots of trees laid horizontally with the ends outward so as to form the face of the building, each bit being cut thro' smooth, and the different woods shewing different colours. They are laid according to the taste of the architect and resemble something like mosaic work.[19]

But the *chef d'oeuvre* was Chambers' Casino, of Portland stone, costing over £60,000, a Greek cross in plan, and of two stories (not one as it appears, for the external stairs lead from the terrace to the *piano nobile*). The entablature is carried by twelve unfluted Roman Doric columns, the whole majestic building being about seventy-foot square and fifty in height. Its proportions belie its size. At the corners of the terrace, carved stone lions by Joseph Wilton lie diagonally couchant.[20]

In plan it is only a few feet smaller than Lord Burlington's villa at Chiswick, but it has no auxiliary building to link it to the main house. Lord Burlington designed his Chiswick villa to work and live in, his library being in the basement. Lord and Lady Charlemont used the Casino for entertaining on a small scale, and in hot weather as a belvedere, Lord Charlemont's considerable library being housed in Marino House or Charlemont House in Dublin. The Casino was much more practical than the Chiswick villa: for example, there were ample servants' quarters and kitchens in the basement which occupied the whole stylobate. Rain water from the roof (not a factor considered by Lord Burlington) is drained by an ingenious system off the pediments to the outer corners, where it falls forty feet through the free-standing columns to the basement level making a fascinating sound in a storm. The handsome urns on the roof, like the Chiswick obelisks, act as chimneys. There is a delicacy in the carving, whether of panels below the lions' paws or in urns and swags, as well as a strength in the boldness of the cornice crowning the frieze. The interior decoration is entirely apt, even to the detail of hay-rakes and figures in plaster symbolizing country tasks near the town. It reflects the character of Charlemont whose life was devoted to the preservation of order and the encouragement of the arts. More than this, it reflects an unusual understanding and exchange of ideas between patron and architect. Chambers has achieved a regularity, order and repose about the whole building, and even the four statues on platforms at the attic ends did not give it a baroque flamboyance.[21] The interchange of letters of architect and patron amply bears out their relationship, as Charlemont fully understood architectural matters and could draw. Another enlightened patriot, Sir John Browne of The Neale, County Mayo, in the course of improving, erected a 'miniature model of the Pyramids of Egypt from a plan and drawing given him by his brother-in-law, the Earl of Charlemont',[22] after he had returned from the East. This nine-tiered pyramid was formerly crowned by a lead statue of Apollo (Plate 161). Another garden building of Sir John Browne's was the classical temple (Plate 162), now ruined, an eye-catcher standing on an arched sub-structure.

On 25 August 1767 Chambers sent designs to Charlemont for the iron gates at the road entrance to Marino, 'done in the manner your Lordship desires. My clerk has misunderstood my sketch and committed a mistake or two in the drawing which I have endeavoured to correct in the margin as there is not time this post for drawing it correctly. I fancy the smith will understand it sufficiently . . .'[23] Then on 9 February 1768 he sent Cipriani's drawing for 'the dragons [griffins] of the gate . . .'[24] and on 30 January 1771 Chambers recommended that the roof vases should be drawn and cut out full size, then put in place to see whether the proportions were right. They should be made of metal and sanded to look like stone. In answer to a query from Charlemont about the size of the statues on the exterior, he pointed out that they were proportioned to the columns and could not be smaller, as they would look taller from below. The interior decoration of the Casino was also established after a consistently amicable exchange of ideas. Chambers sent specimens of the colours he recommended, point-

161 THE NEALE, CO. MAYO. *Pyramid.*

162 THE NEALE. *The temple.*

ing out, however, that colours can be changed by 'want of air' in a box in transit. With regard to the exterior he recommended a flat roof which would 'make a pleasant gazebo' if it had a canvas awning: and he thought that lead would be the 'best Covering . . . Copper is more expensive than lead, poisons all the rain Water, & cannot easily be made tight.' Also in this letter he says he has seen Muntz and 'pressed him to finish your Lordship's design several times'.[25]

The friendship between architect and patron continued throughout the correspondence. In April 1775 Chambers wrote to congratulate Charlemont on the birth of a son, saying that he had heard in Piedmont 'whenever a son is born, his father plants a thousand poplars, which when the young gentleman is of age, are worth just a thousand pounds, and serve as his portion.'[26] There was no need for this expedition in Charlemont's case; but it does seem he grew short of money, and after 1772 there was no more building at Marino. Indeed, in 1779, Chambers had not been paid thirty-seven pounds for work done in 1772. But planting certainly continued as it had for thirty years. In April 1786 Sir Edward Newenham offered Charlemont some rhubarb suckers from plants he had brought from China fourteen years previously, and in September some 'Black Hiccory and Butter nut trees' from 'Colonel Wordsworth of Connecticut'.[27]

With a letter of introduction from Edmund Burke, Arthur Young visited Marino in June 1776. As well as commenting, as was his custom, on the white clover, trefoil and rib-grass of the new lawns 'margined in the higher part by a well-planted, thriving shrubbery', he thought the 'banqueting-room ranked very high among the most beautiful edifices' he had seen anywhere for 'elegance, lightness and effect' as well as commanding a fine prospect. Two years later, John Wesley found it one 'of the pleasantest places he had seen'; high praise from one who had travelled more than 25,000 miles in Ireland:

The water, trees and lawns are so elegantly intermixed with each other having a serpentine walk running through a thick wood on one side and an open prospect both of land and sea on the other. In the thickest part of the wood is the Hermitage, a small room dark and gloomy enough. The Gothic Temple, at the head of a fine piece of water which is encompassed with stately trees, is delightful indeed . . .

He added that 'the most elegant of all the buildings [the Casino] is not yet finished'. Wesley was an admirer of Shenstone's Leasowes, and Marino with its 'lovely mixture of wood, water, and lawns, on which are several kinds of foreign sheep, with great plenty of peacocks' equally pleased him.[28]

From these accounts it is easy to see that Charlemont's landscape was romantic-poetic picturesque as later outlined by Price. It avoided the extremes of Brown or the gloomy, associative picturesque of Payne Knight. In a letter accompanying a copy of 'The Landscape', Edmund Malone wrote: 'Mr. Henry Payne Knight, (the author of that extraordinary book which you had some years since from the Dilettanti Society)[29] has published lately a Poem on Landscape in which he has endeavoured to bear off a wreath from the brows of Capability Brown, and in the opinion of some has succeeded.' To which Charlemont replied on 4 June 1794:

Knight's Landscape I have read, and greatly approve of it. I am happy at length to have seen a modern poem perfectly free from that fashionable verbiage by which our Poetry has for some years past been so sadly infected . . . The Taste also of this new Gardener pleases me much, principally, I suppose, because in most particulars, it nearly coincides with my own – Brown was undoubtedly a Reformer but, like most Reformers, has, in my opinion, carried his System a great deal too far.[30]

This statement is typical of the moderation of variety and intricacy in the disposition of objects as later delineated by Price, which was indeed in the tradition of the romantic gardens at Stourhead, Hagley or Painshill.

The perfection of the Marino landscape coincided with the period of Grattan's Parliament, that high watermark of Irish history before the Act of Union (1800). Like Burke, Charlemont thought there should be no separation between aesthetics and politics; and his life bore this out, whether as Whig leader, commander of the

Volunteers, friend of Sir Joseph Banks and Sir Joshua Reynolds, translator of Petrarch or landscaper at Marino. Unfortunately Burke devoted his life to politics after his initial *Philosophical Inquiry into the Origin of our Ideas of the Sublime and Beautiful* (1757), written before he was twenty-one (see page 104). It was a pity that he never again wrote at length on aesthetics, for his definitions of Sublimity and Beauty, though derived from Longinus, influenced much subsequent thought on landscaping. The qualities of admiration, dread and mystery by vastness of dimension, especially in dark rugged surfaces, were inspired by Sublimity, and produced a 'delightful horror' as the imagination was infinitely extended. Whereas the main inspiration of Beauty was not awe but love, found in smallness and smoothness, delicacy and clear, bright and diversified colours. The antitheses were brilliantly outlined by Burke, and Edmund Malone wrote to Charlemont in 1792 that he wished Burke would devote 'the remainder of his life to literature. I once proposed to him the revival and enlargement of his Sublime and Beautiful, to which at the end of thirty years he cd make most valuable additions: but he pleads that his mind has now taken an entirely different bent, and his studies been long diverted to other objects: yet such is his versatility that I have no doubt he could yet do wonders.'[31] Charlemont, with his inherent spirit of compromise thought both Brown and Payne Knight went 'too far'. So Marino combined the sublimity of forest trees – oak, ash and elm – with the beauty of myrtle, vine and jasmine, or the sublimity of Muntz's Gothic Room with the beauty in Palladian detail of Chambers' Casino. This combination of Gothic, Oriental and classical styles in the Marino garden buildings was probably influenced by Chambers' ideas worked out at Kew.

W. B. Yeats declared his respect for the leaders of Ireland in the 'ten or fifteen years after the declaration of the independence of the Irish parliament'.[32] From them he had inherited a pride which he in turn would pass on:

> The pride of people that were
> Bound neither to Cause nor to State,
> Neither to slaves that were spat on,
> Nor to the tyrants that spat,
> The people of Burke and of Grattan
> That gave, though free to refuse –
> Pride, like that of the morn,
> When the headlong light is loose,
> Or that of the fabulous horn,
> Or that of the sudden shower
> When all streams are dry,
> Or that of the hour
> When the swan must fix his eye
> Upon a fading gleam,
> Float out upon a long
> Last reach of glittering stream
> And there sing his last song.[33]

The last image of the swan and the fading gleam is almost identical with Pope's example of the picturesque which he told to Joseph Spence.[34] Such pride was worthy of such a setting. The people of Burke and of Grattan epitomized for Yeats, in their several ways, the best of Irish patriotism – a depth of imagination, a quality of intellect, a force of leadership and an elegance in creation. Charlemont's landscape at Marino[35] was an abstract of his time: 'the child of patriot, civil wisdom as well as the graces'.[36] Its creation by Charlemont, the President of the Society of Dilettanti, was an example of Roman moderation in politics and taste from a leader of the Irish Volunteers.

Very different is the landscape created by another leader of taste and an Irish Volunteer also – Frederick Hervey, the Earl-Bishop of Derry. Here the vast sweeps of Burke's sublimity reflected the extravagance and grandeur beloved by the Earl-Bishop, producing not the idea of the Roman villa set near the metropolis, wooing the elements and even the inhabitants, but a palace set high on a cliff far from anywhere, aweing visitors to silence and fighting Atlantic salt and winds.

The Irish landscape is littered with ruins of eighteenth-century houses. War, fire, rapine and desertion have taken their toll, and except for the filching of stone for other building, no one seems to have bothered much about the remains. The largest of these ruins must be the Bishop of Derry's house at Downhill near Coleraine in County Derry. It is little decayed as the roof was not removed until 1950: a vast house of local granite with two wings each with twelve bays of 165 feet by 35 feet. It stands on a high, exposed plateau dominating the scene for miles (Plates 163 and 164). A few hundred yards to the north, one-hundred-and-eighty-foot basalt cliffs drop abruptly to the sea, and on a clear day the mountains of Islay and Jura can be seen. To the west, Lough Foyle and the Donegal Mountains; to the east the Antrim coast sweeps up to the Giant's Causeway. Such are the Atlantic gales that no trees have ever grown on the high ground round the house, and none ever will. In the last quarter of the eighteenth century when this house was built, the County of Londonderry had less trees than any other in the British Isles,[37] on account of lavish waste of fuel, the exporting of staves, charcoal smelting of lead and iron and, above all, because absentee landlords had failed to plant. Here is a spot with all the aspects of sublimity: nature untamed, man isolated – dwarfed by solitude and emptiness beside the ocean's infinity. There is a hugeness of dimension in the rugged cliffs that might

163 DOWNHILL, CO. DERRY. *Engraving from J. P. Neale's* Views of Seats . . . , *vol. VI.*
164 DOWNHILL. *Engraving from J. P. Neale's* Views of Seats . . . , *vol. VI.*

have been exemplified by Burke, and an awe-inspiring grandeur, with evidence of man's work. Although the ruin is of a neo-classical building, with a huge and inappropriately castellated wall enclosing its stable yard, the effect is still prodigious, for it seems as if the owner in his pride had demanded a house in a setting where it would majestically defy the elements rather than gently fuse with them. It is not a Gothic ruin, yet it still seems to be (as Michael Sadleir wrote) 'a parable of the victory of nature over man's handiwork'. As such, its *hubris* deserves the fate it has received.

The originator of all this was the richest and most eccentric character ever to set foot in Ireland in the eighteenth century – Frederick Augustus Hervey (Plate 165), an Englishman, eventually Earl of Bristol in 1779 on the death of his brother. In 1754, he took Holy Orders, became chaplain to George III in 1763, then travelled in Europe for two years before being given the bishopric of Derry through the influence of his brother the Earl, who was briefly the Lord Lieutenant. Derry was the richest see in Ireland bringing in about five thousand pounds from land and eventually as much as ten thousand pounds a year from the see in tithes, to which Hervey could add an equally large personal income. It seems initially that he took his pastoral duties seriously for he had soon visited every parish in his diocese with his private chaplain

165 FREDERICK HERVEY, FOURTH EARL OF BRISTOL. *Oil on canvas by Pompeo Batoni.*

(whom he chose unprecedentedly because he was Irish rather than English). At the age of forty, one could have expected much of him: he was rich, had showed exceptional tolerance in religious matters, had demonstrated a taste for art in his travels, and displayed a sympathy for Irish difficulties. But there were two flaws in his character: the first, an inability to follow any project through to its fulfilment, the second, an excessive and compulsive urge to build, and to collect works of art to fill his buildings. So for two-and-a-half years he travelled on the continent with Michael Shanahan, the Cork architect and builder who made detailed drawings of buildings. Many of the places to which he went in 1765 were epitomes, during this period, of the sublime: the Rhine at Schaffhausen, the Harz Mountains, the passes of the Alps, the Montagne du Luberon in Provence, the Grand Chartreuse at Grenoble, and Vesuvius. This may be his reason for choosing a site such as Downhill on which to build and landscape.

But complaints soon reached the King of his absence, which was said to be through amusement rather than illness, so he returned to Derry and started on the building of his house at Downhill. It might be thought that Derry was a remote spot for one as internationally minded as the Bishop to live. Yet in 1785 the large yarn vessels were sailing daily to Derry, Coleraine and Belfast from Liverpool, so that, after two days from London to Liverpool in a coach, in another thirty-six hours or less you could land in the Coleraine river 'under' the Bishop's 'Park Wall'.[38] It is common practice in landscaping to plant before building, but such was not the case here. The 'edifying' Bishop, as he was called, on account of building proclivities rather than moral qualities, started to build, although there were no trees round the site of his house. By August 1776 when Arthur Young went there it must have appeared much as it does now from a distance – walls but no roof: 'the shell of the new house building on the sea-coast by the Bishop of Derry, which will be a large and convenient edifice when it is finished.' No mention of the landscape, which Young usually noted first, nor of the unsuitability of the terrain both from an agricultural and a picturesque point of view. One is apt to forget that Young was a capable artist who illustrated, for example, his *Tour of the North* with scenes, especially of cascades. Had he been some years later to Downhill he would have seen from the house the cascade which had been constructed. Soon the slate roof was on the house, and the stucco applied. The latter was a sensible precaution always followed by the Bishop, even to his last house at Ickworth, Suffolk, where the stucco has been repaired. He wrote at that time that he would 'follow dear impeccable old Palladio's rule, and as nothing ought to be without a covering in our raw damp climate, I shall cover the house, pillars and pilasters, with Palladio's stucco, which has now lasted 270 years'.[39] In comparison, the bishop's horticultural knowledge was limited, and as he was absentee (June to August 1776 on a geological expedition to Staffa; March 1777 to December 1779 in Italy or England) he must have left the landscaping to Michael Shanahan. The house was surrounded by a vast lawn, sixty-four acres on the north, fifty acres on the south, with a ha-ha on the south and east. On the whole, a most unpleasant spot in which to live, exposed to all the winds, no near-by garden nor grounds planted in which to walk, and no landscaping to unite house and country together.

In 1779 the Bishop's brother, the third Earl, died, and soon Shanahan and the Bishop had planned a building to his memory. It was a cenotaph or mausoleum modelled on the Roman Temple of the Julii at St Rémy near Arles, which they had seen together. The mausoleum was not so tall as the Roman original which is about sixty feet, but was similar – a high pedestal supporting Ionic (rather than Corinthian) columns with arched openings between them. Above was a life-size marble statue of the Earl inside a circular story with eight fluted Corinthian columns, and entablature with a high conical roof. The pedestal and the base of the top story alone remain (Plate 166), the tall roof and columns having been blown down in the great gale of 1839, which indicates the force of the Atlantic wind at this spot. The headless and damaged statue was allowed to lie where it fell until recently when it was propped up by the Bishop's Gate; yet the excellence of the sculpture of Van Nost, especially in the earl's robes, can still be seen. The head has presumably been stolen. Shanahan was proud of the mausoleum, which he thought superior to its Roman original, and he may well have been right. It is admirably placed at Downhill as an eye-catcher from the

147

house, and as a constantly recurring feature of the skyline between the trees of the glen.

The east and west glens twist in a horseshoe shape round the rugged basalt plateau on which the house stands. But for this lower ground there would be no possible landscaped area at Downhill, and as it was not started until 1780 the Bishop saw it planted only with young trees. Near the sea at the Port Vantage end, the prevailing north-west wind blights all trees, and twists them away from the sea like straws at a sudden angle after only a few feet of vertical growth.[40] Fortunately the glens curve and vary in height. At the west side of the fishpond or lake at Port Vantage there is a precipitous cliff on which is perched Lady Erne's Seat,[41] a circular building with windows on three sides, now in ruins like the house. Most of the work at Downhill took place between 1780 and 1787, with a concentration in 1783. In that year alone roads were made to stone quarries at the foot of Burren Hill a mile and a half to the south-west, and to lime kilns and quarries which were opened up on or near the beach; acres were levelled east of the house; a boundary wall was built round the demesne; the walks were cut out and levelled in both glens after much blasting, levering, boring, raising or sinking and carting away of rock; the two fishponds or lakes were dug out and drained; and earth was taken to make a walled garden a quarter of a mile from the house. During the spring about fifty labourers were daily

166   DOWNHILL. *The mausoleum.*

employed on trenching, drawing or preparing ground, digging holes and planting twenty thousand forest trees obtained from nurseries in the Inishowen peninsula, County Donegal, north-west of Londonderry,[42] from near Lough Beg or from Lord Enniskillen at Florence Court, County Fermanagh. No English nurseries provided trees for Downhill at this stage. In the east glen, larch, pine and Scotch fir grew among columnar basaltic rocks which formed recurrent points of visual interest. In the west glen a superb bank of trees, including ash, oak, willow, lime, horse-chestnut, spruce and larch were planted in soil which was blue clay for two feet. Soon the cascades and streams flowed into a lake[43] still as glass, along whose side black sallows (*Salix caprea*) were planted; Dunboe Church ruins became picturesquely focused; the banks of the stream by Drumagully Bridge were curved and covered with foliage and, finally, the hilltop with the 'Danish' Fort called the Giant's Grave was opened up to view.

In their finished state the glens possessed all the essential features of the sublime and the picturesque: at different levels, winding walks in which the final objective was seen then lost to sight; tumbling cascades, still lakes, mouldering ruins, an ancient fort, and even a tunnel under the main road so that continuity should not be lost. By the walls of the garden, the dovecot with ice house underneath, was a *point de vue* at the end of a vista. The glens were in fact the descent from the sublime of the plateau to the picturesque of the valleys. Such a scene calmed the political conscience of John Wilkes when he was at the Grand Chartreuse near Grenoble at the same time as, but not in the company of, the Bishop in the summer of 1765. 'The savageness of the woods, the gloom of the rocks, and the perfect solitude, conspire to make the mind pensive, and to lull to rest all the turbulent passions of the soul.'[44] This is what the Bishop hoped to achieve at Downhill.

But the landscaping was no easy nor cheap task, as the hundreds of receipts for money paid to labourers show. A typical small one is that of 'James Neil and Partners' showing the detailed and accurate description of work done:

February the 10th 1783

for enlarging the walk leading to the Caskeard at the uper End of the west
Glen 3 parch

Enlargd, 8 feet at the Bottom of the Rock at 6s 6d per parch	£0 19 6
also 13 parch & 2 yards Enlargd, 2 feet at the Bottom at 1s a parch & 3½d	13 3½
3 pips	3 3
	£1 16 ½[45]

Even twenty-five years later a visitor reported he had never seen 'so bad a house occupy so much ground. It is . . . surrounded by a planted glen, which latter is so low, that until its woods grow up it will remain hid.'[46]

During most of this period, if the Earl-Bishop was not abroad, as in 1781 when he was at Ickworth for a whole year, he was occupied with the Irish Volunteers in their fight for the freedom of the Irish Parliament. At the same time, the west gallery was added to the house, and a start was made on the Mussenden Temple (Plate 167). In late 1778, John Soane, the architect, says that the Bishop commissioned him to make drawings of the Temple of Vesta at Tivoli, the idea being to build a facsimile at Downhill.[47] If this was so, then yet another eighteenth-century garden building derives from this classical temple. The building at Downhill is indicative of the many sides of the Earl-Bishop's character: his taste in conceiving such a splendid building on a scale so right for its position; his pride in siting it on the very edge of the cliff, at a point from which he could survey the sea to infinity and two huge sweeps of broad strand to the far headlands of Inishowen and Kenbane; his lack of discernment in naming it after the beautiful young Mrs Mussenden (thought by contemporaries to be inappropriate conduct in a bishop whose wife had just left him); and his tolerant far-sightedness in arranging for a Catholic priest to hold Mass in it weekly, as there was no Catholic church in the parish.[48] This most elegant but strong building is about three hundred and fifty yards from the house and is forty feet in diameter, of freestone on a basalt plinth, with sixteen engaged Corinthian columns with drapery swags in between capitals supporting an entablature with frieze on which is inscribed in bronze embossed letters (originally gilded) the opening lines from Lucretius' *De Rerum Natura, Book II*:

Suave, mari magno, turbantibus aequora ventis,
e terra magnum alterius spectare laborem.[49]

The hemispherical concrete dome surmounted by an urn has been admirably restored by the National Trust which came on the scene too late to save the interior which originally had a coffered ceiling, but there are traces of the original blue and gilt in the library on the first floor. In the crypt below, where Mass was held, a miraculously constructed brick vaulting, sprung from a single pillar, supports the upper floor. Evidently the library was for use in summer as there is no provision for heating. But in that season, with the sound of the surf from below, and the panorama through three great eighteen-paned sash windows, what finer place to study? Yet the Bishop can have sat there rarely, and certainly not with Mrs Mussenden, for at the age of twenty-two she died, and the temple, which was just being finished, became a memorial to her.

The Earl-Bishop did not watch over the landscaping at Downhill except from a distance in Italy during most of 1785, 1786 and 1787. But it continued under the guidance of the Italian architect and *stuccodore*, Placido Columbani, who was responsible for payments being made to David McBlain,[50] a master-builder, and also to Michael Shanahan. The Bishop's Gate, at the head of the east glen, called the Coleraine Arch in honour of the local Volunteers, was completed in 1784.[51] The actual gate was 'a sort of Chinese wooden one only between two piers . . .'[52] Until 1787 the glens were still being worked on, as there are continual receipts for 'blasting, culling down rock and casting at the head of the Glen, and sinking a watercourse'.[53] In the same year, Shanahan paid Thomas McWilliams, a sculptor, for 'finishing the leopard'. This was the second of the two 'leopards'[54] on top of the Doric piers of the so-called Lion Gate; these lynxes or 'leopards' are taken from the Hervey family arms.

When on a visit to Derry in the summer of 1787, John Wesley reported that the Earl-Bishop had 'utterly forsaken an elegant summer-house in the garden of the Bishop's palace, a room fifty feet long, because it was no longer new'.[55] Dr Beaufort saw the Banqueting House later in the same year and reported that it was not finished, except for one room with a fine prospect up the Foyle. He regretted the garden was 'going to rack', especially as it had cost two thousand pounds which would have to be paid by the next bishop.[56]

In fact, the Earl-Bishop had started on the building of another large house at Ballyscullion overlooking Lough Beg farther south in County Derry, 'in a situation, beautiful and salubrious beyond all description', which he described to his daughter, Lady Erne:

Imagine to yourself then my dear Mary a globular hillock of gravel carpetted with dry green grass whose declivity reaches at the end of half a mile to the Banks of the River Bann or rather of Lough Beg, a small lake; this Lough Beg you may be sure is the Front of my house; the River again, after being decorated by Mr. O'Neill's new Bridge at Tomme, ends in Lough Neagh, & this is finally bounded by an immense ridge of the Conical Mountains of Mourne – such is my Prospect to the South. On the East, wch is the aspect of my Eating Room, the River Bann & the hills of the County of Antrim, together with a few hundred acres of my own estate, & a bridge which I am on the point of building will serve to amuse our eyes when we are not employing our knives and forks: but, on the West, that Phenomenon in the County of Derry, a woodland Country with an elegant Village and the Mansion of Mr. Dawson together with a serpentine River of Two miles length will decorate the view from my drawing-room.[57]

Among other extravagances, he cut this river or canal to 'surround the whole demesne for 360 acres'. In 1788 he 'restrained expenses for 6 months till Xmas to £70 a week'.[58]

The house as designed, with its ellipsis surrounded by twenty pilasters, with an attic story crowned with a domed rotunda, and curved corridors to wings, was the prototype of the family home which he was about to rebuild at Ickworth, Suffolk; but

167 DOWNHILL. *The Mussenden Temple.*

it was only three hundred and fifty feet compared with Ickworth's six hundred feet. Typically also, he arranged for a church spire on Church Island, one of the many islands on Lough Beg, connected with St Patrick, to appear as a focal point in the view from his library, and beyond this spire reared the mountains. He seems to have had no difficulty in obtaining money for further ecclesiastical eye-catchers, as he relates:

The worshipful Company of Drapers in the city of London have in the most obliging & flattering manner given me unanimously £100 towards building a steeple & spire at Bally-nascreen, so that before the end of the year I hope to have 4 or even 5 spires in the sight of Ballyscullion built chiefly at the expense of other people to beautify my prospect.[59]

Before the house was finished he wrote a Latin inscription for the portico which, when translated, becomes:

> Here is a verdant plain,
> I will place a temple of marble
> Beside the waters, where the vast
> Bann strays in sluggish windings
> And clothes its banks with tender reed.

169 BELVIEW. *Buttressed Gothic cottage.*
170 BELVIEW. *Eye-catcher.*

152

The Earl-Bishop never saw either of his houses completed, as he left Ireland in 1791, never to return. Ballyscullion was never finished and was pulled down in 1813. For the last eleven years of his life he continued to collect art treasures for his houses, but there is little mention of Downhill in his letters.[60]

Mr Justice Day, visiting Downhill in 1801, expressed a reaction which shows nature had never been tamed and that it was absurd to imagine it could be in such a wild and exposed spot:

It is impossible, [he wrote] not to regret the misapplication of so much treasure upon a spot where no suitable Demesne can be created, where Trees will not grow, and where the Northern blast and the trade-wind of the West almost forbid all vegetation; where the salt spray begins to corrode this sumptuous Pile of Grecian Architecture, and the imagination anticipating the distant period weeps over the splendid Ruin, a sad monument of human folly . . . in the rear is the Ocean over which upon an elevated abrupt and prominent Cliff the Bishop has built a handsome Grecian temple full of valuable but mouldering books, some on shelves and some piled in disorder upon the floor.[61]

When the Earl-Bishop died in Albano in 1803, Ballyscullion and Ickworth were unfinished, but the trees were established at Downhill and water flowed over the cascades. Although these trees continued to grow until they were felled within living memory, it was undoubtedly a difficult site on which to landscape.[62] Yet it possessed some of the qualities of the sublime which Payne Knight saw in Salvator Rosa's landscapes where 'ruined stems of gigantic trees proclaimed at once the vigour of vegetation . . . and of the tempests that have shivered and broken them'. In September 1803, Edward Wakefield found Downhill uninhabited. Fortunately, his prophecy with regard to the Mussenden Temple has not been fulfilled:

The mausoleum, erected to the late Earl of Bristol's brother, and the Mussenden temple, raised to perpetuate the remembrance of a lady to whom the Earl was much attached, are objects which will attest the vanity of their founder, when the names of those they were intended to preserve are forgotten, and thus serve as proofs, how little connection there subsists between public opinion and private feeling.[63]

Today, when cornfields touch the castellated walls of the stable yard, Pope's prophecy with regard to Timon's Villa has come true.

> Another age shall see the golden Ear
> Embrown the Slope,[64] and nod on the Parterre,
> Deep Harvests bury all his pride has plann'd,
> And laughing Ceres re-assume the land.[65]

But Pope qualifies this by the implicit moral of the 'Epistle' that bad taste, born of excessive wealth, in its unfeeling recreation of ground, requires more expense than good taste's gentle remodelling, and consequently it employs more labour. That is the justification for such landscaping, and it was most valid when applied in practice to the conditions of poverty in which Irish agricultural labourers normally lived. When the Bishop had written from Rome in 1778, to his daughter Mrs Foster, that he hoped 'to winter in Ireland, and if Shanahan will allow us at the Downhill, but the poverty of the country is so extreme, rents have so entirely failed that the poor tenants are not able to pay with daily labour . . .' it was not an unfeeling statement of a situation about which he intended to do nothing. Throughout his life he saved many from starvation, by building and landscaping.

The ruin at Downhill is the only monument in Ireland to his memory. At Ickworth there is a seventy-two-foot obelisk of Ketton stone (in need of repair), which was erected from the subscriptions of people in his diocese of Derry. The final words of the inscription on the Doric pedestal, after declaring his patronage was administered after disinterested principles, show that the Earl-Bishop's religious tolerance was valued in Derry, and as one reads them one cannot but reflect that some of his sentiments might be followed with advantage in Ireland in our own times:

> Grateful for Benefits
> which they can never forget,

the inhabitants of Derry
have erected at Ickworth
where his mortal Remains are deposited
this durable Record of their Attachment.
The Roman Catholic Bishop
and the Dissenting Minister at Derry
were among those who contributed
to this Monument.

1. Christopher Hussey in his excellent and authoritative work, *The Picturesque*, p. 66, described Painshill as a 'glorified *ferme ornée*,' but it seems to us that the main part of a *ferme ornée* should be devoted to agriculture, and this was not so at Painshill which was a combination of park and garden, as at Hagley, Worcestershire.
2. Llanover, *Mrs Delany*, vol. III, p. 566.
3. Some of his interests were correctly anticipated by William Dunkin, Swift's friend, who forecast in his *Epistle to the Right Honourable James Lord Viscount Charlemount* (1744) that Charlemont on his tour would write

    Accounts of Lakes, Volcanoes, Grottoes
    And Monuments with Ancient Mottoes
4. J. Parker to Lord Charlemont, Rome, 24 December 1755. Royal Irish Academy, Charlemont Correspondence, MS 12/R/9.
5. Although the design (slightly altered) does not appear in Chambers' *Civil Architecture* until 1759, he had planned it in Rome as an end pavilion of Harewood House, but it was rejected.
6. Charlemont Correspondence, letter 46.
7. *The English in Ireland in the Eighteenth Century*, London 1872.
8. John D'Alton, *The History of the County of Dublin*, Dublin 1838.
9. Brewer and Neale, *Beauties of Ireland*, gives a figure of a hundred acres, 'finely wooded' and 'sumptuously ornamented', but 'subject to considerable neglect'.
10. He was the father of the Reverend Matthew William Peters, R.A., 1741–1814.
11. Charlemont Correspondence, 12/R/9, letter 67.
12. By 'Stove' is meant a range of heated glass houses against a brick wall supporting the north side; but in this case it evidently refers to an orangery.
13. Charlemont Correspondence, 12/R/12, letter 33.
14. Alnwick Castle, MS Diary, The Duchess of Northumberland.
15. MS belonging to the Christian Brothers, quoted by M. Craig, *The Volunteer Earl*, London 1948.
16. John Harris, *Sir William Chambers*, London 1972, p. 34.
17. For further detail of Muntz's life and work see *The Age of Neo-Classicism*, Arts Council of Great Britain Catalogue, 1972, p. 866.
18. Bowden, *Tour through Ireland* (1791), p. 79.
19. Anon., 'Diary of a Tour in Ireland', National Library, Dublin, MS 194.
20. George Montagu wrote to Horace Walpole that he had seen the incomplete Casino, which 'promises to be very pretty', 1 October 1761. Lewis and Brown, *Walpole's Correspondence*, vol. 9, p. 391.
21. Ceres and Bacchus on the north front alone remain. Venus and Apollo have fallen.
22. Sir William Wilde, *Memoir of Gabriel Beranger*, Dublin 1880, p. 67.
23. Charlemont Correspondence, 12/R/10.
24. Charlemont Correspondence, 12/R/12, letter 52.
25. Charlemont Correspondence, 12/R/12, letter 55.
26. Charlemont Correspondence, 12/R/13, letter 4.
27. Charlemont Correspondence, 12/R/14, letter 65.
28. *Journal of John Wesley* (16 July 1778 and 3 July 1787), London 1827.
29. He means Richard, and refers to *An Account of the worship of Priapus*, London 1786.
30. Charlemont Correspondence, 12/R/8, letters 12 and 13.
31. Charlemont Correspondence, 12/R/17, 7 August 1792.
32. 'Emmet the Apostle of Irish Liberty', *Gaelic American*, 5 March 1904.
33. Collected Poems (1950), 'The Tower', pp. 222–23.
34. See p. 47.
35. Today, it is almost impossible to imagine these scenes. Firstly, the O'Brien Institute (1876) close to the Casino, straddles the landscape with engineering brick, and recently a concrete building has devoured the land at the entrance from the Malahide Road. A few aged horse-chestnut trees and a large yew, under which Charlemont may have sat, alone remain, with a pile of fallen tufa stones from Rosamond's Bower. Over the rest, the woods are felled, the water has dried up. But the negligence had started many years ago. *The*

Irish Farmers' Journal, vol. v, no. XVIII (1846), p. 348, reports with reference to Marino: 'The range of building, known as the Crescent of Clontarf, could not have been more advantageously placed, had the intention of its erection been to injure Marino . . . as well as the Drogheda Railway on an embankment.' The Casino – the only non-functional eighteenth-century building in Ireland to be maintained by the Board of Works under the Ancient Monuments Act 1930 – is watertight and externally in adequate repair. But its interior was neglected and dirty; stone urns, statues and pieces of balustrade lie in the basement, the State Bed is in pieces on the floor; plasterwork falls, walls peel and internal colour fades in the sun – but the Board of Works has now begun work on the interior.

36. Francis Hardy, *Memoirs of the political and private Life of James Caulfield, Earl of Charlemont*.

37. Robert Slade, *Narrative of a Journey to the North of Ireland in the Year 1802*. London 1803.

38. The Earl-Bishop to John Symonds, 25 March 1785. MS 941/51/4, the Record Office, Bury St Edmund's, Suffolk.

39. Downhill, with its pilasters in pairs over a rusticated basement, with projecting three-sided bays on the south front, might well be the work of James Wyatt, as it is very similar to Wyatt's work at Heaton Park in Lancashire. Wyatt's name is mentioned in the correspondence. We are indebted to Mr Peter Rankin for this observation made in his lecture on 20 April 1969 to the Ulster Architectural Heritage Society. See also his *Irish Building Ventures of the Earl Bishop of Derry*. Ulster Architectural Heritage Society 1972.

40. On occasions, the wind on the plateau was so strong that servants could get back to the house only on hands and knees.

41. Mary, his eldest daughter, who married the first Lord Erne.

42. McCracken, 'Notes on Eighteenth Century Irish Nurserymen', lists 110 nurseries in this peninsula; but says it was cheaper in 1800 to get seedlings from Scotland than from local nurseries.

43. Stocked with fish sent by Lord Moira from Montalto, County Down.

44. *Correspondence*, 1805, vol. 2, pp. 183–84.

45. MS DI 514/9/6, PRONI (Belfast). The spelling of James Neil is evidently phonetic.

46. Wakefield, *Account of Ireland*, vol. I, p. 29.

47. *Memoirs of an Architect*, London 1835 (privately printed), p. 15. In the same year he also designed for the Earl-Bishop a 'Canine Residence' or classical dog-kennel. His drawing can be seen in Sir John Soane's Museum, Lincoln's Inn Fields, London.

48. He also provided in his will for food for the priest and his horse.

49. Translated by Dryden as:

'Tis pleasant safely to behold from shore
The rolling ship, and hear the tempest roar.

The next two lines ameliorate the apparent complacency of these:

non quia vexari quemquamst incunda voluptas,
sed quibus ipse malis careas qui cernere suave est.

50. McBlain therefore was in a superior position to Shanahan.

51. Another famous arch to commemorate Henry Grattan's corps of Volunteers is in the demesne of Belview near Lawrencetown, County Galway (Plate 168). As can be seen, it is finer and more elaborate than the Coleraine Gate, having twin lodges and entrances for pedestrians. It was built by Henry Lawrence (1729–96). The urn has gone from the pediment, and one of the sphinxes has been decapitated. All that remains of this splendidly-planted estate (see Appendix B) are a few old cedars, ilexes and ruins. Remarkable eye-catchers and Gothic follies also survive (Plates 169 and 170).

52. Dr Beaufort, op. cit., vol. 3, p. 30.

53. PRONI (Belfast), MS 1514/9/11.

54. The other lies uncared for in the crypt of the Mussenden Temple.

55. Wesley, *Journal*, 4 June 1787, vol. 2.

56. Dr Beaufort, op. cit., vol. 3, pp. 25–26.

57. To Lady Erne, 8 March 1787. Quoted by W. S. Childe-Pemberton, *The Earl-Bishop*, 1924, vol. 2, pp. 399–400.

58. Dr Beaufort, 13 July 1788.

59. To Lady Erne, 12 February 1792.

60. Hotels Bristol on the Continent are named after him on account of his extensive and expensive travelling.

61. Day, *Diary*, 1801, RIA MS 12 W 15.

62. The National Trust is slowly replanting the Port Vantage glen. In 1803 Robert Slade, *Narrative of a Journey*, an accurate reporter, estimated about a million trees on the estate.

63. *Account of Ireland*, vol. 1, p. 29.

64. An eighteenth-century term for ground artificially treated.

65. 'Epistle to Richard Boyle, Earl of Burlington', lines 173–76, *Moral Essays*.

8 The Picturesque Scene at Killarney

A spot whereon the founders lived and died
Seemed once more dear than life; ancestral trees,
Or gardens rich in memory glorified
Marriages, alliances and families,
And every bride's ambition satisfied.

W. B. Yeats, *Coole Park and Ballylee.*

Thackeray, on his way from Kenmare to Killarney during his Irish tour, was much affected by the awe-inspiring sublimity of the view as he passed under the brows of the Mangerton Mountains. For many writers at that time, an association of romantic ideas induced analogies with the other arts – in this case with music. Thackeray thought of 'that diabolical tune in *Der Freischütz'*.[1] The mountains must have terrified him, for the theme to which he refers is evidently that epitome of Gothic horror, played in the Wolf's Glen. This scene from Act II reveals a deep ravine, mountains and waterfall on a stormy moonlit night, while a great owl and ravens perch on blasted trees. Weber's blood-curdling interpolations from violins with wolf-like howls from trombones complement the setting, before we hear the intoning voices of invisible spirits crying that the tender bride will be dead ere dawn. But Thackeray quickly recovered his composure as he dropped down to the level lake and the lime avenue into Killarney.

The towering alps and the spruce-covered mountains of Norway, looming over vast lakes, also have a sublimity in their wild grandeur; but Killarney combines a comparable grandeur with an elegant improvement of nature by man in the form of estates along the lake shores. Killarney's uniqueness lies in man's combining this most savage and wild scene – its mountains, lakes and waterfalls – with lawns and woods of a landscaped scene. A dualism in which, from the cheerful vicinity of a lakeside house, one responds to the stimulus of the sublime in lakes and mountains, with many ruins of ancient chapels and towers, visually and conceptually powerful, as a reminder of the great Irish past. Edmund Burke would have thought that both the Muckross and Kenmare estates at Killarney were ideal in this way, for he fancied that endless sublime scenes, such as many in Switzerland, stunned the mind unless combined with natural textures in a landscape created by man to form an 'artificial infinite'.[2] His concept is only one step removed from the later picturesque of Uvedale Price. Killarney is this perfect mixture of art and nature, even to the landscaping by planting of trees on the many islands of the lakes; and, in the eighteenth century, of permitting nature to adorn medieval ruins. In the second half of the century a lakeside estate did not have too startling an artificiality which would have contrasted violently with the natural environment. The mountains, unchanging and transcendent in contrast with the precariousness of human endeavour, were wooed rather than antithesized. By layout and planting the true picturesque estate conveyed a repose in which one could move round by 'undulating paths' to observe the startling roughness and grandeur of the external natural scene. One would not be distracted, as Price would have said, by 'an open licentious display of beauties' (such as the huge clumps of hot-toned *Rhododendron arboreum* or *Prunus serrulata* planted at Muckross), but would be delighted by a romantic textural intricacy on a smaller scale, both tonally and spatially, which led naturally by its organic form into the larger elements of nature – in fact from the smaller picturesque to the cosmic sublime, the one complementing the other.

One of the first mentions of Killarney in the eighteenth century comes from Lord Orrery in a letter to his friend, John Kempe. This letter deals chiefly with matters concerned with Lord Orrery's estates in County Kerry, but the sentiments expressed at the beginning, in Lord Orrery's inimitable style are repeated with variations by tourists, diarists and travellers for the next one hundred and fifty years.

Dingle: 17th Aug. 1735. Sunday.
I begin this letter without any Regard to the Post-day, but merely as I have leisure. You see by its date how far I am arriv'd in my Territories of Kerry: We left Egmont on Monday, & stay'd at Killarny all Tuesday to see the Slough [*sic*] there. This Llaugh is one of the Beauties of Nature, exclusive of Art; of which She may be justly proud. It is a vast Lake of Water, in which between forty & fifty little Islands, all cover'd with wild Evergreen, stand erect. The high Mountains, that are its Boundaries, are likewise cover'd in the same Manner, with Arbutus, Oak, Holly & Yew. In the midst of one of these Islands, Ross Castle, an old venerable Building, rears its Head. Eccho lives in the Woods; & the Musick of a Pack of Hounds, chasing a Stag up & down the almost perpendicular Hills, made a Harmony much more agreeable to the Ears than one of Handel's best Chorus's. We din'd under an Arbutus, by a River-side, & a Violin in Concert with a Drum sent the Bumpers of Wine with great Pleasure down the Throats of some of my Companions. At Night we return'd to Killarny, where I slept at Lord Killmere's [Kenmare's] House, & lay on Wensday at Mr. Godfrey's the High Sherriff's.[3]

The two families of Browne and Herbert were established by the Crown in Killarney during the Elizabethan Plantation of Munster, displacing the rightful owners, the O Donoghue Mórs, the descendants of the ancient tenth-century Kings of Munster. In 1448, Donal M'Carty Mór had founded the Franciscan friary and church at Muckross on the banks of the Lower Lake, and for two centuries this had been one of the great houses of learning in Ireland. But as a result of Cromwell's sacking, only a ruined nave, belfry, south transept and cloister remain today.

When Arthur Young visited Muckross in September 1776, Edward Herbert had incorporated the ruins into his estate. The broken walls were covered in ivy,[4] giving a picturesqueness which 'that plant alone can confer', and were overhung by old trees including a huge canopied yew in the cloisters. Young says it was the most 'prodigious' yew he had ever seen, having a trunk two feet in diameter. This is obviously an uncorrected error of the printer's, for Young was proverbially accurate, and would never have underestimated the girth of a tree which other eighteenth-century writers[5] thought had been planted about the time of the founding of the abbey. In the early 1930s the circumference of the tree was nine feet six inches at four and a half feet from the ground, so in 1776 it would have been considerably more than two feet.[6] In 1797 the abbey still had a spire but it was ruinous.[7] Young noted many skulls and bones lying in this burial place of Irish chiefs; and, apart from these and a hermit,[8] the scene is much the same today (Plates 171 and 172). In his practical fashion Young also commented on the difficulties which Edward Herbert had overcome in his landscaping. It must have been a tremendous task to reclaim one hundred and forty acres round the house, in an area which had been covered in rocks, brambles and furze. If of limestone, some of the six-feet-square rocks had been drawn off by thirty bullocks; if of sandstone, they were removed by first lighting fires on them, then cracking them by blows from a sledge hammer. In addition, Edward Herbert drained many acres of bog to make productive pastureland for sheep.

Charles Smith in his *History of County Kerry* (1756) somewhat belittles Herbert's initial work, evidently failing to appreciate the manner in which abundant nature would complement art.

These natural gardens therefore wanted little assistance to beautify them, except an enclosure towards the land, and the lopping away part of their luxuriance to form avenues and walks through them; besides the addition of such exotics, as have been of late years introduced to *Ireland*: among which there have been planted a considerable number of vines, which are now spreading their branches, and crawling up sloping rocks of variegated marble.

The lake washed the lawns round his house, *domus ultima* lying in ten thousand acres set on a narrow peninsula between the Lower and Middle Lakes (Plate 173); and he constructed a Gothic bridge to Brickeen Island. Dr Beaufort in 1806 was impressed by the fact that the rocks on one side of this bridge were limestone, on the other of 'brown' stone (sandstone), the former being 'perforated and excavated into a variety of the more grotesque forms, like the rocks in Chinese drawings'.[9] Mr Herbert also built a three-mile carriage road rising and falling through mixed woods of sorbus, acacia, holly, juniper, sycamore, oak, ash, beech and *Arbutus unedo* (Killarney strawberry tree). This last, a Mediterranean native, grows at Killarney and elsewhere

171 MUCKROSS ABBEY,
CO. KERRY. *Oil on canvas
by G. Nairn, 1829.*

172 MUCKROSS ABBEY.
*Exterior with hermit:
watercolour by William
Pars (1742–82).*

173 KILLARNEY, CO.
KERRY. *Aquatint map of
lakes by Jonathan Fisher,
1794.*

to about twenty feet,[10] with deep green leaves, red stalks, lily-of-the-valley-like blossoms, and berries (from which it gets its name) of insipid taste which turn from green through yellow to scarlet in November.

Muckross is an area favoured by nature. Sheltered by the McGillicuddy Reeks, the highest mountains in Ireland, there is no exposure as along the coast, so there is a natural growth of oak and, under it, evergreens – arbutus, ilex and deciduous betula and corylus; below them, ferns, mosses and liverworts. It combines mild winters with a heavy rainfall (eighty-seven inches on the Upper Lake) giving a uniformity of temperature with heavy mists, which when they clear, reveal the picturesque calluna, the shaggy heather, above the tree limit. All the works of Edward Herbert seen by Arthur Young – the building of new roads and bridges through the peninsula and the planting of trees – must have been achieved at Muckross after 1760, for when Samuel Derrick went there in that year the abbey had not yet been incorporated in the grounds, and the gardens were 'neglected and out of repair'.[11] But another visitor in the summer of 1763 was more impressed:

> Mr. H. Showd us an Abby of His at the Bottom of the Lake most sweetly placed with a Cloister entirely perfect tho very ancient & so large a Yew Tree in the Center of the Cloisters that the Branch extended to the Eaves of every side, which formed the most solemn Gloom I ever beheld. I saw near there an Yew grown in appearance from solid rock out of the Body of which at [indecipherable] feet height grew a very fine Birch 14 feet high & a large Holly . . . At Mr. H.'s house we took some romantic rides and had most noble Views of Cascades in abundance, the lakes and all their Islands and the country . . . having Mongarti [Mangerton] over our Heads and Brandon in full view which are by much the 2 highest mountains in this kingdom.[12]

Samuel Derrick also visited a larger but less picturesque estate, that of the Browne family, whose head, Lord Kenmare, lived in a house on the Killarney side of the Lower Lake. During his time there Derrick wrote[13] to 'James Boswell Esq., of Auchenleck [sic], North-Britain' that Lord Kenmare had done little improving to his park of six hundred and fifty acres along the lakeside; but that he was obviously the dominant and benevolent influence in the neighbourhood. His ancestor, Sir Valentine Browne, in 1622 had received a grant from the Crown including 'The Lakes of Killarney, with all the islands of or in the same and the fisheries of the said lakes and the soil and bottom thereof'. In the mid-eighteenth century, Thomas Browne, fourth Lord Kenmare (1726–95), an 'easy, affable and polite man', took his responsibilities seriously. All boats were rowed (sails were prohibited through loss of life in squalls), and were his monopoly; but he never refused to provide them for travellers who asked for them in suitable weather. In a short time he raised the town 'from nothing' by introducing woollen and linen manufactures, established charities and subsidized agriculture. His house, superior then to Muckross House,[14] had been built by his father, 'a plain, un-adorned oblong of dark hewn stone, three stories high with eleven front windows in each of the upper stories',[15] a mile from the lake with fine views to the mountains opposite but no view of the lake except from garrets. His planting was extensive, and, as can be seen from an examination of Plate 173, a straight avenue[16] with a vista to Ross Island, and two radial avenues at forty-five degrees led from a rectangular parterre on the east front of the house, showing the lack of 'improvement' noticed by Samuel Derrick in 1767. Some old oaks and limes individually marked on Fisher's map can be seen today in the avenue which makes a fine arch over the Muckross road, as well as standing isolated in the park. In the western side of the park Lord Kenmare provided rustic seats and pavilions, for the entertainment of the Killarney townsfolk, in a glen through which the Flesk dropped over dark rocky ledges.

This account of Lord Kenmare's work is borne out by Richard Pococke who visited Killarney in 1758,[17] the year in which he became Bishop of Ossory. He was a much travelled man, having been to Ireland twice before, and toured extensively in the British Isles and Europe, as well as to Alexandria and Rossetta. His writing is impersonal and matter-of-fact yet accurately observant of material detail (except for place names, which he did not hear well). He had evidently been to Killarney in 1749, although no diary nor letters have been found of that tour. From his and Derrick's accounts one can date the opening up of Killarney for tourists as between 1750 and 1758. Yet it certainly had been known about earlier. When trying to persuade Bishop Clayton and his wife (Plate 149) to accompany him there, Lord Orrery had written: 'There is a Llough worth a thousand burning Rivers. There are Hills that will employ our visive Faculties during the Time we stay. They vie in Beauty with Libanus, in Height with the Apenines . . .'[18] On Bishop Pococke's second visit in August 1758 he stayed for four days and wrote with unusual enthusiasm of Lord Kenmare and the scene; having seen Killarney in 1749 when it was a 'miserable village'

It is wonderful to see what Lord Kenmary [sic] has done in about nine years. He has made a walk round the Isle of Innisphalen at a mile distance on the lake & built a house there for company to dine in. He has built a Tower and Steeple to the church, market house, caus'd many roads to be made & some at his own expence, allotting the profits of a Salmon fishery to public works; he has variety of boats to attend all strangers, & what is more extraordinary, he has raised such a town without any manufacture; in a word, he is a pattern for a most noble public spirit conducted by an excellent understanding & an unprejudic'd judgement. The Park chiefly hanging grounds to the north east is finely wooded, there are beautiful ridings in it, & it commands a charming tho' I think distant view of the Lake.

In the next year Edward Willes corroborates the Bishop's account, but is more accurate about the size of the hermitage on Innisfallen:

Inesfallen, hermitage, 'salmon fish caught in the Lake and broiled on the coales . . . The hermitage did not admit room for more than one servant to wait inside so the side board was out of Doers and the wine served to us through the windows . . . My Lord proposes building a room or two in the old Abbey style to retire to and spend a day when he pleases. I don't mean in the old Monkish Reverie and indolence, but with sensible cheerfulness accompanied with his friends.

Grass walk round the islands' openings to the lake. [Kenmare] planted whole island with potatoes this year to kill the Bryars and Thorns and proposed having the whole next year in turf under the grove of Oak trees. There is likewise a large Rookery which adds greatly to the Beauty of the place. The whole Spot appears like Fairy Ground or the Inchanted Island, The ruins of the Abbey, The Hermitage cover'd with ivy as old as the Reformation. The Crawking of the Rooks, The different Romantic Scenes and views can't fail at putting me in mind of
> In these deep Solitudes and Awful Cells
> Where Heavenly pensive contemplation dwells etc.[19]

It seems that Lord Kenmare's and Mr Edward Herbert's successors at the beginning of the nineteenth century were absentee, for Lady Bessborough wrote from Killarney to Lady Granville on 11 October 1808 that the boatmen lamented the Killarney woods which had 'all gone to England' as 'Ld Kenmare and Mr. Herbert live in England; they make the most of Estates they never see; the trees are all to be cut down for timber, and the money sent to them . . .'[20] A poem by 'J.A.' printed in *The Irish Farmers' Journal*, vol. IV (Sept. 1815–Aug. 1816) laments the loss of these trees:

> Where is the wilderness of ancient trees
> Our wand'ring vision now no longer sees,
> That o'er yon *mountain* tower'd in pomp sublime.
> Where are they gone; ah! whither are they flown?
> Are they decay'd by time, or man o'erthrown?
> By *ruthless man*, a *hermit's voice* exclaims,
> But prudence now the past destruction blames;
> And nature still an infant stock supplies,
> Which from the relics of their parents rise
> In pride elate, and spreading fame to live
> A future forest to Glena to give.

One of the most famous Killarney trees, *Arbutus unedo*, is often mentioned by Shelley in his poetry. In 1813, as a young man, he was in need of a rest after seeing an apparition, and spent a few weeks with Harriet in a cottage on Ross Island. He never forgot the arbutus or the exceptional beauty of Killarney which he later thought was more lovely than Lake Como.

By 1822 the formal layout of the Kenmare estate had been allowed to get out of hand. The vista to Ross Island was obscured by woods which had so grown up that there remained only

a narrow telescopic view of the waters, and of the lesser hills which trend away beyond the Lower Lake. In the evening, the line of water, seen over the tufts of trees which bound the lawn, forms merely a streak of light in the landscape, totally inadequate to counterpose the overpowering masses of shadow, which everywhere surround it; during other parts of the day it is generally in obscurity, owing to the reflection of the mountains, – and at such times the whole scene is tame and unattractive.

There are several stations in these grounds from which admirable prospects of the Lower Lake might be opened, so as to allow a view of the mountains in all their grandeur and sub-limity, which at present are only partially visible. Instead of this, the pedestrian is hemmed in, during the remainder of his walk through the grounds, by quaintly trimmed hedges, flanking smooth gravel walks, as monotonous as art can render them. Sometimes the fatigued eye is relieved from the irksome repetition of these unvarying promenades, by an occasional shrub, the light foliage and pliant boughs of which may have escaped the Vandal touch of perverted taste, and retained their natural luxuriance.[21]

It is not to be expected that the author of the above with an eye for the picturesque could appreciate any attempt at a formal garden so he also makes fun of the planting of the parterre: 'It is impossible to resist smiling at the trimly-shorn hawthorns which are disposed in front, like so many wig-blocks on a green carpet – a simile which is most appropriate in the months of May and June, when nature confers upon them a luxuriancy of curls.'[22]

In *Legends of the Lakes* by Thomas Crofton Croker, London 1829, one of the local fishermen asks the author whether he thinks Killarney is not a fine place, and he adds:

it was'nt always so, it's myself remembers or if I don't, sure my father does well enough, when the ground we're triding on, was a wild boggy spot, all full of running strames; but the ould Lord Kenmare, the Lord rist his sowl in glory, gave good incouragement to the people to build; and sure enough, many a jackeen would'nt be walking the pavements like gentlemen today, if it wasn't for the ould lord's giving farms to their fathers and grandfaders, for little or nothing, and all because they were the good lords, that did'nt go out of the country, but staid at home and minded the poor people . . .

This opinion had been earlier stated by Dr Beaufort who reported that the late Lord Kenmare was much beloved but that his son lived in London, 'spent money and cut trees'.[23]

Crofton Croker also relates a boatman's account of a brief visit by Sir Walter Scott and Maria Edgeworth in the summer of 1825: 'the part of the lake Sir Walter likes the best, was the river under Dinis there; but, sure, he didn't stay half long enough to see anything worth spaking about.'[24] Maria Edgeworth wrote to her friend Joanna Baillie, the Scottish authoress, on 19 August 1825:

We spent 3 days at Killarney and during that time saw in perfection and quite at ease all that is to be seen – Lower and Upper lake – Innisfallen – Ben Turks – Mouse Island &c. My brother William who has been employed as an engineer in laying out a new road on the banks of the lake and who is well acquainted with the place and the people in the neighbourhood came from Valentia . . .

You need not be afraid of my giving you a description of Killarney . . . All I shall say is that it surpassed Sir W Scott's expectations, satisfied and delighted him.[25]

Evidently the Herbert family continued to plant, as in 1806 Colt Hoare noticed Scotch fir, recently planted in Muckross which he complimented by calling it a 'wes-tern Tempe'. Today, Muckross is the more interesting estate in landscaping terms, but it is evident from travellers' accounts that it was developed later than Lord Kenmare's. The gentle undulating parkland with a drive leading from Kenmare estate to Killarney town is still undramatic, and the small town as undistinguished now as then.[26] It is entirely tourist-geared and commercialized, but fortunately never en-croaching upon the lake shore, which is guarded by miles of stone walls – in fact much the same as when, in the summer of 1849, Thomas Carlyle wrote that 'the lake tho' we are close to it, cannot be seen. I tried on all sides, found it everywhere padlocked under walls, and grated gates, beset with guides, whom in my spleen I determined not to employ.' Then reacting to the exaggerated accounts he had heard of it, he commented: 'don't bother me with audibly admiring it'.[27]

It is still possible to see the lakes and Muckross approximately as in the eighteenth century, for no motor vehicles are allowed in the estate, the journey being taken in an Irish horse-drawn jaunting car. By this means and by walking one sees the abbey and Muckross House, then the Lower Lakeside (Lough Leane) and the Torc Waterfall, a splendid mass of water bouncing and splashing over huge glacial boulders, deeply inlaid in a chasm and permanently in spate, being fed from a dark pool called the Devil's Punchbowl high on Mangerton Mountain. In the eighteenth century the Torc Waterfall was visible from the house, but today it is hidden in deep wood of larch and fir.[28] Thackeray's description of this waterfall is still one of the best written: 'Evergreens and other trees, in their brightest livery; blue sky; roaring water, here black and yonder foaming of a dazzling white; rocks shining in the dark places, or frowning black against the light, all the leaves and branches keeping up a perpetual waving and dancing round the cascade.'[29] Early travellers have given us enraptured accounts of the scene, and even the dyspeptic Richard Twiss[30] wrote in hyperbole of the ruins of the abbey, the old yew tree (then said to be nearly 350 years old) and the craggy rocks. Many people hired boats knowing that by this means the variety of the lakes was best seen, by curving silently round rocky promontories, through straits, by islands, with ever-changing views of towering mountains, picturesque bays and sparkling waterfalls. There is no such concentration as Killarney in the rest of Ireland, or so great a variety within an area smaller than Windermere; in fact what Louisa Conolly called 'the sublime, the romantic, the gay and the improved scene' rapidly succeed one another. The travellers embarked amid the wild and sublime grandeur of the Upper Lake with its many islands and tremendous mountains; then they passed between the perpendicular cliffs called Coleman's Eye, under the Eagles Nest, a rugged cone-shaped mountain, towering over the river, thickly wooded at the base[31] (Plate 174). In this three-mile strait between the lakes, unearthly echoes of horn and trumpet can be made to ring round, especially on a summer's evening when the winds are still. For this purpose Lord Kenmare used to provide a trumpeter for his guests (Plate 175). Mrs Delany expressed a desire to see the 'enchanted place' when told by Mrs Wogan, Lord Kenmare's sister, of the effect of music there 'such as trumpets, French horns and hautboys'.[32] She went there and sketched in 1767. Like everyone else she found the echoes eerie because they become lower and fainter in the distance, then suddenly after a pause gain renewed power, generating on all sides strange harmonies in ensemble as they die off. By Tennyson's time bugles were blown:

174 KILLARNEY. *The Eagles Nest: oil on panel by William Sadler.*

175 KILLARNEY. *Ron-ayne Island, Upper Lake: aquatint by T. Medland after J. Carr.*

The splendour falls on castle walls
And snowy summits old in story;
The long light shakes across the lakes,
And the wild cataract leaps in glory.
Blow, bugle, blow, set the wild echoes flying,
Blow, bugle; answer, echoes, dying, dying, dying.

Lord Kenmare also provided ammunition for a cannon which when fired sounded like prolonged peals of thunder rolling among the mountains.

After these diversions, travellers passed into calmer water by the tiny coves of the romantic Middle Lake to the open elegance of the Lower Lake. On the north side lies the twenty-acre island of Innisfallen which until the present century was covered in wood, chiefly large hollies, beeches and yews. One of these fine trees, a holly, was noted by Samuel Hayes in 1794 as fifteen feet in circumference with a stem the same height. The twelfth-century chapel with its Romanesque door, once concealed by trees, is now cleaned and stripped of ivy. All round are superb views – immense mountains, the lake dotted with wooded islands and rocks on one side, a wide sweep of water to the cultivated shore on the other. After heavy rain, the lower part of O'Sullivan's Cascade at the foot of Tomies Mountain can be seen on the opposite shore as it splashes down under arched trees to a dark pool (Plate 176). A contemporary writer describes a visit:

Here [on Innisfallen] Ld Kenmair has built a Room in which We dined that day having a compleat View of that Lake & many of the Islands, but before dinner We were rowed to the upper Lake two full leagues from the former through a Channel about 50 yards wide between mountains all wooded as the former, & at proper places Cannon were fired to salute us, the Noise of which no Thunder I ever heard surpast & the Echoes of Them among those vast mountains no Pen can express.[33]

It seems always to have been a place for the locals to trap tourists. In the summer of 1788 Dr Beaufort's party, on landing, found a 'crowd of apple women and nutsellers' assembled there, 'just as if it was a fair, or rather like the savages coming down to barter with our Ships on distant Islands'.

In early October 1777, Louisa Conolly journeyed from the Lower to the Upper Lake, describing the scene in picturesque terms:

Beyond these beautifull highhills you see monstrous rocky mountains, you then turn round an Island into Muckross Lake, where you coast along a rocky shore, that the water has made so beautifull that every rock pleases you. Mr Herbert (happy man) has his House upon that shore, and his garden is dressed very nicely down to these rocks; he has also a fine old Abby, and beautifull lying grounds that you would admire anywhere, with Wood, and all this backed by

163

176 KILLARNEY.
*O'Sullivan's Cascade: en-
graving by V. Picot after
Jonathan Fisher.*

177 KILLARNEY. *Ken-
mare House: formal
garden, 1860.*

178 KILLARNEY. *Kill-
arney and Lord Kenmare's
house, watercolour by
William Pars.*

enormous high mountains down one of which rolls a cascade 200 feet high in sight of the house. You then go thro' a narrow channel into the Upper Lake, where you have the sublime in perfection. The Eagles' nest is glorious, tis a very steep rock covered in parts with wood . . .[34]

On this visit to Killarney, Tom and Louisa Conolly were accompanied by Lord John Townshend and Charles James Fox, her nephew, who bathed in the Devil's Punch Bowl, but apparently suffered no ill effects from the extreme cold of the water.[35] A tale is told of Fox that, when he arrived at Killarney in heavy rain, Lord Kenmare assured him it was only a shower. It rained all the time Fox was there so he never saw the views. Three years later Fox greeted Kenmare in London with 'Well, my Lord, is the shower at Killarney over yet?'

The mountains forming the amphitheatre in which Muckross lies are still clothed in wood dropping steeply to the lake; and as the light fades rapidly from warm purple to deep grey, or is diffused in the vast Atlantic clouds which float transparently across, one knows that the basic essentials of the picturesque and the sublime are present – but never more intensely than when the purple tone of the mountains is increased by the flowering of *Erica cinerea*. In addition, many of the ruins stand at key-points on promontories or islands: Ross Castle, the original seat of O Donoghue Mór, near the town; Castle Lough, McCarty Mór's castle, on a rock headland on the eastern side; and the round tower at Aghadoe.[36]

Bishop Berkeley visited Killarney in the summer of 1750, a year before his death. It is not surprising that he was sensitive to the beauties of Muckross, and it is related that he said that 'the King of France might lay out another Versailles, but that with all his revenues he could not lay out another Muckross.'[37] He was right, for at Muckross art and nature complement each other in a way in which they have not been allowed at Versailles. However, at the back of his mind he must have been thinking of the straight avenues and parterre at Kenmare House (Plate 177) which can be seen in William Pars' watercolour (Plate 178).

Muckross today holds the same secret which Edmund Spenser may have seen in Elizabethan times in the gardens and orchards of the Franciscan abbey on Innisfallen and the friary of Irrelagh (Muckross Abbey). Killarney was no great distance from Spenser's home, Kilcolman Castle, County Cork, at the end of a fine lake with the 'mountains of Mole' to the north. There he wrote much of *The Faerie Queene* and had both leisure and means for travel. His poem has many references to the type of ideal landscape exemplified by Killarney – woods, water, islands and mountains intermingled with the work of man – scenes rare in England though common in Ireland. Sir Guyon on his way to the 'Bowre of blisse' describes one such scene:

There the most daintie Paradise on ground,
It selfe doth offer to his sober eye,
In which all pleasures plenteously abound,
And none does others happinesse enuye:
The painted flowres, the trees upshooting hye,
The dales for shade, the hilles for breathing space,
The trembling groves, the Christall running by;
And that, which all faire workes doth most aggrace,
The art, which all that wrought, appeared in no place.

One would have thought, (so cunningly, the rude,
And scorned parts were mingled with the fine,)
That nature had for wantonesse ensude
Art, and that Art at Nature did repine;
So striving each th'other to undermine,
Each did the others worke more beautifie;
So diff'ring both in willes, agreed in fine:
So all agreed through sweete diversitie
This Gardin to adorne with all varitie.[38]

In the 1580s, whether the Brownes and Herberts had been granted lands of the McCarty Mór or not, the abbeys of Innisfallen and Irrelagh remained in the monks' occupation, and had not yet been put to secular uses despite the Queen's command to that effect, so these abbey lands and the environs of the McCarty Mór's Castle Lough by the lakeside (now the grounds of the Lake Hotel), as well as the demesne and lands of Ross Castle, must have presented a scene in which the shores of the lake showed much evidence of man's handiwork in the development of gardens, orchards and planting.

Neither Herberts nor Brownes still own much of the Muckross or Kenmare estates, yet they have left us enough of art in the natural scene to give Killarney its world-wide reputation. In the last two hundred years, the many 'Guides' for visiting travellers, often written in the hyperbole of Louisa Conolly's picturesque style, usually say at length that words fail the writers in trying to describe this enchanted spot. The anonymous *Compleat Irish Traveller* (1788) is no exception, but it concludes with some finely balanced writing in the William Gilpin manner. The sentiments remain valid.

There is such an artless disposition of the several beauties, such an entertaining variety, such a sublimity throughout, as will be superior to the most laboured portrait. The finest subjects in the world for painting and drawing in the rural or romantic taste, are here exhibited in the richest perfection from nature, the sovereign mistress of these ingenious arts.

1. *Irish Sketchbook*, vol. I, p. 196.
2. *A Philosophical Inquiry into the Origin of our Ideas of the Sublime and Beautiful*, London 1757.
3. See The Knight of Glin, 'Lord Orrery's Tour of Kerry', *Journal of the Kerry Historical and Archaeological Society*, vol. IV, 1972.
4. Ivy was a major ingredient of the picturesque scene. An advocate for it, one James Kearney, the owner of Garretstown, County Cork, a large wooded estate near the sea, wrote in his *Essays on Agriculture and Planting* (1790):

Among the Romans it was held in great esteem, and planted round the trees in their pleasure grounds. I know it is said that ivy prejudices the growth of trees; I cannot say that it does not, but this I know that some of the largest trees I ever saw, were covered with ivy. Allowing, however, what I much doubt, that it injures in some small degree the growth of trees, is it unusual with men of fortune to sacrifice something to ornament? Can suffering a few trees, which stand in view of a house, or on the skirts of a wood, to clothe themselves with ivy be attended with any loss that should make us deprive ourselves of one of the finest verdures, that any climate can produce?

5. Such as Richard Twiss's, *A Tour in Ireland in 1775*, and *The Compleat Irish Traveller* (1788).
6. See Forbes, 'Tree Planting in Ireland during Four Centuries'. *R.I.A. Proc.*, 25 August 1933.
7. See G. Holmes, 'Sketches of some of the Southern Counties of Ireland in 1797', *British Tourist's Pocket Companion*, vol. IV, London 1809.
8. Like Charles Hamilton's hermit at Painshill he did not fulfil his role, and, on being found drunk one day by Colonel Herbert, was dismissed.
9. Dr Beaufort, *Irish Travels, 1806*, vol. I, p. p. 59. The connection between Chinese landscaping and the picturesque is well discussed in Osvald Sirén's *China and the Gardens of Europe in the Eighteenth Century*. New York 1950.
10. Hayes, *Treatise on Planting*, Dublin 1794, reports on an arbutus at Mount Kennedy which was a hundred years old with a girth of thirteen feet nine inches.
11. *Letters from Leverpoole, Chester, Corke, Killarney etc.* London 1767. He came of an Irish family, and later succeeded Beau Nash as Master of Ceremonies in Bath.
12. Yorke MSS. Letter from Owen Salusbury Brereton to Simon Yorke of Erddig, Clywd, September 1763.
13. *Letters*. Compare Pococke's account, see p. 160.
14. In 1787, according to Dr Beaufort it was 'a very mean and ruinous structure'. Op. cit., part IV, p. 3, Trinity College MS, K.6.60 (4030).
15. Derrick, *Letters*.
16. Originally a canal but converted to grass.
17. *Tour of South and West Ireland in 1758*, Bodleian MSS, Top Ireland d.I. Some of the earliest poems and descriptions of Killarney are in the Bradshaw Collection in Cambridge University Library. For instance, Richard Barton, 'Some Remarks on Upper and Lower Lough Lene' (1751); Anon., 'The Masterpiece of Nature' (1750); Anon., 'A Description of Killarney' (1748).

18. Orrery, *Orrery Papers*, vol. I, p. 196.
19. Edward Willes to Lord Warwick, BM. Add. MS 28 252 70517557, pp. 67 and 69.
20. Lord Granville, *Leveson Gower Private Correspondence. 1781–1821*, 1916, vol. 2, p. 336.
21. G. N. Smith, *Killarney and the surrounding Scenery*, London and Dublin 1822, pp. 19–21.
22. Smith, *Killarney*, p. 105.
23. *Irish Travels, 1806*, vol. I, p. 58.
24. Sir Walter Scott, 'Essay on Landscape Gardening', *Miscellaneous Prose Works*, vol. XXI, shows his taste for the Picturesque.
25. Quoted by Colvin in *Studia Neophilogica*, 1971, vol. XLIII, no. 1, pp. 252 ff.
26. Except for St Mary's Cathedral by A. W. Pugin, opposite the entrance to the Kenmare estate.
27. To his wife, 18 July 1849.
28. When walking one can still notice *Saxifraga aizoides*, fuchsias and ferns, perhaps including the rare *Trichomanes radicans*.
29. Thackeray, *Irish Sketchbook*. He also noticed Mr Herbert's 'Elizabethan house' being built to the design of William Burn: the fourth to be on the site, and standing today.
30. *A Tour of Ireland in 1775*, p. 129. He was so unduly critical of everything Irish that a few years after the publication of this book one could buy chamber pots in Dublin decorated with his portrait inside.
31. The Golden Eagle was common there until about a hundred years ago.
32. Mrs Delany to Mrs Dewes, Delville, 20 October 1750. Llanover, *Mrs Delany*, vol. II, p. 605.
33. Yorke MSS.
34. Desmond Guinness MSS.
35. *Memorials and Correspondence of Charles James Fox*, edited by Lord John Russell, London 1853, vol. I, p. 156.
36. Under a Covenant established by the Bourne family from New England, who presented Muckross to the Irish nation in 1929, it was laid down that no trees might be sold for gain, and no motor vehicles enter the estate, except immediately to the house.
37. Quoted by I. Weld, *Illustrations of the Scenery of Killarney*, Dublin 1812, p. 12.
38. *The Faerie Queene*, Book II, Canto XII, 58 and 59.

9 The Wicklow Tour and Picturesque Landscape

These woods have been well loved, well tended by some who came before me, and my affection has been no less than theirs. The generation of trees have been my care, my comforters. Their companionship has often brought me peace.

Lady Gregory, *Coole*

The Wicklow Mountains grew into another centre for travellers intent on viewing both the picturesque and the sublime. By the 1780s a well-worn itinerary from Dublin led to Powerscourt with its mansion and waterfall, to the Glen of the Downs, that deep pass between two long ranges of mountains, and to the Devil's Glen and Glendalough where the early Christian remains enhanced the landscape both visually and conceptually.

In 1753, a three-hundred-acre estate on this route, backed by the Glen of the Downs and fronting the sea, was bought by David La Touche of the famous Huguenot banking family in Dublin. Here La Touche built a house costing £30,000 and started to lay out a landscape garden, calling his new-found elysium 'Bellevue'. In this landscape one could visit ornamental buildings by following an ascending serpentine path, first to an octagon house (1766) with stained glass, shells, minerals and books as well as a stuffed tiger; then the visitors could climb to a Gothic banqueting room (built in 1788 to a design of Francis Sandys) on a pinnacle of rock at the summit of a mountain with a fine view up the Glen of the Downs, over the sea north to Howth and Lambay Island and south to Wicklow Bay. These views perfectly illustrated the quality of surprise in landscaping, for one did not see them while walking up to the banqueting house through the trees.

> He gains all points who pleasingly confounds
> Surprizes, varies and conceals the Bounds.[1]

Thus does the romantic-poetic landscape of Pope develop into a cheerful picturesque in a setting like Bellevue, and on a princely scale. Although Pope condemned false magnificence – 'the first grand Error of which is to imagine that *Greatness* consists in the *Size* and *Dimension*, instead of the *Proportion* and *Harmony* of the whole'[2] – yet he would have enjoyed Bellevue and its banqueting house, as nature had done much, and art had not 'been sparing of its embellishments'.[3] Indeed, the advocacy of surprise as a delightful quality in landscaping was restated by Montesquieu later in the century: 'Cette disposition de l'âme, qui la porte toujours vers differens objets, fait quelle goute tous les plaisirs qui viennent de la surprise; sentiment qui plait à l'âme par le spectacle et par promptitude de l'action; car elle aperçoit on sent une chose qu'elle n'attend pas, où d'une manière qu'elle n'attendoit pas.'[4] The interior of this banqueting house was as if excavated from solid rock. In addition at Bellevue there were a rustic temple composed entirely of wood, with Gothic arches and rustic seats overlooking a fine prospect, and a Turkish Tent (1793) also to the design of Francis Sandys, a 'pretty seat, consisting of drapery and ornaments in the style of an eastern pavilion', and a root house with roof thatched in purple heather.

When La Touche died in 1785, his second son, Peter, inherited the property and continued the embellishments both architectural and horticultural. John Carr went there in 1804 and was surprised by its unrivalled glass houses (Plate 179), one of which was 650 feet in length, for vines, oranges, peaches and cherries, as well as for plants from 'sultry regions' of Asia, Africa and America which 'filled the air with the most voluptuous perfume'.[5] Carr had seen many princely conservatories, but thought Bellevue's was surpassed only by Prince Potemkin's at St Petersburg, and by that 'only in

179 BELLEVUE, CO.
WICKLOW. *One of the*
glass houses: wash drawing
by Anne La Touche.

its prodigious magnitude'.[6]

It was Peter La Touche who discovered the lake and valley of Luggala, about nine miles south-west of Bellevue, further and deeper in the romance of the Wicklow Mountains. He probably bought Luggala in about 1790, as the first edition of *The Post Chaise Companion* (1786) catalogues all the beauties of Wicklow without mentioning Luggala. However, ten years later, John Ferrar, in his fascinating *A View of Ancient and Modern Dublin . . . To which is added a Tour To Bellevue in the County of Wicklow*, notes that Mr La Touche 'has another modern house at Lugala . . . agreeably situated between two mountains and extremely romantic'. Ferrar goes on to describe a well-executed rustic bridge 'in a spot which is diversified with rocks curiously shaped, wood and waterfalls', and then with enthusiasm exclaims: 'But what is most remarkable, frequent rumblings and roarings are heard in the bowels of the mountains, sometimes as loud as a cannon shot, probably occasioned by the firing of sulphureous and bituminous matter.' La Touche's 'modern built house' dates then from about 1790, and though the architect of this 'cottage mansion' in the 'pointed style' is unknown it is not unlikely that it was Francis Sandys.[7] He also practised as a landscape gardener, which further supports the supposition he may have designed Luggala, for the whole arrangement of the house, plantings, serpentine drive and Gothic hut, with the mountains and lake, has the imprint of an architect professionally attentive to late eighteenth-century landscape gardening before the full onslaught of picturesque theory.

By the early nineteenth century the lake and grounds were a three-star attraction in the constellation of delights that made up the Wicklow tourist route. Pückler-Muskau described it in much detail after his visit in 1828.[8]

The valley forms a nearly regular long oval basin. The lake occupies the immediate foreground to the mountain's foot; the middle-ground is meadow-land, studded with groups of trees, and watered by a meandering stream; and in its centre backed by a solitary rock, is an elegant 'shooting lodge'. The mountains surrounding the valley are very high and steep, and rise on every side, in a bare and unbroken line from the perfectly level plain. On the left are naked rocks of imposing aspect, only here and there overgrown with heath-plants; the three other sides are clothed with thick and varied vegetation, whose foliage hangs into the very lake. At the spot where the mountain streams flow through bright green herbage into the lake, it forms a broad waterfall. It is indeed a lovely spot of earth, lonely and secluded; the wood full of game, the lake full of fish, and nature full of poetry.

N. P. Willis has a description typical of the melancholy of this period. He incorrectly makes an interpretation of the name as Lough Hela, or the Lake of Death in Danish mythology, whereas Luggala simply means a hollow in the hills; but, he continues,

169

the title must have been peculiarly appropriate to this dark lake before the hand of cultivation had softened the wild horrors of the valley . . . In the outline of one of the precipitous rocks, is definitely traced a gigantic resemblance of a human face, looking gloomily on the lake below. The eyebrows, broad and dilating, are marked by moss and heath and the prominent cheeks and deep-sunk eyes perfectly formed by clefts in the rock . . .[9]

When Joseph Atkinson eulogized it to Mrs Peter La Touche in 1807, it must have been one of the most important examples of a romantic wonder.

> In this sequester'd, wild, romantic dell
> Where nature loves in solitude to dwell,
> Who would expect 'midst such a lonely park
> The charms of fancy and the plans of art,
> Whilst the neat mansion, formed with simple taste,
> Amidst a wilderness for comfort plac'd,
> Adorns the scene and hospitality shews
> The seat of pleasure and serene repose . . .[10]

Many tourists were impressed by Luggala (Plate 180) 'the elegant little structure' in the deep valley with its rustic bridge (Plate 181) alongside the dark Lough Tay, as William Smith referred to it when he went there with his eight companions on the first day of his five-day tour in July 1815.[11] In this brief period he and his companions visited an astonishing number of estates, commenting briefly on each in the language of the picturesque. On the first day they saw Stillorgan, passing through Bray to the entrance of the Dargle, the 'Glen of the Downs', on the Dublin-Wicklow road, Luggala, Mount Kennedy and Dunran (Plates 182 and 183) in a romantic glen with much rocky scenery and hills clothed in wood, but with a 'stiff formal canal through the valley, ill-according with the scenery'. It was a clear day and from the top of the valley they saw the Welsh Mountains, and also beyond Ballycurry House into the

180 LUGGALA, CO. WICKLOW. *The Gothic lodge.*

181 LUGGALA. *The rustic bridge.*

182 MOUNT KENNEDY,
NEWTOWNMOUNT-
KENNEDY, CO. WICK-
LOW. *Engraving by
Thomas Milton after
William Ashford.*

183 DUNRAN, CO.
WICKLOW. *Engraving by
Thomas Milton after
William Ashford.*

Devil's Glen, two miles north-west of Ashford. At the entrance of the glen they
glimpsed, but did not visit, Mr Synge's Glenmore, a castellated building (Plate 184)
commanding a prospect of the glen.[12] Evidently William Smith and his party, on
account of the speedy tour which they were undergoing, did not have time to look at
Glenmore thoroughly. The estate was chiefly famous for the growth of trees in a very
mild climate, as well as for superb views of sea, mountains and river. After passing
Glenmore they continued along the 'awful grandeur' of the Vartrey river and Mr La
Touche's Bellevue, to Mount Usher for the first night.[13]

On the second day their initial visit was to Mr Tighe's Rosanna, through which the
Vartrey also flowed. Here they saw the remarkable Spanish chestnut tree which then
had a circumference round the extreme branches of 210 feet. By now they were in
'tame and domestic scenery' with no mountains, but parkland with fine trees. In the
evening they walked through Hollymount where they drank water from 'the limpid
brook', and watched a crane feeding her young in the top of an old Scotch fir.

The next day they entered Avondale belonging to Mr Parnell Hayes who had inherited the estate from the great forester, Samuel Hayes (Plate 185). In the woods
were a 'pretty cottage' and rustic gates (Plates 186 and 187) which, although out of
repair, were set in a valley contributing much to their picturesqueness:

a wilderness of sweets, and from an association of ideas the mind is led to imagine that there is
a peculiar sadness in the scene as if inanimate nature could partake of the sorrows of real life –
the gently murmuring Avon, the sighing of the wind through the woods and the solemn stillness that pervades the entangled pathways, where 'Many a garden flower grows wild', all
forcibly press upon the imagination and call the feeling heart to mourn in sympathy with the
sorrows that give rise to the sweet desolation of the scene.

This estate, with its extensive planting by Samuel Hayes, and with the Avonmore
meandering through the grounds, sometimes in a shallow channel tumbling over
masses of rock, was a goal for picturesque travellers. 'The sides of the river,' wrote
Anne Plumptre, 'are sometimes fringed with close thickets of wood, sometimes with
fine lawns having majestic forest-trees scattered about; in parts the dell is quite
inclosed, having only majestic rocks covered in ivy and rock-plants on each side; then
again it expands, forming for three miles the most varied and beautiful scenery
imaginable.'[14]

A mile or two further on, Castle Howard (Plate 188) looked down on them in its
mock-castellated grandeur, and they visited an elegant cottage in its grounds. J. N.
Brewer's *The Beauties of Ireland* (1825) describes it in detail which is little altered
today:

A
Practical Treatise
ON
PLANTING;
AND
The Management of
Woods and Coppices.

By S.H. Esq. M.R.I.A. and

Member of the Committee of Agriculture,

of the

DUBLIN SOCIETY,

&c. &c.

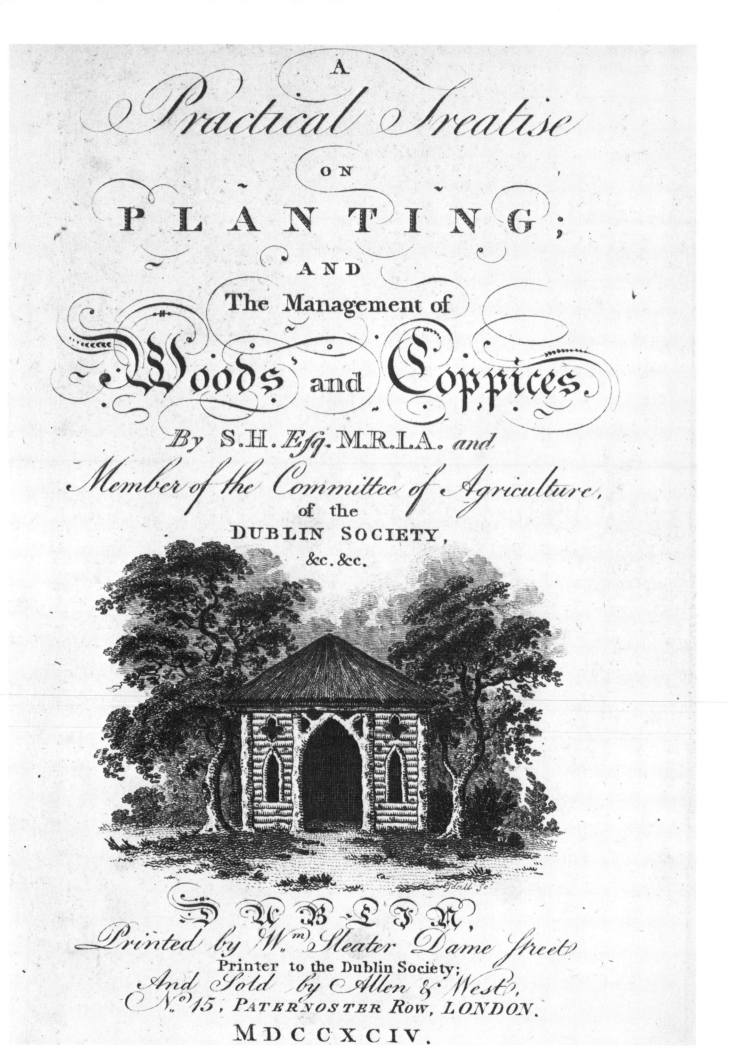

DUBLIN,

Printed by Wm. Sleater Dame Street

Printer to the Dublin Society;

And Sold by Allen & West,

Nᵒ 15, PATERNOSTER ROW, LONDON.

MDCCXCIV.

AVONDALE WOODHOUSE
Designed & by S:H:

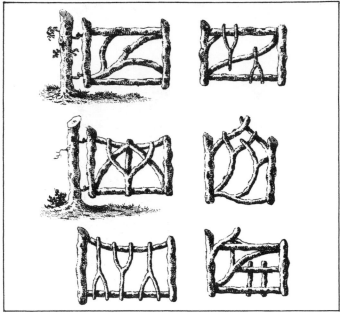

A carriage-road, nearly one mile in length, winds up the sides of the mountain, resembling in every respect, except excellence of construction, the circuitous progress to the embattled castles of time long past . . . The mansion is composed of stone, and its design by Morrison involves the representation of a castle, or rather a castellated house, and an attached ecclesiastical structure. The whole is happily imagined for the attainment of picturesque effect . . . The adoption of the ancient English style of architecture is peculiarly judicious in a mountainous and romantic country, like Wicklow. The towers of this elevated building, so beautifully circumstanced by nature, afford conspicuous ornaments of the fairest vale which Ireland produces, and which is, perhaps, not to be excelled in any other part of Europe.

186 AVONDALE. *The woodhouse from* A Practical Treatise on Planting . . .
187 AVONDALE. *Rustic gates from* A Practical Treatise on Planting . . .

William Smith and his party then dropped down to the Meeting of the Waters (Avonmore and Avonbeg) made famous by Tom Moore. After this they went on to Mr Symes' Ballyarthur in the Vale of Arklow, thirty-six miles from Dublin. Again they saw a 'moss house built of birch and fir handsomely interspersed; sides and seats of which are inlaid with moss; it has a tesselated pavement of sea pebbles and the roof is formed of the cones of Fir and Larch in a most fanciful and elegant manner'. From the mile-long terrace on the northern side of the vale, splendid views across thick oak forests to the sea opened up, and the river, encircling the estate in the wooded valley, was especially attractive.

Day four included Glendalough and down to Luggala again where they had trout for supper. William Smith was lost 'in the sublimity of rocky cliffs rising to the clouds, or meliorated to tranquillity by the softer beauties of the vale . . . here all the sterner passions should melt into stillness, and each thought bend in submission to Him, the magic of whose mighty hand drew from primeval silence the wonders of the scene.' After a night at the Enniskerry Inn (where a rat gnawed William Smith's candle and shoes), before returning to Dublin the next day, they went up the Dargle Glen from Powerscourt House (Plate 189). The climax of the four-mile walk was the waterfall where the Dargle slips and swirls four hundred feet off the mountain with a white spray into an amphitheatre of oaks and lawn below (Plate 190). By 1815 it had received visits from tourists for many years, and pages had been written of its beauties – in fact more than about any other spot in Ireland, including Killarney. As early as 1741, the Reverend Edward Chamberlayne's eulogistic couplets echo the prevailing Augustan taste with regard to art and nature, and exhibit the customary sycophancy towards the owner:

> While Nature smiles, obsequious to your Call,
> Directs, assists, and recommends it all.
> At last she gives (O Art how vain thy Aid)
> To crown the beauteous Work, a vast Cascade.

188 CASTLE HOWARD, CO. WICKLOW. *Engraving by T. Matthews after J. P. Neale.*

189 THE DARGLE, CO. WICKLOW. *Watercolour by Mrs Delany, 1765.*

190 POWERSCOURT, CO. WICKLOW. *The waterfall: watercolour by William Pars, 1775.*

. . . .
Thus in Improvements shines the Attick Taste,
Thus Eden springs where once you found a Waste.[15]

Pococke on his tour in 1752 admired the scene; and a picturesque traveller who had seen both Killarney and the Giant's Causeway as early as 1761 was so charmed by the waterfall that he doubted whether he was 'awake or in some scene of enchantment'.[16] John Bushe in his *Hibernia Curiosa* (1764) devoted pages 66–72 to the demesne. Richard Twiss was as critical as ever in dubbing it picturesque but not grand, and no equal of Terni or Tivoli.[17] Arthur Young was unusually picturesque in his response: 'The shade is so thick as to exclude the heavens: all is retired and gloomy, a brown horror breathing over the whole. It is a spot for melancholy to muse in.'[18] *The Post Chaise Companion* (1820), as usual, repeats Arthur Young, so we again read the above passage verbatim. Philip Luckombe, during his tour in 1779, writes of the walks, the octagon room, the moss house, the wooden bridge and seats which all feature in the improvements of the Viscounts Powerscourt. The octagon room seems to have been ingeniously constructed for keeping out the wind, yet preserving a view, and was viewed as:

. . . 25 feet in diameter and fifteen feet high, built with bricks, plaistered and rough cast on the outside. The floor is mosaic work of different colours, the ceiling stucco, and the roof covered with straw. This elegant room is so contrived, that there may be five openings at once, or any less number, having windows arched to fill up these vacancies from top to bottom, and doors for the same if necessary; both which, by springs, fly up and down with greater expedition. Within a few yards of this Octagon, there is a very near kitchen of twelve feet square, furnished with every convenience for dressing victuals; and what is worthy notice, the time from laying the foundations to completing these buildings did not exceed five weeks . . .

The comforts of visitors were cared for by Lord Powerscourt who had made walls, in such a way that the public might see the beauties of the glen, and also placed along them alcoves, chairs and tables

with every convenience for the curious and fatigued traveller. On the side of a hill, is an hexagon pavillion [Plate 191] of about seventeen feet in diameter floored with red tiles, the roof covered with straw, supported by six pillars of grown trees, incased with their natural bark; two sides of this apartment are lined with moss, and the other four open, from which there are many rich and delightful prospects. Next to the moss in this rustic building are placed benches to sit on, chairs in other parts, and a table in the centre, to rest the weary, and regale those who bring their food with them.[19]

John Carr thought the moss house was 'suspended, like an aeronautic car, from some vast impending oaks, which spread over it an umbrella of leaves'.[20] But by 1827 G. N. Wright wrote in a spirit which seems singularly modern that 'the defacing hand of the uncultivated intruder' had invaded the glen, as Lord Powerscourt had constructed a road through it in order that George IV's carriage might pass that way. As it happened, George IV did not have time to visit the waterfall, so the large reservoir, which was also constructed for the occasion in order that an impressive amount of water should be falling for His Majesty, was also redundant.

Two miles from Bray on the north bank of the Dargle was Joseph Cooper Walker's[21] small estate called St Valery. The house was on a considerable slope above the river, and had a marvellous view up the Dargle, the Wicklow Mountains to the skyline, and a bridge taking the Bray road in the middle distance (Plate 192). His use of *Populus nigra* (Lombardy poplar) for vertical emphasis is an interesting feature, which is similar to the use of cypresses in Italy. But he does not try to hide the distant bridge, inn and coaches passing, for he was evidently of the same opinion as Horace Walpole who had written to the Countess of Upper-Ossory on 26 September 1793: 'I have an aversion to a park, and especially a walled park in which the capital event is the coming of cows to water.' Humphry Repton also liked the enlivened scene when great houses were opened to the public, commenting with pleasure on the gaiety of Longleat in his time. Cooper Walker placed a granite Rood Cross of a Cornish type, a holy-well or

191 THE DARGLE. *The Moss House: aquatint by T. Santelle Roberts.*

192 ST VALERY, CO. WICKLOW. *Aquatint by J. Carr.*

'font' at focal points in the garden landscape, and 'some very elegant verses . . . on Saint Colman's Well' in his glen.[22] Dr. Robert Anderson wrote to his friend, Bishop Percy of Dromore, after a visit to St Valery in 1802:

I went directly to St Valeri . . . where I spent ten days very agreeably in the society of a very amiable and interesting circle of friends. St Valeri is delightfully situated at the confluence of three rivers, near the entrance of the Dargle, about a mile from Bray, opposite to the two Sugar Loaves, the most beautiful mountains in Wicklow. The grounds, which do not exceed eight acres, are laid out with great taste. The lawn before the house, sloping to the river, was laid out this year in wheat, for the purpose of some further improvement.[23]

William Smith's is a typical tour by a writer who was not bound by the exaggerated tenets of the picturesque like Dr Syntax, but who had an eye for a romantic-poetic setting such as that at Rosanna, and a philosophy of the association of ideas derived from David Hartley. On this Wicklow tour, many of the estates they visited were set in the Wicklow Mountains or in deep glens, but *en route* they could not fail to be impressed by Rosanna, set as it was in grounds of great natural beauty with a river flowing through them. Its creation by an ancestor of Mr Tighe's was commented on by Mrs Delany and was very typically Irish in its emphasis on the romantic-poetic.

177

By the time she went there in May 1752 Mr W. Tighe had seen Charles Hamilton's Painshill and Philip Southcote's Wooburn Lodge, and had come back to Ireland dissatisfied with the landscape around Rosanna. It must have been an ancestor of Mr Tighe's who planted the Spanish chestnut tree which A. C. Forbes in 1733 estimated as the largest tree in Ireland, having a girth of thirty feet at four-and-a-half feet. There were also older trees on the estate including a milltown oak which Samuel Hayes noted as showing a canopy of thirty-six yards over a clear stem nineteen feet round when he visited Rosanna in 1794. A typically picturesque estate, also belonging to the Tighe family, was at Woodstock. It had one of the finest eighteenth-century houses (built by Francis Bindon, destroyed 1922) in County Kilkenny, set above the banks of the river Nore. On the south side, a mountain stream ran through a wooded glen, crossed by two or three rustic bridges, constructed of unbarked timber, which gave them 'the appearance of trees which had fallen across by accident, rather than of works raised by the hand of man'. Perched on the summit of rock above a precipice was a cottage *à la Suisse* designed by Mrs Tighe.

At Woodstock's namesake in County Wicklow, Lord Robert Tottenham had difficulty with the planting of trees. *The Irish Farmer's and Gardener's Magazine*, 1834, vol. 1, p. 135, reported that

indeed it is not a little extraordinary that the very persons sent by Sir Henry Steuart to this country for the purpose of transplanting large trees, either through ignorance (which is hardly to be supposed) or a want of proper subject made use of in some places (as at Woodstock . . .) of those quite unfit for the purpose, and the failures have been proportionate to the want of judgement displayed in the selection.

Plate 193 taken from Sir Henry Steuart's *The Planter's Guide*, shows his methods which appear to have been generally successful elsewhere.

The previous owners of Woodstock, County Kilkenny, Sir William and Lady Fownes (see page 19) had become the guardians of Sarah Ponsonby, orphaned at the age of thirteen in 1768, and a distant relation. After ten years at Woodstock, Miss Ponsonby and her friend, Lady Eleanor Butler of Kilkenny Castle, caused something of a scandal by eloping together and fleeing to Wales where, despite opposition from both their families, they settled at Llangollen. The setting these two aristocratic ladies created round a small cottage, which they named Plas Newydd, became famous throughout the islands. Ireland and Wales have similar picturesque qualities – mountains, streams, lakes – and the romantic river Dee at Llangollen reminded Sarah Ponsonby of the Nore at Woodstock. Despite being acutely short of money they managed to create a picturesque setting in the five acres round their little four-roomed cottage. A small ravine, with dashing mountain stream, and the towering cone of Dinas Bran with its ruined castle perched on the skyline were the delightful natural elements to start with; and by planting extensively 'every shrub and Perennial that was admired at Woodstock' as well as a new thicket of 'Lilacks, Laburnums, Seringas, White Broom, Weeping Willow, Apple Trees, poplar . . .' they made a most attractive setting. Elizabeth Mavor, in her *Ladies of Llangollen* (1972, pp. 104–7), describes it:

Neither there, the kitchen garden, nor in the whole precincts, can a single weed be discovered. The fruit trees are of the rarest and finest sort, and luxuriant in their produce, the garden house and its implements arranged in exact order.

Nor is the dairy house for one cow the least curiously elegant object of this magic domain. A short declivity shadowed over with tall shrubs, conducts us to the cool and clean repository . . .

The wavy and shaded gravel walk which encircles this Elysium, is enriched with curious shrubs and flowers. It is nothing in extent and everything in grace and beauty and in variety of foliage; its gravel smooth as marble. In one part of it we turn upon a small knoll which overhangs a deep hollow glen. In its tangled bottom a frothing brook leaps and clamours over the rough stones in its channel. A large spreading beech canopies the knoll and a semicircular seat beneath its boughs admits four people. A board, nailed to the elm [*sic*] has this inscription 'O cara Selva! e Fiunicello amato.'

193 MOVING A TREE. *From* The Planter's Guide *by Sir Henry Steuart, 1828.*

For fifty years the 'Ladies' embellished this picturesque setting, rarely going out, but being visited by such diverse friends as the Duke of Wellington, Charles Darwin, Wordsworth, Lady Caroline Lamb, Sir Walter Scott and many of the Irish nobility and gentry on their way to and from London. Their fame spread, and Pückler Muskau described them as 'the most celebrated Virgins in Europe'.

One of the finest sites for a castle is at Lismore, County Waterford, above the Blackwater. With its fine trees, ivy-grown towers and ruinous aspect (Plate 194) it was even more the epitome of a William Gilpin picturesque scene before it was 'restored' (1812–22) with heavy battlements and turrets. After the time of the Earl of Burlington, the architect, the estate passed to the fourth Duke of Devonshire on his marriage to Lady Charlotte Boyle in 1753. There have always been criticisms of absenteeism: Edward Wakefield (1812) found the Devonshire estates 'in a disgraceful condition to a civilized and cultivated country' and he quoted Arthur Young's earlier account: 'The landlord at such a great distance is out of the way of all complaints, or, which is the same thing, of examining into or remeddying evils; miseries, of which he can see nothing, and hear as little of, can make no impression.'[24] However, the 'bachelor' Duke rebuilt the castle and did much to reorganize the estate in Victorian times.

The arch of Irish yews, said to be eight hundred years old, is the most interesting feature in an otherwise horticulturally ordinary garden. The principal part of the estate adjoins Ballysaggartmore with its fantastic gateways and bridge built in the early nineteenth century (Plates 195 and 196) for Arthur Kiely by his gardener, Mr Smith.[25] They cost so much that the house was never built; but the gates are habitable.

Another mecca for the sublime was the five miles of dark sandstone cliffs in County Clare, known as the Cliffs of Moher. Since 1835 the best viewpoint has been Cornelius O'Brien's Tower (now restored) nearly six hundred feet above the sea (Plate 197). From there one can see, as James Fraser described in his *Handbook for Travellers in Ireland,*

179

194 LISMORE CASTLE, CO. WATERFORD. *Water-colour by William Pars.*

196 BALLYSAGGART-MORE. *The bridge.*

the awfully impending cliff, deep ravine, resounding cavern, and detached island-rock, arched and pinnacled in a thousand grotesque forms, which the cliffs here, in common with all those composed of clay-slate rock, exhibit, when exposed to the ceaseless fury of a heavy sea. To hear the deep sounds of the ocean surge; to look from the dizzy heights, and see its billows breaking and foaming against the rugged basement; the myriads of sea-fowl breasting the wave, wheeling in mid-air, or congregating on the pinnacles of the time-worn rocks, at once fills the mind with awe and admiration . . .

The scene has not changed as one looks over Galway Bay and the Aran Islands towards Connemara.

The maker of the excellent drives and walks along the cliffs was Cornelius O'Brien, M.P. who lived at castellated Birchfield nearby.[26] The house is now part of a farm, but the large central archway with flanking curtain walls and end towers is still visible. Half a mile from the house is a stone column topped by an urn, which was paid for by tenants during O'Brien's lifetime. An unusual idea, perhaps, yet if the words on the inscription are rightly interpreted, they do not deserve the sneer in the comment of a recent guide book, 'O'Brien compelled his tenants to pay for it':[27]

This testimonial
has been erected by public subscription
to
Cornelius O Brien Esqre
The Representative of This County in Parliament
for more than twenty years
as a lasting record of his public conduct
and private worth
in admiration of the energy and success
that characterized his many labours
to promote the prosperity of his people
and
as a tribute
to his warm hearted liberality and forethought
in providing for the accomodation
of strangers visiting
the magnificent scenery of this neighbourhood
signed on behalf of the committee
Colman O Loghlen Bart. Chairman
Mich. McNamara Sec^y
4 October 1853

195 BALLYSAGGART-MORE, CO. WATERFORD. *The gateway.*

O'Brien was a model, if somewhat scandalous, landlord, building comfortable houses for tenantry, constructing roads and a bridge across the river Dealagh, and reclaiming and draining waste land. Near to this monument is Daigh Bhrighde (St Brigid's Well) and, over where the holy water comes out of the rock, O'Brien built a small white-washed building. It has been a place of pilgrimage on the last Sunday in July, attended by the local people and Aran islanders for many hundreds of years. A mixture of Christian and ancient pagan ceremony – this was *Lughnasa*, the festival at the end of summer, still common in remote parts of Ireland.

A similar type of union of Christian and pagan mythology at Coole Park, County Galway, has been described in verse and prose by W. B. Yeats. Once again this was an estate owned by a family who cared for their tenants. Soon after Robert Gregory, a native of Galway city, purchased the Coole estate he was visited by his friend, Arthur Young. By then Gregory had 'built a large house with numerous offices, and had taken 5 or 600 acres of lands into his own hands, which I found him improving with great spirit. Walling was his first object, of which he had executed many miles in the most perfect manner; his dry ones 6 feet high, 3 feet and a half at bottom, and 20 inches at top.' Young also saw 'a noble nursery from which he will make plantations which will be a great ornament to the country'.[28] After Robert Gregory's death in 1802 successive generations of Gregorys continued to plant in difficult ground where the limestone lies near the surface and the sea winds from the Atlantic blow across the rocky Burren hills. But, on the positive side, there was a romantic river (Plate 198) which flowed into a wild and natural lake edged in brown and velvet moss and in sight of the house. This river which comes from nearby Lough Cutra plunges into the ground several times: first after passing through a deep ravine where it sweeps under a perpendicular rock, then reappearing before finally going underground in Coole park on its way to Galway Bay.

Lough Cutra castle is picturesquely situated high above the banks of the lough, whose waters lash the terrace walls. Of the four John Nash Gothic castles[29] in Ireland it is the most picturesquely sited, with extensive and deep planting of woods and plantations, and wooded islands with ruins of churches and mountains in the back-

197 CLIFFS OF MOHER, CO. CLARE. *O'Brien's Tower.*

198 COOLE, CO. GALWAY. *Lady Gregory by the Natural Bridge.*

ground. No pigmy parterres chequer the turf in the vicinity, and long, sweeping approaches traverse the woods. As the first Lord Gort visited and liked John Nash's East Cowes Castle, and the architect visited Lord Lorton at Rockingham (see below) in 1809,[30] it is fair to assume he also visited Lough Cutra at the invitation of Lord Gort, in the year 1809 when he 'travelled in the three kingdoms 11,000 miles . . . and in that time had expended £1,500 in chaise hire'.[31] In 1835, there was a range of glass-houses (about three hundred feet long) which were poorly constructed so that little sun and light entered because of flues on the south side.[32] Had Mr Sutherland, the well-known landscape gardener who laid out the estate so skilfully, forgotten this practical detail? It sounds more like the result of Nash's shoddy work.

At Coole no professional landscapers were employed, yet throughout the nineteenth century seven woods were planted round the house. There was a wild and picturesque grandeur in the deep shades, the romantic river, and the setting, by tradition, of the birth of St Colman, whose mother had been miraculously saved from drowning in the Coole lake. It was a landscape saturated with the Christian and pagan mythology of Ireland, and its Georgian house, neither grand nor imposing but a simple three-storied cube, lay in a small park bounded by deep woods. Both the library in the house, and the garden ornaments showed treasures collected by eighteenth-century Gregorys; Evelyn's *Silva* in a superb Irish binding and a bust of Maecenas set under ivy boughs at the end of a walk. The walled gardens for years possessed abundance of 'flowers, fruit, shade and water',[33] those essentials recommended by Sir William Temple, himself related to the Gregorys.

Another landscape with Christian and pagan interwoven, as is common in the tapestry of Irish folk tales, was Rockingham, County Roscommon, overlooking Castle Island in Lough Key (Plate 199). The gently undulating lawns of the demesne stretch down to the water's edge over which graceful trees dip; close to the house, there is a ruined nineteenth-century castle, further off a ruined medieval one. The shores of the lough are indented with many coves and its surface dotted with numerous islands. In the Castle of the Heroes[34] on the rock on Castle (Rock) Island, W. B. Yeats dreamed of a mystical Order which would meet in this castle of the MacDermotts (Plates 200 and 201) where, in the sixteenth century, Tadhg MacDermott had entertained the poets of all Ireland. These ruins, seen from Rockingham House in the early nineteenth century, must have been the most picturesque of their kind in all the country and could be dramatic still; they have all the overtones of the picturesque: the confusion, delight and oppression of the imagination which for Hannah More at Cheddar 'darted back a thousand years into the days of chivalry and enchantment'. On Trinity Island, the White Canons compiled the *Annals of Loch Cé* in about 1589, and the ash trees entwine their branches across the graves of the star-crossed lovers, Una MacDermott, daughter of the last Chieftain of the Rock, and the MacCostello of Moygara.

The first Lord Lorton, whose creation the demesne was in the 1820s, strangely insulated the house in a sea of lawns, no offices being visible: the kitchens, as was customary, in the basement and a subterranean passage leading to the stables, conveniently hidden by a screen of trees.[35] Turf for fuel was brought by boat over the lough to the mouth of another underground passage, so that 'the appearance of movement near the mansion' was prevented.[36] This seems to have been the external equivalent of the alcoves built into the staircase in the house in Lansdown Crescent, Bath, belonging to William Beckford, in order that he could pass unmolested by the sight of the servants. Such an attitude would have been abhorrent to Swift when staying at Gaulstown, or with Grattan at Celbridge, or Charlemont at Marino, who were never out of touch with the local community.

If demesnes such as Rockingham, embracing much of both early Irish history and eighteenth-century landscaping traditions, are to be cared for by public ownership, it is possible that they may have a future as public parks. But it will require imagination and judgement on the part of the State, both aesthetic and horticultural, to adapt them so that they do not lose those qualities which inspired the love and appreciation of visitors in the past. The moral is obvious by comparing two nineteenth-century

199 ROCKINGHAM, CO. ROSCOMMON. *General view of MacDermott's Castle and Rockingham: painting by James Arthur O'Connor.*
200 ROCKINGHAM. *MacDermott's Castle before restoration: engraving by J. Hooper, 1792.*
201 ROCKINGHAM. *Fishing house and view towards Castle Island.*

castle-style residences: Killua Castle, County Westmeath (Plate 202) and Johnstown Castle, County Wexford (Plate 203). The former was, according to James Fraser, 'a handsome, modern castle, and the grounds extensive, beautifully diversified and well planted'[37] in the 1840s. Yet the Chapman family who owned it were eventually bankrupted by the expense of its conversion to the Gothic style and the maintenance of its enormous demesne. Had they not felt the necessity to keep up with their neighbours in this fashion, the castle today might be the excellent eighteenth-century house shown in Plate 204. The latter, Johnstown Castle, was 'modernized' at the same date, and presented to the nation in 1944 when the upkeep of the extensive grounds became too much for its owners. Today it is a research station of the Agricultural Institute with lake, lawns and ancient trees in a demesne of over a thousand acres open to the public. Many such estates in England and Scotland have been saved by being converted for use as schools and colleges; but this is rare in Ireland where civil war, absenteeism and poverty have taken their toll.

Curragh Chase, County Limerick, like Rockingham, has been imaginatively converted into a forest park, and recently a more enlightened attitude has been taken by the Forestry and Wild Life Division of the Department of Lands. The trees, demesne walls and gates at Doneraile Court (Plate 205) are carefully looked after; only a few

184

202 KILLUA CASTLE,
CO. WESTMEATH. *Castle
ruin and obelisk.*
203 JOHNSTOWN
CASTLE, CO. WEXFORD.
View across the lake.

204 KILLUA CASTLE.
*Oil on canvas by William
Sadler.*
205 DONERAILE
COURT, CO. CORK.
*Entrance gates : photo-
graph, 1968.*

years ago the beeches would have been felled and the demesne turned into a commercial forest or divided up. Woodstock, County Kilkenny has recently been designated as an arboretum, and Fota Island with its unique arboretum had a narrow escape before University College, Cork stepped in where the present government refused to tread. If this book with its many photographs can show something of Ireland's past glories and the destruction that has ensued during the last eighty years, it may indicate to our legislators, whatever their politics, the necessity of not repeating the sins of our fathers. Then we would feel our study has been worthwhile. That special Irish unity of house, lawns, trees, water and mountains might again be, in W. B. Yeats's words, 'sheer miracle to the multitude'.

1. Pope, *Moral Essays IV*, 'Epistle to Lord Burlington', lines 55–56.
2. *Moral Essays*, Epistle IV 'Argument'.
3. Wakefield, *An Account of Ireland*, p. 52.
4. Montesquieu, 'Sur le Goût', *Oeuvres posthumes*. London 1783.
5. John Carr, *The Stranger in Ireland*, pp. 123–24.
6. It is of interest to see the construction of a small wooden frame greenhouse connected to 'Belleview' (Plate 179).
7. Sandys was probably the son of another Francis who had built the Gothic dining-room at Bellevue. Sandys *père* died in 1785, and his son evidently worked for Peter La Touche for, according to Ferrar, he constructed the Turkish Tent at Bellevue in 1793.
8. *A Tour in England*, p. 337.
9. *The Scenery and Antiquities of Ireland*, London 1842, vol. 2, pp. 169–70.
10. 'Luggilaw, written on a late excursion to the County of Wicklow', *The Magazine or British Register*, XXIV, 1807, pp. 365–66.
11. William Smith, *Journal of an Excursion to the County of Wicklow*. 1815. Nat. Lib. Dublin, MS 678.
12. By Francis Johnston for Francis Synge. Recently rebuilt in part.
13. The Vartrey is a larger river than the Dargle and its valley was deeper and more covered by thick wood in 1840. Thus it was more sombre and pleasing to nineteenth-century travellers in search of the picturesque.
14. *Narrative of a Residence in Ireland*. London 1817, pp. 182–83.
15. 'A Poem occasioned by a View of Powers-court House, the Improvements, Park etc.' Inscribed to Richard Wingfield Esq. Dublin 1741.
16. R. Masham to Francis Naylor. Hist. MSS Comm. 14th Report. App. IX, p. 264.
17. *A Tour in Ireland in 1775*. London 1776, p. 55.
18. C.f. Pope, 'Eloisa to Abelard' (1717) lines 163–70:

> But o'er the twilight groves, and dusky caves,
> Long-sounding isles, and intermingled graves,
> Black Melancholy sits, and round her throws
> A death-like silence, and a dread repose:
> Her gloomy presence saddens all the scene,
> Shades ev'ry flow'r, and darkens ev'ry green,
> Deepens the murmur of the falling floods,
> And breathes a browner horror on the woods.

19. According to the Duchess of Northumberland, the moss house 'kitchen' consisted of 'two stoves in the open Air upon the Rock'. Alnwick MSS.
20. *Stranger in Ireland*, pp. 87–88.
21. The author of 'The Rise and Progress of Gardening in Ireland'. Dublin 1791.
22. J. B. Nichols, *Illustrations of the Literary History of the Eighteenth Century*, London 1848, vol. VII, p. 153.
23. Ibid., p. 105.
24. Wakefield, *An Account of Ireland*, vol. 1, pp. 278–79.
25. *London's Gardener's Magazine*, 1837, vol. XII, p. 583.
26. In 1844, according to James Fraser, these walks were infinitely superior to the footpath made by the Earl-Bishop to the Giant's Causeway (see p. 49). Yet inaccessibility in the case of the Causeway may have been an advantage.
27. *The Shell Guide to Ireland*, London 1962, p. 355.
28. Young, *Tour in Ireland*, vol. I, p. 284.
29. The others are Kilwaughter Castle, County Antrim; Killymoon Castle, County Tyrone

where the landscaping was carried out by George Repton, Humphry Repton's younger son, who was then working in John Nash's office; and Shanbally Castle, County Tipperary (gutted 1958). The Victorian additions (1856) to Lough Cutra Castle have now been demolished. See Terence Davis, 'John Nash in Ireland', *Quarterly Bulletin of the Irish Georgian Society*, April–June 1965, vol. VIII, no. 2, pp. 55 ff.

30. Lord Lorton to James Stewart of Killymoon, 2 July 1809. Marcus Clements MS.
31. Statement to Joseph Farington. *Diary*, edited by James Grieg, London 1928.
32. *Irish Gardener's and Farmer's Magazine*, vol. II (1835), p. 74.
33. Lady Gregory, *Coole*. Dublin 1971, p. 102. Some years after Lady Gregory's death (1932) the house was demolished by a building contractor for the value of the stone. Then the garden was planted with spruce trees by the Department of Agriculture who owned the property. But successful and worthy attempts have recently been made to restore the garden to something like its original condition. Considering that the house was a setting for gatherings of many of the leaders of the Irish literary and dramatic renaissance it is surprising that the government of the time allowed it to be destroyed. J. M. Synge was one of many writers who stayed at Coole with Lady Gregory, and the County Wicklow garden he describes in the essay we quote may well be taken as an elegy for many such demesnes.

A stone's throw from an old house where I spent several summers in Co. Wicklow, there was a garden that had been left to itself for fifteen or twenty years. Just inside the gate, as one entered, two paths led up through a couple of strawberry beds, half choked with leaves, where a few white and narrow strawberries were still hidden away. Further on was nearly half an acre of tall raspberry canes and thistles five feet high, growing together in a dense mass, where one could still pick raspberries enough to last a household for the season. Then, in a waste of hemlock, there were some half-dozen apple trees covered with lichen and moss, and against the northern walls a few dying plum trees hanging from their nails. Beyond them there was a dead pear tree, and just inside the gate, as one came back to it, a large fuchsia filled with empty nests. A few lines of box here and there showed where the flower-beds had been laid out, and when anyone who had the knowledge looked carefully among them many remnants could be found of beautiful and rare plants.

All round this garden there was a wall seven or eight feet high, in which one could see three or four tracks with well-worn holes, like the paths down a cliff in Kerry, where boys and tramps came over to steal and take away any apples or other fruits that were in season. Above the wall on the three windy sides there were rows of finely-grown lime trees, the place of meeting in the summer for ten thousand bees. Under the east wall there was the roof of a greenhouse, where one could sit, when it was wet or dry, and watch the birds and butterflies, many of which were not common. The seasons were late in this place – it was high above the sea – and redpolls often used to nest not far off late in the summer; siskins did the same once or twice, and greenfinches, till the beginning of August, used to cackle endlessly in the lime trees.

Everyone is used in Ireland to the tragedy that is bound up with the lives of farmers and fishing people; but in this garden one seemed to feel the tragedy of the landlord class also, and of the innumerable old families that are quickly dwindling away. These owners of the land are not much pitied at the present day, or much deserving of pity; and yet one cannot quite forget that they are the descendants of what was at one time, in the eighteenth century, a high-spirited and highly-cultivated aristocracy. The broken green-houses and mouse-eaten libraries, that were designed and collected by men who voted with Grattan, are perhaps as mournful in the end as the four mud walls that are so often left in Wicklow as the only remnants of a farmhouse.

'A Landlord's Garden in County Wicklow'. *Collected Works*, vol. 2. London 1966, pp. 230–31.

34. Plate 200 shows it as it was before the castle had been 'restored'.
35. The house, remodelled by John Nash, has now been demolished, having been burned down in 1863 and again in 1957. George Repton, Humphry's younger son, worked at Rockingham and a splendid watercolour by him is in the possession of Sir John Summerson. Illustrated in Sean O'Faolain's *The Story of Ireland*. London 1943, p. 25.
36. Isaac Weld, *Statistical Survey of the County of Roscommon*. Dublin 1832, p. 233.
37. *Handbook for Travellers*. Dublin 1844, pp. 507–8.

Appendices

APPENDIX A *Planting in County Kerry, 1801–1812*

In the early nineteenth century, the lack of trees in Ireland was ameliorated by consistent planting by the great landlords. The work of three such in County Kerry at this time is worth looking at in detail.

(a) MR HERBERT OF MUCKROSS

Under the direction of his Scottish gardener, Mr Andrew Donnan, a comparatively small nursery produced healthy and profitable plantations. Mr Herbert's memorandum book shows how much was achieved for woods of about four thousand acres.

1801. Planted 16 acres of Turk mountain, with 97,000 Scotch fir, oak, ash, and sycamore, and 22 pecks of acorns dibbled.
Transplanted 98,000 forest trees.
1802. Planted 9 acres of Turk mountain, and 13 acres of Rusneagarry, with 131,000 trees of the above kinds.
Transplanted 184,000, amongst them 70,000 larch from Scotland, all the rest reared at home.
1803. Planted 16 acres in various directions, with 104,000 forest trees.
Planted in the nursery, 131,000 seedlings, principally oak.
1804. Planted 16 acres in detached pieces, with 114,000 forest trees.
Planted in nurseries 336,000, 300,000 of which were oak, reared at home.
1805. Planted 10 acres with oak, &c. so as to obtain a premium from the Dublin Society.
Replaced the wood of Tomis, 1500 acres, by 49,000 three year old oak.
Planted 52,000 in nursery.
1806. Repaired the planting of the years 1801, 1802, and 1803, also planted about three acres.
Transplanted in nursery 68,000 forest trees.
1807. Repaired the planting of former years, planted small pieces, and planted in the nurseries 68,000 forest trees.
1808. Planted 10 acres with 70,000 trees, chiefly oak.
Repaired the wood of Caiarnabawn.
Planted the fall of the last year, with 16,000 oak of 8 years old.
Planted in nursery 76,000 forest trees. Sold 50,000 seedlings.
1809. Planted the fall of the last year, with 22,000 oak.
Planted in nursery 40,000 seedlings.
Sold 30,000 seedlings.
1810. Planted the fall of the last year, with 12,000 oak.
Planted in nursery 32,000.
Sold 35,000.
1811. Planted the fall of the last year, and a large tract copiced in, with 40,000 oak and Scotch fir.
Planted in nursery 32,000.
Sold 35,000.
1812. Headed down all the oaks in the planting of 1808, and planted amongst them 10,000 Scotch fir, as nurses.
Finished planting Cairna wood, of 1,300 acres.
Planted in nursery 30,000.
Sold 35,000.

The entire planting for the twelve years, (except 130,000 seedlings, brought at first from Scotland) was performed from a small seminary of half an acre, in which are at present 200,000 seedlings.

Quicks, shrubs, and fruit trees, have also been raised for the use of the tenantry.

This nursery of about seven acres was started in August 1811. The following details were given by Mr Wright, his gardener. The period is from August 1811 to April 1812 only.

547,000	two and three years seedling beech and ash, from the old woods.
10,500	one year's seedling holly, collected from the old woods.
40,000	one year's seedling larch.
20,000	two years seedling larch.
60,000	two years seedling Scotch fir.
20,000	two years seedling Norway spruce.
7,000	one year's seedling witch or Scotch elm.
1,000	elm suckers, taken from the roots of some old English elm trees.
1,500	lime suckers, taken from the roots of some old lime trees.
2,000	lilacks, taken from the old plants.
2,000	mountain ash seedlings, 2 feet high, collected from the old woods.
3,000	birch seedlings, 3 feet high, collected from the old woods.
11,000	sycamore, one year's seedlings, collected from the old woods.
500	sycamore, from 2 to 3 feet high, collected from the old nursery.
1,000	ash, from 2 to 3 feet high, collected from the old nursery.
300	laurels, taken from old plants.
100	laurestinus, taken from old plants.
400	honey-suckle, taken from old plants.
4,400	sallows and oziers of different sorts, from cuttings.
500	fly honey-suckle, from cuttings.
500	Carolina dogwood.
100	platanus.
100	timber ozier and weeping willow.
1,700	privet.
200	sweet bay.
100	Portugal laurel.
100	laurestinus.
1,000	laurestinus layers.
2,500	cuttings of laurel.
156,000	birch, from seeds.
231,000	sycamore, from seeds.
4,000	alder, from seeds.
2,000	oak, from acorns.
2,000	arbutus, from seeds.
20,000	Scotch fir, from seeds.
15,000	wild pine or pineaster, from seeds.
36,000	ash, from seeds.

1,204,500

Lord Lansdown's registry shows planting on a larger scale than either Mr Herbert or Lord Kenmare. His nursery of ten acres was surrounded by a nine-foot stone wall, and subdivided by beech hedges. The details are provided by his Scottish gardener, Mr Irwin.

A Registry of Trees removed annually to the forest, out of the Marquis of Landsdown's nursery, from Spring 1801, to Spring 1812, inclusive.

Years	Laburnum.	Oak.	Willow of kinds	Syca- more.	Ches- nut of kinds.	Ash.	Plata- nus.	Fir Scotch	Wild or M. Pine	Beech.	Lime.	Fir Larch.	Alder.	Birch.	Elm.	Poplar of kinds.	Fir Spruce.	Horn Beam.	TOTAL.
1801.	26		109	300		687		1012					68	172	1009	97			3480
1802.	208	8602	60	1200	10	1805	10	100		642		200	20	1558	1120	180		100	15815
1803.	1700	9860		14559		16658		8200		7438		8370		620		360			70765
1804.	100	18300		8706		18400		13450		11000	60	5250		16000	100	570	300		90236
1805.		131080	1150	15660		9160		2700		25560		3000	360	7560		600		1206	198336
1806.		67500	200	11850		16500		1400		20240		1050				2460	760		121960
1807.		87360	2056	2500		19620		37160	1500	13620		3880		6900			1660		176256
1808.		48600				6200		46400											101200
1809.		40160	2770	2050		5310		40620				6020		3030					99960
1810.		21120				6590		28060		15870		28328					7400		105368
1811.			2800					44400		5900		30000						300	83400
1812.			4320					25660	6600							520			37100
	2034	432582	13465	56825	10	100930	10	249162	8100	98270	60	85098	448	35840	2229	4787	10120	1606	1,103 876

These details for County Kerry are taken from Rev. T. Radcliff, *A Report on the agriculture and livestock of the county of Kerry*. Dublin 1814, pp. 77 ff.

The detailed account, *A statistical and agricultural survey of the County of Galway* (Dublin 1824), by Hely Dutton, a practising nurseryman and landscape gardener, firstly shows the trees planted in the 1760s at Bellevue, with the methods employed; and, secondly, demonstrates how by bad forestry many of these deteriorated.

Many gentlemen have planted extensively, but still they have not planted *forests*. I have scarcely ever seen one that a quarter of an hour's ride would not bring you from one end to the other. The late Mr. Lawrence of Bellevue planted a great extent of *screens* and *clumps*,* upwards of 370 acres; but from their narrowness, want of timely thinning, and a deficiency of underwood, they admit the light to be seen through them. This is the general fault of the Irish planting, and if we may judge from different publications, of English planting too. When, some years since, by an order from the court of Chancery, I thinned the plantations of Bellevue, I advised them to be carefully copsed, and an additional breadth, and more varied outline to be given to the screens and *clumps*. These would in a few years have shut out the light, and relieved them from that wretched tameness that Mr. Lawrence, in conformity with the fashion of the day, adopted, and would have converted his *clumps* into *groups*. I regret to say that none of these ideas have been adopted; cattle have been admitted into most of the plantations, and something like an *American* improvement has been pursued.

It was the late Mr. Lawrence's intention to have added considerably to those screens, and I am informed he often wished his demesne extended seven miles, that he might have *planted it all*. The study of the demesne of Bellevue would, however, be well worth the attention of the lovers of this charming art; exclusive of those very general faults he would learn to avoid, he would perceive some of the best oak trees growing in several feet of turf bog, badly drained; whilst in dry ground, apparently more appropriate to their growth, they have made little progress. Here also may be seen (or *might have been seen*) some of the most beautiful ash trees growing luxuriantly in upwards of three feet of turf bog, completely surrounded by stagnant water within a foot of the surface; and what is very remarkable, there are *Scotch fir* and *alder* amongst them, greatly inferior in growth and health. In the servants' hall there is a table made of pineaster, planted and cut down by the late Mr. Lawrence. The first length of the tree was nine feet, cut into boards *nineteen inches broad*; another length nine feet also, cut into boards *sixteen inches broad*, exclusive of a considerable top; the wood beautiful, and of excellent quality. There was a Weymouth pine of about forty-four years growth, (planted by Mr. Lawrence,) cut down for a pump stick; the circumference was four feet ten inches; the timber was very fine, *very red at the heart*, and full of turpentine: the top was decayed, which caused its conversion to this use; until then, I had been always led to think that Weymouth pine was a *soft, white, worthless timber*. Balm of Gilead fir uniformly decayed in every part of this demesne when about fourteen feet high. Indeed I do not recollect to have seen a flourishing tree of this species of considerable age, in any part of Ireland.

Pineaster invariably flourishing at the *west side* of every plantation, whilst on the *south* and *east* they have mostly decayed. I cut down many hundreds in that state. Larch, Scotch fir, and sweet chestnut, bent by the westerly winds; but oak, spruce and silver fir, and Weymouth pine, not bent; beech a little bent. The following dimensions of trees, (if they have not been cut down) will show, in a forcible light, the spirit of planting Mr. Lawrence possessed; and, in addition to what I have just detailed, the profit of planting. That has been so often doubted by those who are eager to lay hold of every excuse to hide their *indolence*, that I give it with more pleasure than hope. They were all planted by the late Mr. Lawrence. They were measured in 1808, and were in circumference, at three feet from the ground, and about forty-four years growth, as follows:

			Ft.	In.				Ft.	In.
Acacia	-	-	5	4	Copper beech	-	-	5	4
Cedar of Libanus	-	-	6	8	Occidental plane	-	-	9	6
Scotch elm	-	-	10	0	Evergreen oak	-	-	5	0
Sweet chestnut	-	-	7	6	Horse chestnut	-	-	5	9
Oak	-	-	8	6	Scotch fir	-	-	4	4
Silver fir	-	-	7	3	Ash (sold for four guineas)			6	1
Portugal laurel	-	-	4	7	Pineaster	-	-	5	7
Weymouth pine	-	-	5	0	Beech	-	-	7	5
Tulip tree (60 feet high at least)		5	10	Hornbeam	-	-	6	2
Common laurel	-	-	3	9	&c. &c. &c.				
Larch	-	-	6	3					

* But ah! how different is the formal lump,
Which the improver plants and calls a clump.
                    Knight's Landscape.

The late colonel Hayes of Avondale, (dear to the memory of every lover of planting and polished manners,) measured the sweet chestnut in 1790; it was then, at six feet from the ground, four feet eight inches: as there is very little difference in the girth at six feet or three feet from the ground, there has been an average of two feet ten inches in eighteen years, *nearly a foot diameter in so short a period*. If this statement is correct, what an immense loss must be sustained by the *premature* and *indiscriminate* cutting at Bellevue since the death of Mr. Lawrence. The late colonel Hayes, in his admirable treatise on planting, sets this in a very clear light. "The timber of an oak tree of fifty years growth, is worth from *twelve to twenty shillings*: a tree of seventy-five years growth may be worth from *four to seven pounds*." – Note, I beg most earnestly to recommend an attentive perusal of this treatise to every person possessing woods. I cannot suppose any one who has either a taste or a love of planting can be without it. The mistaken idea of planting trees of very inferior value for nurses, has been practised at Bellevue, as well as in every plantation in Ireland, England, and a recurrence to my Survey of the County of Clare, p. 279, will show it has been also adopted in Scotland. When thinnings of plantations are to be sold, the money received for those of larch, when compared with that of beech, alder, and many others, will throw a strong light on my position. The country people are all perfectly sensible of the superiority of larch over every other except ash, to which they are very partial, that any quantity of those can be sold, whilst beech, alder, or Scotch fir, may remain long on hands.

Mr. Lawrence shewed great judgment in selecting hardy trees for the west side of his plantations; they are very much beech, hornbeam and sycamore. Many people, I have been informed, thought him a little deranged when he planted such a quantity of his demesne as 370 acres; but if his views had been seconded during the minority of his son, there would be an *immense* property coming to him and his children. He planted 100,000 oaks at the distance at which they were intended to stand for timber, and filled up the spaces with other trees for nurses. He calculated that each oak tree in forty years would be well worth at least 20s.; and had they been properly thinned *in time*, this calculation would have been greatly below the value. Some progress was made for this purpose when I *commenced* the thinning; and if it had been *gradually* carried on for a few years, his judicious intentions would have been more than realised. If I am rightly informed, since that period, oaks and nurses have nearly all disappeared. I made a valuation of what value the entire plantations of this demesne would be at a future period of thirty years, when they would be about seventy-four years old, and supposing the trees to stand twelve feet asunder, which is sufficient for trees not intended for ship timber, and even at twenty shillings each, they would be worth £181,300. but they would be more likely worth £3. each, when they would be worth £543,900. besides the value of the thinnings in the mean time. I am aware it will be said that there must be deductions for failures; I grant it; but I am convinced that it is more probable that many trees of this age (seventy-four years), will be worth from £5. to £10. each. It proves, amongst numberless instances in Ireland, that one or more sworn superintendants of the plantations of minors, under the control of the court of Chancery, (as my operations at Bellevue were) would be a most useful officer, and would prevent the gross frauds and dilapidations committed frequently by guardians and executors on the property of wards of chancery.*

* I took the liberty, some time since, to address a letter on this subject to the Lord Chancellor. As I have never been honored with an answer, I presume his lordship did not approve of the idea. I can only regret it, without having had any reason since to change my opinion.

A further mention of the ingenious Hely Dutton occurs in *The Irish Builder*, Vol. XXIV, 15 August 1882, p. 235 under 'Adversaria Hibernica': 'Mr. Hely Dutton, in his Survey of the county tells us that in this burial-ground (Fort Hill near Galway town) lies interred "Mr. Thomas Leggett, a very celebrated landscape gardener, who after beautifying almost every demesne in the County, is most ungratefully suffered to lie here neglected, without even a *Hic Jacet*. I proposed," says Mr. Dutton, "some years since, to receive subscriptions, to enable me to raise an humble monument to his memory, but, alas! I felt a freezing indifference, except from one gentleman, who would give 20 guineas, *provided it was erected in his own demesne*." '

We would like to know where Mr Hely Dutton himself is buried, and in what year he died. He, too, was a noted landscape gardener and agriculturist, as well as author. He wrote three volumes of surveys, under the auspices of the Royal Dublin Society, the first, *Observations on Mr. Archer's Statistical Survey of Dublin*, about 1802. Some years afterwards, Mr Dutton published his *Survey of the County Clare*, and, in 1824, issued his *Statistical and Agricultural Survey of the County of Galway*. The preface of Mr Dutton's last survey is dated from Mount Bellew, Castle Blakeney. Towards the close of the last century, Mr Dutton and his father appear to have been engaged in the business of seed merchants in Dublin, and the name of 'Hely Dutton, Seed Merchant and Florist, 59 Dorset-street', appears in the Dublin Directory.

In *The Irish Builder* of 15 October of the same year, an article, 'Planting for Shelter and timber purposes in Ireland', mentions Dutton with Shanly and Leggett as being employed extensively around the turn of the century in the west of Ireland; Dutton, it further states, was employed 'generally over the four provinces'. An interesting discussion about pruning trees and the age of pineasters follows.

APPENDIX C   *Planting at Lyons, County Kildare, 1813*

The following notice appeared in the *Dublin Gazette* 14 to 16 January 1813:

I Hereby give notice that I have planted or caused to be planted, within 12 Calendar Months past, on the Lands of Lyons and Clonoclis, in the Parish of Lyons and Clonoclis, in the County of Kildare, the following trees:– 20,000 Oak, 15,000 Ash, 15,000 Larch, 10,000 Beech, 10,000 Elm, 10,000 Spruce Fir, 10,000 Scotch Fir, 10,000 Dutch Alder, and 5,000 Canada Poplar, and that it is my Intention to register the said Trees pursuant to the Acts of Parliament* in that Case made and provided.

Dated January 16, 1813   CLONCURRY.
To all whom it may concern.

---

* An Act to amend the Laws for the Encouragement of Planting of Timber Trees', twenty-third George III, which, among other clauses, laid down that notice must be made in the *Gazette* of planting, as well as 'reciting' the details before a Justice of the Peace.

On 22 October 1745, Dr and Mrs Delany were visited at Delville by their friend, Lord Chesterfield, the Lord Lieutenant, 'who could not have said more pleasant things had it been my Lord Cobham's Stowe'. Lord Chesterfield was a most successful Viceroy with humanitarian ideals like the Delanys, and he soon realized that Ireland had more to fear from poverty than the papacy, so he initiated schemes for the employment of the poor. One of these was the extensive replanting of the royal deer park to the north-west of Dublin, and he was also responsible for the design and erection of the fluted stone column of the phoenix burning in her nest. In 1747 he opened the Phoenix Park (then the largest city park in the world) to the public, a popular action which typified his period of office in Ireland.

As one can guess, Chesterfield's ideal landscape was an enlargment of the Twickenham pattern of Pope, largely informal, ungeometric and naturalized. This he tried to achieve in the Phoenix Park by frequent clumps of trees somewhat formally sited, but with a freedom in the planting of avenues by not having to centre them on any particular building or obelisk, except for the Phoenix Column. This can be clearly seen in Thomas Wright's drawing* (Plate 206), from his *Sketches and Designs of Planting*, of the formal planting of a semi-circular ring of trees at the end of a straight avenue. As yet the Viceregal Lodge was not *in* the Park but on Kilmainham Priory lands to the north. In the early 1750s the park ranger, Mr Nathaniel Clements, an amateur architect in the eighteenth-century tradition, built a modest redbrick house, round which he started to landscape. Faulkner's *Journal* of 21 September 1754 records 'a very great variety of curious small Figures and Statues were landed at the Custom House to ornament the fine Gardens of Nathaniel Clements, Esq, in the Phoenix Park.'

206   PHOENIX PARK, DUBLIN. *The Phoenix Column: pencil drawing by Thomas Wright, c. 1746.*

---

* Thomas Wright visited Ireland in 1746–47 and, in the companion volume, *Sketches and Designs of Buildings*, in the Avery Library, Columbia University, New York (Phillipps MS 13448 & 13451), his drawings include Castletown House, Tower of Waterford and Change of Waterford.

By 1782 Mr Clements had made such improvements that his house was considered to be worthy as a residence for the Viceroy, and was duly bought by the government for that purpose. In that same year landscaping improvements for the whole park were put forward by Mr James Donnell, who had worked with Lady Masserene at Leixlip. Austin Cooper gives an account of an examination of this gardener's plans, with Mr. Clements. 'He therein proposed to plant it in many places, to remove some of the clumps of trees planted by Lord Chesterfield in order to abolish regularity . . .'* Mr James Donnell also planned new roads, a masked bridge across the pond near the Dublin gate, and to build a rectangular tower or observatory with round towers. Although Lord Chesterfield's original plan had not been influenced by the geometricality of French gardens, his symmetrical though loose clumps were evidently similar to William Kent's design for Euston Hall, Suffolk (c. 1740). These were criticized by Horace Walpole as 'sticking a dozen trees here and there till a lawn looks like the ten of spades. Clumps have their beauty; but in a great extent of country, how trifling to scatter arbours where you should spread forests!'

The Phoenix Park has suffered from never having had an overall landscape designer, and there was little done in the 1780s except for the planting of alternate groups of elm on each side of the road, and scattering hawthorns prolifically. The park's general flatness is relieved by its narrow ravines with streams, handsome lodges, a stone wall seven miles in circumference, and fine views to the Dublin Mountains, especially from the rising ground on which the Wellington Testimonial stands. This is a brilliantly chosen site, as the great obelisk, designed by Robert Smirke, can be seen from far down the Dublin quays. But at the beginning of the nineteenth century the park was obviously in a very neglected state. Hely Dutton in *The Irish Agricultural Magazine*, p. 339, writes of the open drains 'very aptly called breaknecks' and adds:

One fourth at least is waste, or the produce so bad to be little better. If it was properly drained, judiciously planted, the briars, furze etc. etc. eradicated, the useless ditches levelled, and other improvements made, an increase of surface and produce, equal, at very moderate calculation, to £6000 per an. might be obtained at an expense comparatively small, and be at once an honor to the country, an ornament to the city of Dublin, and a lasting monument of the taste and spirit of the Board of Works, in whose department I understand such expenditures are.

By 1816, when Francis Johnston enlarged and plastered over the Viceregal Lodge,** the enclosure had grown to one hundred and sixty acres with a lake and fine ornamental trees, as well as oaks and elms. Some years later Decimus Burton was commissioned to design a formal garden for the Viceregal Lodge. To the north-west of this was the Under-Secretary's official residence, now the Papal Nunciature, with its landscaped garden. Between 1813 and 1831 Mr William Gregory of Coole Park, County Galway, was Under-Secretary. Like many of his family he was a keen gardener, and his enclosure was reputed to be neat and well wooded.

The park's 1752 acres have been admirably adapted to modern conditions: People's Gardens, Zoological Gardens, the Polo Ground, hundreds of acres of playing fields for hurling, football and cricket, and a racecourse. Although the Earl of Chesterfield may have failed as a patron of Samuel Johnson's *Dictionary* in 1747, in that same year he permanently benefited the inhabitants of Dublin.

---

* *Dublin Penny Journal*. 2 August 1902.

** Now Áras an Uachtaráin, residence of the President of the Republic.

The Right Honourable the Earl of Clancarty
Boylan, Mr. M., Gardener to the Earl of Kenmore [*sic*], Killarney, Ireland
Fraser, James, Esq., Landscape Gardener, etc., Ireland
Grant, Mr., Gardener to Charles Purland, Esq., Bray Head, Ireland
Johnston, Mr. A., Gardener to the Right Honourable the Earl of Clancarty
Leningan, James, Esq., Castle Fogarty, Tipperary, Ireland
Mackay, J. T., Esq., Cottage Terrace, Dublin
Matheson, Mr. J., Gardener, Hibernian School, Phoenix Park, Dublin
Mc Gregor, Mr. J., Gardener to His Grace the Archbishop of Tuam
Mc Lean, Mr., Forester to the Right Honourable Viscount Powerscourt
Millikens, Messrs., Dublin
Niven, Mr., Gardener to the Chief Secretary, Phoenix Park, Dublin
Pullock, Matthew, Esq., Oatlands, near Dublin
Robson, Mr., Gardener to His Excellency the Lord Lieutenant of Ireland
Ross, Mr., Gardener to the Right Honourable Viscount Powerscourt
Russell, Mr. M., College Botanic Garden, Dublin
Wilkie, Mr. W., Under Ranger, etc., Phoenix Park, Dublin
Young, Mr. W., Gardener to the Right Honourable the Earl of Enniskillen

Bibliography

ADAMS, C. L. *Castles of Ireland*. London, 1904.

AHERON, John. *A General Treatise on Architecture*. London, 1754.

ANON. *The Compleat Irish Traveller*. London, 1788.

ANON. *Journal of a Tour in Ireland performed in 1804*. London, 1806.

ANON. *The Pleasure Tour in Ireland*. Edinburgh, 1825.

ARCHER, Joseph. *Statistical Survey of the County of Dublin*. Dublin, 1801.

ATKINSON, A. *The Irish Tourist*. Dublin, 1815.

ATKINSON, Joseph. *Killarney: a poem*. Dublin, 1790.

BAGSHAWE, W. H. G. *The Bagshawes of Ford*. London, 1886.

BALL, Dr. F. Elrington. *The Correspondence of Jonathan Swift*. Dublin, 1912.
    A History of the County of Dublin. Dublin, 1902.
    Howth and its owners. Dublin, 1917.

BARROW, John. *Tour round Ireland*. London, 1836.

BERKELEY, George. *The Works of . . .*, ed. George Sampson. London, 1897.

BOND, R. Warwick (ed.). *The Marlay Letters 1788–1820*. London, 1937.

BOWDEN, Charles T. *A Tour through Ireland in 1790*. Dublin, 1791.

BOYLAN, Lena. *The Early History of Castletown*. Dublin, 1967.

BRERETON, Sir William, Bart. *Travels*. Chetham Society, 1844.

BREWER, J. N. and NEALE, J. P. *The Beauties of Ireland*. London, 1825.

BRUCE, H. J. *Silken Dalliance*. London, 1946.

BUDGELL, Eustace. *Memoirs of the Lives and Characters of the Illustrious Family of the Boyles*. London, 1754.

BURKE, Rt. Hon. Edmund. *A Philosophic Inquiry into the Origin of our Ideas of the Sublime and Beautiful*. London, 1757.

BUSHE, John. *Hibernia Curiosa*. London, 1764.

BUTLER, H. J. *The Family of Edgeworth*. London, 1927.

CAMPBELL, Gerald. *Edward and Pamela FitzGerald*. London, 1904.

CAMPBELL, The Rev. Thomas. *A Philosophical Survey of the South of Ireland*. London, 1778.

CARLYLE, Thomas. *Reminiscences of my Irish Journey in 1849*. London, 1882.

CARR, Sir John. *The Stranger in Ireland . . .* London, 1806.

CHAMBERS, Sir William. *A Treatise on Civil Architecture*. London, 1759.

CHETWOOD, William R. *A Tour through Ireland*. 1748.

CHILDE-PEMBERTON, W. S. *The Earl-Bishop*. New York, 1924.

COLVIN, Howard and CRAIG, Maurice. *Architectural drawings in the library of Elton Hall by Sir John Vanbrugh and Sir Edward Lovett Pearce*. Oxford, 1964.

COOK, Thomas. *Pictures of Parsonstown*. Dublin, 1826.

COOPER, George. *Letters on the Irish Nation*. London, 1800.

COOTE, Sir Charles. *General View of the Queen's County*. Dublin, 1801.
    Statistical Survey of the King's County. Dublin, 1801.

CORKE AND ORRERY, The Countess of (ed.). *The Orrery Papers*. London, 1903.

COWPER, William. *Poetical Works*, ed. H. S. Milford. Oxford, 1967.

COYNE, Joseph Stirling. *The Scenery and Antiquities of Ireland*. 1846.

CROKER, Thomas Crofton. *Legends of the Lakes . . .* London, 1829.

CURRAN, C. P. *Dublin Decorative Plasterwork of the seventeenth and eighteenth centuries*. London, 1967.

D'ALTON, John. *The History of the County of Dublin*. Dublin, 1838.

DELANY, Mrs. *The Autobiography and Correspondence of Mary Granville, Mrs. Delany*, ed. Lady Llanover. London, 1861.

DERRICK, Samuel. *Letters from Leverpoole, Chester, Corke etc*. London, 1767.

DOWNES, G. *Killarney and the surrounding Scenery*. Dublin, 1822.

DUBOURDIEU, John. *Statistical Survey of the county of Down*. Dublin, 1802.

DUTTON, Hely. *Observations on Mr. Archer's statistical survey of the County of Dublin*. Dublin, 1802.
    A statistical and agricultural survey of the County of Galway. Dublin, 1824.
    Statistical Survey of the County of Clare. Dublin, 1808.

EDGEWORTH, Maria. *Memoir*. London, 1867.
    Tour in Connemara and the Martins of Ballynahinch. London, 1952.

FAHEY, Dr Jerome. *History and Antiquities of the Diocese of Kilmacduagh*. Dublin, 1893.

FARINGTON, Joseph. *Diary*, ed. James Grieg. London, 1928.

FIENNES, Celia. *The Journeys of . . .*, ed. Christopher Morris. London, 1949.

FISHER, Jonathan. *Scenery of Ireland*. London, 1795.

FITZGERALD, Brian (ed.). *The Correspondence of Emily, Duchess of Leinster, 1731–1814.* Dublin, 1949–57.

FORDHAM, Sir H. G. *Roadbooks: Itineraries of Ireland, 1647–1850.* Dublin, 1923.

FRASER, James. *A Handbook for Travellers in Ireland.* Dublin, 1844.

FROST, James. *The History and Topography of the County of Clare . . .* Dublin, 1893.

FROUDE, James Anthony. *The English in Ireland in the Eighteenth Century.* London, 1872–74.

GAMBLE, John. *Sketches of history, politics and manners in Dublin and the North of Ireland in 1819.* Dublin, 1826.

GAUSSEN, Alice. *Percy: Prelate and Poet.* London, 1908.

GILBERT, Sir John Thomas. *A History of the City of Dublin.* Dublin, 1861.

GILPIN, The Rev. William. *Three Essays: On Picturesque Beauty; On Picturesque Travel; On Sketching Landscape.* London, 1792.

GILPIN, William Sawrey. *Practical Hints on Landscape Gardening.* London, 1832.

GÖTHEIN, Marie Louise. *A History of Garden Art,* trans. Mrs Archer Hind. London, 1928.

GRANVILLE, The Lord. *Leveson Gower Private Correspondence, 1781–1821.* London, 1916.

GRAVES, Richard. *The Spiritual Quixote.* London, 1773.

GREGORY, Lady. *Coole.* Dublin, 1971.

GREGORY, Vere R. T. *The House of Gregory.* Dublin, 1943.

GROSART, Alexander B. (ed.). *The Lismore Papers.* London, 1886.

GUINNESS, The Hon. Desmond and RYAN, William. *Irish Houses and Castles.* London, 1971.

HALL, Samuel Carter and HALL, Anna Maria. *Ireland: its Scenery, Character etc.* London, 1841–43.

HAMILTON, The Rev. William. *Letters concerning the Northern Coast of the County of Antrim.* Dublin, 1790.

HANMER, Sir Thomas. *Correspondence of . . .,* ed. Sir Henry Bunbury. London, 1838.

HARDIMAN, James. *A History of the Town and County of Galway.* Dublin, 1820.

HARDY, Francis. *Memoirs and political and private life of James Caulfield, Earl of Charlemont.* London, 1810.

HARRIS, John. *Sir William Chambers.* London, 1972.

HARRIS, Walter. *The ancient and present State of the County of Down.* Dublin, 1744.
The History and Antiquities of the City of Dublin. Dublin, 1766.

HAYES, Samuel. *A Practical Treatise on Planting . . .* Dublin, 1794.

HICKEY, William. *Memoirs.* London, 1913.

HOARE, Sir Richard Colt. *Journal of a Tour in Ireland A.D. 1806.* London, 1807.

HOGARTH, William. *The Analysis of Beauty.* London, 1753.

HOLMES, George. *Sketches of some of the Southern Counties of Ireland.* London, 1801.

HUSSEY, Christopher. *English Gardens and Landscapes 1700–1750.* London, 1967.
The Picturesque. London, 1967.

HYDE, H. Montgomery. *The Rise of Castlereagh.* London, 1933.

INGLIS, Henry David. *A Journey throughout Ireland in 1834 . . .* London, 1834.

JOHNSTONE, J. *Works of Samuel Parr.* London, 1828.

JONES, Henry. *Poems on Several Occasions.* London, 1749.

KNIGHT, Richard Payne. *An analytical inquiry into the principles of Taste.* London, 1805.
The Landscape. London, 1794.

LANGLEY, Batty. *Gothic Architecture improved . . .* London, 1747.
New Principles of Gardening. London, 1728.

LEDWICH, Edward. *Antiquities of Ireland.* Dublin, 1790.

LENNOX, Charles, Earl of March. *A Duke and his friends.* London, 1911.

LESLIE, John. *Killarney: A Poem.* Dublin, 1772.

LEWIS, Richard. *The Dublin Guide.* Dublin, 1786.

LEWIS, Samuel. *A Topographical Dictionary of Ireland.* London, 1837.

LEWIS, W. S. and BROWN, R. S. (eds.). *Horace Walpole's Correspondence.* New Haven, Conn., 1941.

LONDONDERRY, The Marquess of (ed.). *Memoirs and Correspondence of Viscount Castlereagh.* London, 1848.

LOUDON, J. C. *Encyclopedia of Gardening.* London, 1860.
Observations on the formation and management of useful and ornamental plantations. Edinburgh, 1804.

LOVEDAY, John. *Diary of a Tour through . . . Ireland.* London, 1890.

MACLYSAGHT, Edward. *Irish Life in the Seventeenth Century.* Cork and Oxford, 1950.

MACPHERSON, James. *The Poems of Ossian.* London, 1807.

MALINS, Edward. *English Landscaping and Literature 1660–1840.* Oxford, 1965.

MANT, Walter. *Memoirs of R. Mant.* Dublin, 1857.

MASON, George. *An Essay on Design in Gardening.* London, 1768.

MAXWELL, Constantia E. *Country and Town in Ireland under the Georges.* Dundalk, 1949.

M'EVOY, John. *Statistical Survey of the County of Sligo.* Dublin, 1802.

MILLER, Philip. *The Gardener's Dictionary.* London, 1732.

MILTON, Thomas. *Views of different Seats of the nobility and gentry.* London and Dublin, 1783.

MONTAGU, Lady Mary Wortley. *Letters of . . .*, ed. Robert Halsband. Oxford, 1966.

MONTESQUIEU, Charles Louis de. *Oeuvres posthumes*. London, 1783.

MOORE, George. *The Lake*. London, 1905.

NEALE, J. P. *Views of Seats of Noblemen and Gentlemen . . .* London, 1823.

NEALE, J. P. and O'NEILL, H. *Picturesque Sketches of some of the finest Landscapes . . . of Ireland*. Dublin, 1835.

NEWENHAM, Thomas. *A View of the natural, political & commercial circumstances of Ireland*. London, 1809.

NICHOLS, John Bowyer. *Illustrations of the Literary History of the Eighteenth Century*. London, 1848.

O'LAVERTY, James. *An Historical Account of the Diocese of Down and Connor*. Dublin, 1878–84.

OTWAY, Caesar. *Sketches in Ireland . . .* 1827.

　　Tour of Connaught. 1839.

PASQUIN, Anthony. *An Authentic History of the Professors of Painting . . . in Ireland*. Dublin, 1796.

PETRIE, George and WRIGHT, G. N. *A Guide to the County of Wicklow*. Dublin, 1822.

PLUMPTRE, Anne. *Narrative of a Residence in Ireland*. London, 1817.

POCOCKE, Richard. *Pococke's Tour in Ireland*, ed. G. T. Stokes. London and Dublin, 1891.

POPE, Alexander. *The Correspondence of . . .*, ed. George Sherburn. Oxford, 1956.

PRICE, Sir Uvedale. *A Dialogue on the distinct characters of the Picturesque and the Beautiful*. Hereford, 1801.

　　An Essay on the Picturesque. London, 1794–98.

PÜCKLER-MUSKAU, Prince Hermann. *A Tour of England, Ireland . . .* London, 1832.

RADCLIFF, The Rev. Thomas. *A Report of the Architecture and Live Stock of the County of Kerry*. Dublin, 1814.

RAIT, Robert. *The Story of an Irish Property*. Oxford, 1908.

RAND, Benjamin (ed.). *Berkeley and Percival*. Cambridge, 1914.

REED, William. *Remains of William Reed, late of Thornbury*. Bristol, 1815.

RICHARDSON, Ethel M. *Long-forgotten Days*. London, 1928.

RITCHIE, Leitch. *Ireland picturesque and romantic*. London, 1832.

SADLEIR, T. U. and DICKINSON, P. L. *Georgian Mansions in Ireland*. Dublin, 1915.

SAMPSON, The Rev. Vaughan. *Statistical Survey of the County of Londonderry*. Dublin, 1802.

SIRÉN, Osvald. *China and the Gardens of Europe of the Eighteenth Century*. New York, 1950.

SLADE, Robert. *Narrative of a Journey to the North of Ireland*. London, 1803.

SMITH, Charles. *The ancient and present State of the County of Kerry*. Dublin, 1756.

　　The ancient and present State of the County of Waterford. Dublin, 1746.

SMITH, G. N. *Killarney and the surrounding Scenery*. London and Dublin, 1822.

SPENCE, Joseph. *Anecdotes . . . from the conversation of Mr. Pope*. Oxford, 1966.

SPENSER, Edmund. *A View of the Present State of Ireland*, ed. W. L. Renwick. Oxford, 1970.

STEUART, Sir Henry. *The Planter's Guide*. Edinburgh, 1828.

STRICKLAND, W. G. *A Dictionary of Irish Artists*. Dublin and London, 1913.

SWIFT, Deane. *An Essay on the Life and Character of Dr. Jonathan Swift*. London, 1755.

SWIFT, Jonathan. *The Correspondence of . . .*, ed. Harold Williams. Oxford, 1963.

　　The Poems of . . ., ed. Harold Williams. Oxford, 1958.

SWITZER, Stephen. *Ichnographia*. London, 1718.

　　The Nobleman's, Gentleman's and Gardener's Recreation. London, 1715.

　　The Practical Fruit Gardener. London, 1724.

TEMPLE, Sir William. *Upon the Garden of Epicurus*. London, 1685.

THACKERAY, William Makepeace. *The Irish Sketchbook of 1842*. London, 1895.

THOMPSON, R. *Statistical Survey of the County of Meath*. Dublin, 1802.

TIGHE, William. *Statistical observations relative to the County of Kilkenny*. Dublin, 1802.

TOWNSHEND, The Rev. H. *Statistical Survey of the County of Cork*. Dublin, 1810.

TWISS, Richard. *A Tour in Ireland in 1775*. London, 1776.

WAKEFIELD, Edward. *An Account of Ireland*. London, 1812.

WALKER, J. Cooper. *Essay on the Rise and Progress of Gardening in Ireland*. Dublin, 1791.

WALPOLE, Horace. *Anecdotes of Painting in England*, ed. R. N. Wornum. London, 1862.

WEBSTER, Charles A. *History of the Diocese of Cork*. Cork, 1920.

WELD, Charles R. *Vacations in Ireland*. London, 1857.

WELD, Isaac. *Statistical Survey of County Roscommon*. Dublin, 1832.

WESLEY, John. *The Journal of . . .* London, 1827.

WHATELY, Sir Thomas. *Observations on Modern Gardening*. London, 1771.

WILDE, Sir William. *The Beauties of the Boyne and its tributary the Blackwater*. Dublin, 1847.

WILSON, William. *The Post-Chaise Companion . . . through Ireland*. Dublin, 1786.

WRIGHT, The Rev. G. N. *Ireland illustrated from original drawings of E. Petrie*. London, 1836.

WRIGHT, Thomas. *Universal Architecture*. London, 1755.

YEATS, William Butler. *The Collected Poems*. London, 1950.

YOUNG, Arthur. *A Tour in Ireland . . .* London, 1775.

Index